BEERS

OF
NORTH AMERICA

BEERS
OF
NORTH AMERICA

Revised & Expanded Edition

Bill Yenne

GALLERY BOOKS
An imprint of W.H. Smith Publishers Inc.
112 Madison Avenue
New York, New York 10016

Published by Gallery Books
A Division of WH Smith Publishers Inc.
112 Madison Avenue
New York, NY 10016

Produced by
Brompton Books Corp
15 Sherwood Place
Greenwich CT 06830

ISBN 0-8317-0723-2

Printed in Hong Kong

Designed and produced by Bill Yenne

2 3 4 5 6 7 8 9 10

ACKNOWLEDGMENTS

The author would like to express his special
thanks to the following people: *Jose Paz
Aguirre* of Cervecería Moctezuma; *Tom Allen* of
North Coast Brewing; *Katie Bates* of Tied
House; *Peter Blum* of Stroh Brewing; *Carl Bolz*
of Anheuser-Busch; *Michael Buckner* of
Albuquerque Brewing; *Paul Camusi* of Sierra
Nevada; *Mark Carpenter* of Anchor Brewing;
Charles Cooney, Jr, Curator, Milwaukee
County Historical Society; *Hugh Coppen* of
Molson Breweries; *Alan Davis* of Catamount
Brewing; *Jeff Davis* of Fleishman Hillard;
Harley Deeks of Molson Breweries; *James
Degnan* of Degnan Associates; *Roman De
Wenter* of Cold Spring Brewing; *Peggy
Dudinyak* of the Vernon Valley Brewery; *Lilo
Eckert* of Upper Canada Brewing; *Charles
Finkel* of Merchant du Vin; *Jim Ford* of Widmer
Brewing; *Steven Forsyth* of Miller Brewing;
Bert Grant of Yakima Brewing; *Steve Harrison*
of Sierra Nevada; *Stephen Hindy* of the
Brooklyn Brewery; *Robin Hinz* of Bridgeport

Brewing; *Michael Jaeger* of Dubuque Star;
Thomas Jones of Genesee Brewing; *Jim Koch*
of Boston Beer Company; *Suzanne Lanza* of
Rex Communications; *Mike Lanzarotta* of the
Crown City Brewery; *Barry Lazarus* of Pacific
Coast Brewing; *Joanne Lazusky* of Yuengling;
Fritz Maytag of Anchor Brewing; *Philip Merrit*
of Manhattan Brewing; *Alan Paul* of San
Francisco Brewing; *Marie Peacock* of Brick
Brewing; *Robert Peyton* of Basso & Associates;
Lynne Piade; *Gail Rolka*; *Pat Samson* of
Carling O'Keefe; *Stacy Saxon* of the Saxon
Brewery; *Greg Schirf* of Schirf Brewing; *Chris
Sherman* of the *St Petersburg Times*; *Joe
Shields* of the Oldenberg Brewery; *Don Shook*
of Adolph Coors; *Lori Smith* of Moosehead;
Paul Summers of Blue Ridge Brewing; *Mary
Thompson* of Reinheitsgebot; *Catherine Van
Evans* of Carling O'Keefe; *Jeff Waalkes* of
Miller Brewing; *Jeff Ware* of Dock Street;
George Westin of Anheuser-Busch; and *Judy
Wicks* of the White Dog Cafe.

CONTENTS

INTRODUCTION

Beer is one of mankind's oldest prepared foods. It certainly predates wine as an alcoholic beverage, and a good case can be made for the fact that grain was domesticated to brew beer before it was domesticated to bake bread. The ancient Egyptians and Sumerians brewed a great deal of beer, and it was common not only on the table of the average family, but in the tombs of the most exalted god-kings. Baking and brewing went hand in hand during those times when mash was prepared in the form of loaves, which then could either be eaten as bread or brewed for beer.

The history of brewing in North America began with the Indians of Mexico and the American Southwest, but most of our present traditions arrived with the European immigrants. The English brought their top-fermenting ale yeasts with them and immediately established breweries in the Colonies. By the time of the American Revolution, ales and porters were well developed as part of daily life, and most landowners were as likely to have a brewhouse on their grounds as a stable. Both George Washington and Thomas Jefferson were brewers.

In 1840 the first wave of German immigrants introduced bottom-fermenting yeasts to North American brewing, and we soon became a continent of lager drinkers. By the end of the nineteenth century there were 4000 breweries located in nearly every small town and city neighborhood, each with its own special style of beer. The idea of a town or neighborhood brewer was no more unusual than a town baker or neighborhood butcher.

By the turn of the century, the advent of a continental railroad network and invention of artificial ice making made

Above: **The author and a selection of North America's finest.** ***Facing page:*** **A 1947 view of beer's place in world history, featuring the world's most popular brand.**

possible the rise of megabrewers like Schlitz, Pabst and Anheuser-Busch, who became large, regional brewers, and by World War II were in a position to launch truly national brands. With the rise of the national brands, however, small local and regional brewers suffered, and many disappeared as nearly everyone attempted to create pale lagers that would appeal to as wide an audience as possible.

Since the beginning of the 1980s, however, the brewing industry in North America has been enjoying a renaissance. After four decades of decline in the number of brewers, over one hundred microbreweries and brewpubs have opened their doors. Compared to what was available as late as 1980, the spectrum of beer styles being brewed on this continent today is nothing short of incredible. Not only do we have the best selection of lagers in over half a century, but we are able to

choose from ales and wheat beers, whose character is more indicative of true ales and true weissbiers than imitative of lager (as had been the case for many years). Many American brewers are producing distinctive stouts and have even helped to revive the art of porter brewing, which had all but died out even in England. American brewers are also developing more esoteric beer styles. The cherry lager brewed at the Lakefront Brewery in Milwaukee is reminiscent of the kriek lambic beers of Belgium, while Alaskan Brewing produces a porter from barley roasted over an alder wood fire that recalls the rauchbiers of Bamberg in Bavaria. Anchor Brewing in San Francisco, already famous for its unique Steam beer, even went so far as a limited introduction of a beer based on a 4000-year-old Sumerian recipe.

The renaissance in North American brewing in the late 1980s is not unlike that of the American wine industry two decades earlier. Suddenly, North America has many world class beers in wide circulation that are being taken seriously by connoisseurs. Some of the continent's finest restaurants now have beer lists along with their wine lists, and most of these show a great deal of thought and planning, and a true consideration of beer's ability to accent and complement fine dining. Best of all, North America now has fresh local brands again the way we did in the nineteenth century, and brewpubs the way we did as early as the sixteenth century—places where beer, good company and a convivial atmosphere were the center of attention.

Brewing in North America has a long and rich tradition, a heritage that has come full circle. And herein lies the tale.

THE HISTORY OF BREWING IN NORTH AMERICA

THE EARLY DAYS

Beer came to America on the *Mayflower* but did not remain with the pilgrims to warm them during their first trying year in the New World. Instead, the crew retained these noteworthy casks to be tapped on their return voyage to England. John Alden, the cooper who had been hired to look after the beer, did stay nonetheless, and became one of Plymouth's more notable citizens.

This colorful story, however, by no means chronicles the first arrival of beer in America. When Captain Christopher Newport arrived at Jamestown on the cold winds of winter 1607 with the 'first supply,' beer (then spelled beere) was prominent on the ship's manifest. Indeed the English were attentive, keeping their Virginia and Caribbean colonies well supplied with this beverage that was considered to be essential to health. It has been suggested that ale was brewed in Virginia as early as 1587, and by 1609 the colony was actively soliciting London brewers to come to the New World. Even before the English arrived in Roanoke and Jamestown, however, Alonso de Herrera had established North America's first commercial brewery in Mexico in 1544.

Also, before the first European beer made landfall in the New World, the brewing art was well es-

Above: The first beer in the New World was imported from Europe. *Right:* Peter Stuyvesant was governor of New Amsterdam, the New World's first brewing center, and a city of beer connoisseurs *(far right).*

tablished on the Atlantic's western shores. Throughout the Caribbean basin, across Mexico and up into the American Southwest the Indians had been brewing maize (corn) beer —in fact two distinct types—for perhaps centuries. In the Caribbean region the corn was simply chewed to begin fermentation, then placed in a container of water—a practice also common to the early beer-making of South America.

In northern Mexico and the Southwest, moistened corn was allowed to sprout, then ground and boiled into what is today called a wort. The subsequent fermentation period was

relatively short, producing a beer known as *tesguino* with a four to five percent alcohol content within a couple of days. It is not known when this more sophisticated brewing method developed in the present-day United States, but it was still in practice among the Apaches as late as the nineteenth century. For the most part, though, the alcoholic beverages most frequently produced by those Indians first encountered by European settlers were various fruit wines such as the persimmon wine known to have been introduced to John Smith at Jamestown.

The tastes of the European settlers developed in the opposite direction. While in Mexico and the Caribbean demand for wine and distilled spirits, such as rum, exceeded that for beer, in Virginia and the English colonies to the north, beer was the drink of choice. Most of the beer drunk in the English colonies during the early seventeenth century was imported from England, but small attempts at domestic brewing were made almost as soon as the first log cabins were completed. In his history of early Virginia John Smith recorded two breweries established there by 1629. These first European brewers in America, like the Indian brewers before them, used maize rather than barley, and the beer was generally unhopped as had been the earliest beer in England.

NEW AMSTERDAM

The early English breweries in North America usually existed to satisfy a local demand, and their output only supplemented the beer imported from England. Indeed, most breweries in English North America were and continued to be home breweries.

Quite the opposite was true in the Dutch colony of New Netherlands and its capital, New Amsterdam, which became North America's first major commercial brewing center. Beginning in 1632 with the Netherlands West India Company Brewery on Brouwer's Straat (Brewer's Street), a large number of Dutch breweries sprang up, taking advantage of natural wild hops, a resource that the English generally had

ignored. One of these early breweries was that of the Bayard brothers, Nikolas, Balthazar and Peiter, who were nephews of Governor Peter Stuyvesant. Many of the early breweries were associated with individual taverns, while others brewed beer for many taverns. A choice of draft beers was not uncommon in New Amsterdam's watering holes. In 1660 the people of this bustling city welcomed North America's first name-brand beer. It was brewed by the Red Lion Brewery, which was established by Isaac de Foreest on a site just north of present-day Wall Street. The Red Lion Brewery continued in business until it was destroyed by fire in 1675.

NORTH AMERICAN
BREWING COMES OF AGE

Even after New Amsterdam was sold to the English in 1664 and renamed New York, the city maintained its prominence as a brewing center. The English even promoted the industry by levying taxes on wine and rum while exempting beer and cider. By this time commercial brewing had begun to flourish in the other English colonies, and the city of Philadelphia was well on its way toward becoming the New World's second major brewing center. Many Philadelphians entered the brewing business in the late seventeenth century following the lead of William Frampton in 1685. Philadelphia beer began to show up as a popular item among the goods the city exported to such places as New Jersey and Maryland where fewer breweries had been established.

William Penn, the founder of the colony of Pennsylvania, like many of his fellow Quakers was fond of beer and featured it prominently in his 1683 treaty with the Indians. At roughly the same time Penn had a 20-by-35-foot brewery built on his own estate and, although his house was later taken by fire, the brewery stood until 1864.

Each of the colonies developed its own perspective on the new industry. New York and Philadelphia brewers affected tastes in their immediate areas but places like Massachusetts and Virginia saw a proliferation of smaller brewers. The

Above: **William Penn was one of America's first well-known brewers.** *Below:* **A map of seventeenth-century New Amsterdam, highlighting the Netherlands West India Co Brewery.** *Right:* **George Washington was both a statesman and a home brewer who was especially fond of porter.**

first brewery recorded in Massachusetts had been that of a Captain Sedgewick in 1637. It was followed by Sergeant Baulston's in Rhode Island (1639). South of Virginia there was little brewing activity, although a dark beer made with molasses appeared in Georgia in the seventeenth century. In Massachusetts the legislature tried with little success to control its many small brewers, while in New York legislation was passed in 1700 to stimulate the local industry in the face of beers imported from England and from other colonies.

Technically, the beers brewed the English colonies and imported from the mother country were typical dark English top-fermented ales and stouts rather than the lighter, paler bottom-fermented beers favored on the continent. The typical commercial brewery in the early eighteenth century was roughly 70 by 50 feet in size with a copper brew kettle having about a 23-barrel capacity. Most of the output was indeed sold in barrels. Bottled beer had been imported on rare occasions in the seventeenth century, but it was not until after 1760 that any meaningful quantity of North American beer was bottled. Even then it was not until the next century that the domestic glass industry could support beer bottling on a wide scale.

The original draft beer that came to the colonies was drunk from black leather jugs known as 'black jacks.' By the 1600s in New Amsterdam and elsewhere these were replaced by pewter tankards of the type seen in Dutch genre paintings of the era. It was not until the eighteenth century that it became common for a beer drinker to enjoy his favorite beverage from a glass.

Throughout this period, as the means of brewing, marketing and drinking beer became more sophisticated, the classifications of beer remained roughly intact. Though the beers were all generally in the class of top-fermented brews (today called ales or stouts), they were rated by strength of alcohol content on a four-part scale. Their names give us

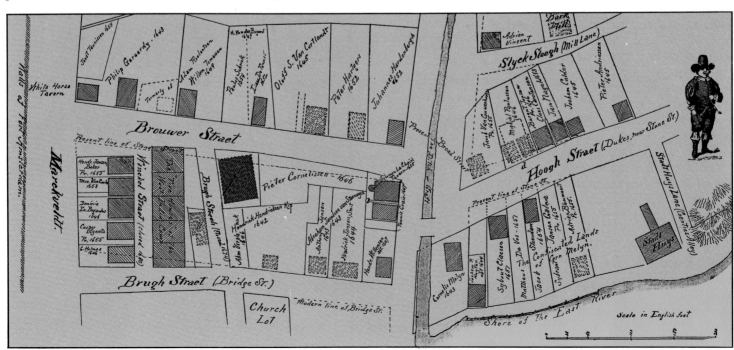

a good idea of how the grades were perceived: (1) small beer, (2) ship's beer, (3) table beer and (4) strong beer.

In 1720 another English top-fermented beer was introduced. Called 'porter' because it was favored by London porters, this new dark sweet beer was made with roasted unmalted barley. Despite its immediate popularity in England porter enjoyed only limited success in the colonies. It is worth mentioning, however, because it came to be the favorite drink of a certain officer in His Majesty's army during the latter third of the eighteenth century.

BEER AND THE
AMERICAN REVOLUTION

George Washington was but one of the fathers of the American Revolution who loved beer, but he was himself a brewer, and his recipe for small beer is still preserved in the New York Public Library. He also went out of his way to promote porter. Washington had a particular fondness for the porter brewed by a Mr Robert Hare of Philadelphia. Hare had arrived on the eve of the Revolution in Philadelphia where he began brewing the New World's first porter in 1774.

Above: In the Revolutionary War US warships confiscated beer from British supply ships. *Below:* Enjoying a beer before a warm fire in an early American home.

Above: During his term as president James Madison considered but rejected Joseph Coppinger's scheme to establish a government-run National Brewery.

In a July 1788 letter, the first president wrote to Clement Biddle in Philadelphia requesting 'a gross of Mr Hare's best bottled porter if the price is not much enhanced by the copious drafts you took of it!' Apparently Washington was satisfied because he ordered a second gross of porter two weeks later.

In 1790, Washington recommended Hare's porter as the 'best in Philadelphia,' indicating that other breweries were producing the beverage by that time. It is unfortunate to note that 1790 was also the year that Hare's brewery burned. Hare rebuilt immediately and took his son into the business in 1800. The Robert Hare & Son name survived Hare Sr's death in 1810 by seven years. The brewery was taken over by the Philadelphia brewing family of Frederick Gaul in 1824, and in 1869 it passed to John F Betz under whose name it survived (except during Prohibition) until 1939.

George Washington's affection for beer was not unmatched. Both Samuel Adams Jr and Samuel Adams Sr were well-known amateur brewers. The celebrated Boston Tea Party of 1773 was a milestone in the struggle against English taxation, but the affair might very well have happened three years earlier as a Boston Beer Party. In 1770 George Washington had joined with Patrick Henry, Richard Henry Lee and others in recommending a boycott of English beer imports in support of the American brewing industry. It was fortunate for Washington that Robert Hare arrived on the domestic scene a few years later, bringing with him the art of porter.

During the Revolutionary War, the Continental Congress actually specified a one-quart beer ration for the troops. With restrictions placed on other, harder alcoholic beverages during the winter of 1777–78, beer became even more popular. The British army in America contracted with London brewers to produce beer for their personnel, but American raiders intercepted the British supply ships at sea and captured much of this beer before it reached Cornwallis and his thirsty legions.

YEARS OF CHANGE AND THE NATIONAL BREWERY SCHEME

In 1770, America's founding fathers had called for a boycott of British beers. Fifteen years later, there were no more British beers to boycott and the American industry faced a sagging market alone. In 1789 Massachusetts began promoting the healthful qualities of its local beer and three years later New Hampshire, which had seen its first brewery established by Samuel Wentworth in 1670, made its brewers tax exempt. In 1796 James Boyd established a 4000-barrel brewery in Albany, New York that survived in one form or another until 1916.

It was against this backdrop that one of the most interesting characters in the history of early American brewing arrived on the scene. Joseph Coppinger arrived from England in 1802 ablaze with the same sort of entrepreneurial fire that drove so many nineteenth-century schemers and dreamers to the Western Hemisphere's first democracy. Among the baggage Coppinger brought to New York was an invention for processing meat and vegetables for preservation 'without the aid of salt,' the customary method of the day. Shortly after his arrival Coppinger wrote directly to President Thomas Jefferson requesting a patent for his invention. Jefferson replied personally telling him to apply for a patent, but apparently the idea went no farther.

Above: Thomas Jefferson brewed more beer than any other American president. Had he served for another term, the US might have had a National Brewery.

Eight years later James Madison was in the White House and another, even grander, scheme was brewing in the fertile mind of Joseph Coppinger who had spent several of the intervening years as a brewmaster at the Point Brewery in Pittsburgh. Coppinger proposed to Madison a National Brewery, a government agency whose purpose would be to brew beer. As he pointed out in his letter, 'The establishment of a brewing company in Washington as a national object, has in my view the greatest importance as it would unquestionably tend to improve the quality of our malt liquors in every point of the Union and serve to counteract one baneful influence of ardent spirits on the health and morals of our fellow citizens . . . .'

He went on to outline a plan for making the National Brewery self sustaining: 'I hesitate not to say that under prudent and good management 100 percent can be securely made on the active capital of $10,000, on all the beer, ale and porter which may be brewed for this company and disposed of in the cask; whilst that which may be sold in bottle will leave 200 percent.'

For a person to administer this new government agency (a secretary of the Brewery), he suggested a man who had 'followed the brewing trade for nearly twenty years in (which) time (having) built two breweries on

Left: An early American manor house with a home brewery attached at the right.

Right: John Molson began brewing in 1786 in Montreal. The Molson Brewery is North America's oldest brewing establishment.

(his) own account . . . two distinct establishments with success in both.' The man, of course, was Joseph Coppinger himself.

The Madison administration, consumed with other affairs of state, did not take up the idea, but the president shared the proposal with former president Jefferson who became an advocate of the idea. Despite the support of a highly regarded former president, the Coppinger plan was soon overshadowed by national concern for survival when the War of 1812 began. Though Coppinger raised the idea again after the war, it was clear that its time had passed. As for Coppinger himself, he went on to some notoriety as the author of the *American Brewer and Malster.* Published in 1815, it was one of the first major books on brewing published in America. One is left, however, to contemplate what might have been if the idea had been proposed a few years earlier when Jefferson was in the White House. Would amber bottles marked Brewery of the United States line our supermarket shelves today? Would the Brewmaster General hold a cabinet post? Would history have immortalized the first secretary of the Brewery as it had the first secretary of the Treasury: Hamilton on 10-dollar bills and Coppinger on 11-ounce beer bottles?

Thomas Jefferson, Coppinger's advocate, took more than a passing interest in the art of brewing. America's third president was a long-time beer drinker and even operated his own brewery on his estate at Monticello. With the help of Captain Joseph Miller, an English brewer stranded on this side of the Atlantic by the war, Jefferson began brewing in earnest in September 1813. By January 1814 Jefferson and Miller were ordering quart and half-gallon bottles by the gross, so the enterprise was evidently successful. Miller, however, seemed to have a bit of trouble keeping his mind on the project. At one point a cork-buying trip to Norfolk turned into a nine-month absence. Nevertheless, Jefferson seemed to take his friend's inattentiveness with a grain of salt, even once helping him to avoid deportation as a spy. Eventually the city lights got the best of Miller and he settled in Norfolk permanently where he began his own brewery in September 1815.

Meanwhile, farther north in Poughkeepsie, New York another famous name was successfully plying the brewer's trade. Matthew Vassar's father had operated a brewery in this city between 1798 and 1810 when it was destroyed by fire. Young Matthew rebuilt the Eagle Brewery in 1813 (some sources say 1810) and went on to develop a brewing empire that lasted until 1896 and which supplied the bankroll for the founding, in 1860, of the women's college in Poughkeepsie that bears Vassar's name.

Despite these activities, tastes were changing in the United States, and both the consumption and production of English-style beers was in decline. It was not until 1810 that the first official tally was made, but it was generally accepted that the figures represented a drop off since the days before the turn of the century. In 1810 there were recorded to be 132 breweries in the country (48 in Pennsylvania, 42 in New York and 13 in Ohio) but their total annual production of 185,000 barrels was less than some individual breweries in England. The Anchor Brewery in London, for example, brewed 235,100 barrels in 1810.

Between 1810 and 1820, a decade that straddled the War of 1812, American beer production collapsed to barely 10 percent of its earlier level. The drop had as much to do with changing tastes as it did with the war, and signaled an end to the English brewing tradition upon whose ashes a new American tradition would be born.

EARLY CANADIAN BREWERS

As the new United States was beginning to grapple with forming its identity as a nation, life continued as before in that vast tract of land to the north called British North America and which one day would be called Canada. Early home brewing had followed similar patterns in the more sparsely populated north, but the first big name in Canadian brewing was Mr John Molson. From the English county of Lincolnshire, Molson arrived in Montreal in 1782 armed with a copy of John Richardson's *Theoretical Hints on an Improved Practice of Brewing.* The people of Quebec, predominantly French, preferred wine, so there was little brewing tradition in this province. Since imported English beer sold for more than rum in Montreal, the city's beer drinkers welcomed John Molson's first brewery which began brewing in 1786. As Stephen Leacock would later say: 'Molson built his brewery a little

downstream from the town, close beside the river. Archeologists can easily locate the spot, as the brewery is still there.' In testament to John Molson's choice of sites, the Molson brewery celebrated its 200th anniversary in 1986 at the original location, though by that time there were Molson breweries in eight other Canadian cities from Vancouver to St John's.

During his first season Molson, along with his lady friend and co-worker Sarah Insley Vaughan, produced 4000 gallons of beer. Over the course of the next century, production increased 175-fold. The brewery formed the foundation upon which Molson built an empire that included Canada's first railroad (1836) and the Molson Bank (1855) which became part of the huge Bank of Montreal. Molson's brewery went on to share the success of his other ventures and today is one of the three largest brewers in Canada and its beer the second-largest-selling imported brand in the United States (after Holland's Heineken).

The second major Canadian brewer was Irishman Eugene O'Keefe of County Cork. He arrived in Canada in 1832 at age 5 and established himself as a brewer of ale and porter in 1862. O'Keefe was among the first to see a future in Canada for lager brewing and built such a brewery in Toronto in 1879. By the turn of the century, O'Keefe had built his operation into the largest brewery in Canada. O'Keefe eventually merged with the firm established in 1840 by Thomas Carling in Ontario, forming the Carling O'Keefe consortium, Canada's largest brewer, with brew-

Three great names in nineteenth-century Canadian brewing *(left to right):* John Carling, Eugene O'Keefe and John Labatt.

ing operations in England and the United States.

The third of Canada's three largest brewing companies was started in 1832 in London, Ontario by John Balkwell and sold to the Labatt & Eccles partnership in 1847. In 1866, upon the death of his father, John Labatt assumed control of the firm that still bears his name. Since then Labatt's breweries have been established in every Canadian province except Prince Edward Island.

NEW BREWING CENTERS IN THE UNITED STATES

When the nineteenth century began, New York and Philadelphia had been America's major brewing centers for over 150 years, but other cities were developing their own traditions, traditions that would help them challenge the primacy of the big eastern brewery towns. George Shiras had started Pittsburgh's first commercial brewery, the Point (that later employed Joseph Coppinger) in 1795, and the Embree brothers began Cincinnati's first in 1805. Jacques Delassus de St Vrain, a relative of the last lieutenant governor of Spanish Louisiana, is said to have established and operated the first commercial brewery in St Louis in 1810, but he may have been preceded by a Mr John Coons who is recorded as having operated a brewery in St Louis between 1809 and 1811. St Louis is important to the history of brewing because it is

now home to Anheuser-Busch, the company which became in the latter twentieth century the world's largest brewing empire. St Louis was not, however, the first city in Missouri to host a brewery. This distinction goes instead to the Sainte Genevieve, 50 miles down river, where Francois Colman, probably from Alsace, was brewing prior to 1779.

Farther north, in 1833 William Lill & Company became the first commercial brewery in Chicago, another city destined to become a major brewing center. Until that time Chicago's tavern owners brewed their own stocks. Lill's Company, determined to change the pattern, brewed 600 barrels of ale during the first year and went on to be a major part of Chicago's brewing history for the next 40 years. Even after the lager revolution that swept the Midwest a few years later, Lill and partner Michael Diversey continued to brew ale and porter until an 1871 fire destroyed the brewery.

In 1829 a young German brewer named David Yuengling established a small brewery on North Center Street in Pottsville, Pennsylvania, a town noted for its mountain spring water. The event was notable not because it was the first brewery in Pottsville (many small towns throughout eastern Pennsylvania were getting their first breweries during this period) but because, while the other breweries soon faded from the scene and were replaced by newer breweries who would themselves fade, the Yuengling Brewery continued. It survived the consolidations of the end of the nineteenth century, it survived Prohibition

The brewery premises of Howard and Fuller in Brooklyn. Ale and porter dominated American brewing until 1840.

and it survives today as the oldest brewery in the United States. It is still owned by the Yuengling family. While Canada's (and North America's) oldest brewer, Molson, went on to become one of the continent's largest brewers with national as well as international distribution, Yuengling remained a relatively small, family-owned brewery content with regional distribution.

THE LAGER REVOLUTION

Brewing in North America, the Indian tradition not withstanding, had begun with the arrival of the first settlers and grew steadily until the American Revolution, after which the growth cycle came to an end. Despite the establishment of new breweries over a wider geographical area, production began to decline. Between 1812 and 1840 as tastes changed, the market for English style ales and porters dropped off, and the American brewing industry declined dramatically.

In 1840, however, a Bavarian brewer named Johann Wagner ar-rived in Philadelphia with the most important innovation since the American brewing industry had begun more than two centuries before. The arrival of Johann Wagner in Philadelphia was to the history of American brewing what the invention of the automobile was to the history of travel.

What Wagner brought with him was a bottom-fermenting yeast that was to soon make Munich, in his native Bavaria, the world's beer capital. The bottom-fermenting yeast not only revived the American brewing industry but made it the biggest in the world.

Lager was the right beer at the right time. It found an immediate popularity with the American public that persists to this day. It has, in fact, become the beer of choice throughout the entire world, with the notable exception of England, where top-fermented beers still hold sway. For the most part lagers are clear and pale, ranging from amber to light gold, whereas ales and stouts are darker, thicker and less transparent. Lager yeast is active at temperatures down to freezing. Lager beers, especially in the United States, are drunk cold, while the English still drink their brews at room temperature, a practice that some Americans find hard to believe. This difference in habit led English humorist John Cleese to parody the American view of English beer as 'nasty warm sticky stuff with odd forms of pond life growing in it.'

In 1840 the golden lagers were just beginning to come into fashion in the area where lager was born, that central European golden triangle whose area encompassed both Bavaria and parts of the Austria-Hungarian Empire, and whose corners lay at Munich, Vienna and Pilsen (now in Czechoslovakia) near Prague. The beers that came forth from this region included the amber Munich beers as well as the especially light and pale Pilsen beers, or Pilseners. Wagner, having little comprehension of the scope of what he

had done, simply brewed small quantities for limited distribution. It took George Manger, who bought some of Wagner's yeast, to set up Philadelphia's (and America's) first commercial lager brewery. By 1844 there were several lager breweries in Philadelphia and lager brewing had spread to other cities. In the years leading up to 1848, the revolution and unrest that swept Germany and much of central Europe resulted in a massive wave of emigration from this region to the United States. Among the emigres were the brewers who would change the face of American brewing and ensure that lager would be its dominant feature.

THE TOWN THAT MADE AMERICAN BREWING FAMOUS

Probably no town is more often identified with the American brewing industry than Milwaukee, Wisconsin. While the beer of the Joseph Schlitz company would be described as 'the beer that made Mil-

Above, left to right: **Joseph Schlitz, Valentin Blatz and Frederick Pabst.** *Below and previous page:* **Early Pabst brewery wagons. The scene below shows the early morning routine in the shipping yards in 1900. Pabst was one of the breweries that put Milwaukee on the map, and at the turn of the century was the nation's largest.**

waukee famous,' it was not alone. The fact that so many major breweries evolved there is what probably accounts for Milwaukee's fame. Nearly 75 breweries came and went over the years. There were four giants whose German brewmasters made Milwaukee into America's brewing capital. These included the empire of Joseph Schlitz, of course, but also Valentin Blatz, Frederic Miller and Captain Frederick Pabst as well.

Among those who established the first Milwaukee breweries in 1840 were Richard Owens, William Pawlett and John Davis. Davis's Milwaukee Brewery eventually became

Powell's Ale and survived until 1880. Other early brewers included Stolz and Krill, whose brewery evolved into the Falk, Jung & Borchert Brewing Company and lasted until 1892, and Herman Reuthlisberger, whose German brewery eventually became the South Side Brewery which closed in 1886. The Eagle Brewery was founded in 1841 and was followed by the brewery of Conrad Muntzenberger in 1842; they survived until 1867 and 1847, respectively.

The first brewery that evolved into one of the big four was the Empire Brewery established on Chestnut Street in 1844 by Jacob Best and his four sons, Charles, Lorenz, Jacob Jr

Above, left to right: **Jacob Best, whose Empire Brewery eventually became the Pabst Brewing Co, Philip Best and Frederic Miller. The Plank Road Brewery *(below)* was built in 1850 by Charles Best, son of Jacob, and bought out by Frederic Miller in 1853 for $8000. Miller's eventually became the world's second-largest brewing company.**

and Phillip. Phillip Best, serving as brewmaster for his father, made the first lager to be brewed in Milwaukee in 1851. Two years later Jacob Best retired, selling his shares to Phillip and Jacob Jr, as Charles and Lorenz had departed from the family firm to start their own brewery in 1850. Phillip Best took over full ownership of the Empire Brewery in 1860. Four

years later he took on a new partner, the husband of his daughter Maria, a former Great Lakes steamship captain named Frederick Pabst. Best sold out his interest in the Empire Brewery in 1866 to Captain Pabst and another son-in-law, Emil Schandein, who soon faded from the scene. In 1873 the brewery was incorporated, using the Phillip Best name, and in 1889 it became the Pabst Brewing Company. By that time, the annual output of the brewery was 585,300 barrels.

The second of Milwaukee's big four was begun as the City Brewery by Johann Braun. Five years later Braun died and his widow married a

This vintage metal tray shows the old Joseph Schlitz brewery in Milwaukee with exquisite and intricate detail.

24

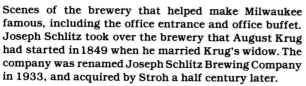

THE BEER
THAT MADE
MILWAUKEE
FAMOUS

Scenes of the brewery that helped make Milwaukee famous, including the office entrance and office buffet. Joseph Schlitz took over the brewery that August Krug had started in 1849 when he married Krug's widow. The company was renamed Joseph Schlitz Brewing Company in 1933, and acquired by Stroh a half century later.

former employee named Valentin Blatz who took over the brewery. The Valentin Blatz Brewing Company grew into one of Milwaukee's majors and between 1889 and 1911 was affiliated with Michael Brand's United States Brewing Company of Chicago. In 1958, 107 years after Valentin Blatz had gone to the altar with the widow of Johann Braun, the company was purchased by Pabst. The following year, the Blatz name was eliminated and the big four became three.

The third in the order of their founding was Schlitz, perhaps the most famous name of all. In 1856 Joseph Schlitz married the widow of brewer August Krug, the man whom Schlitz had served as bookkeeper. It is an interesting coincidence that the men who built two of America's greatest brewing empires had entered the business by marrying their boss's widows in the same town within the space of five years. The brewery that August Krug had started in 1849 retained his name until 1858 when it became the Joseph Schlitz Brewery. The company was

incorporated under Schlitz's name in 1874 and continued as such until 1920 when it was renamed the Joseph Schlitz Beverage Company for the duration of Prohibition. Joseph Schlitz himself was lost at sea in 1875 during a trip back to his native Germany. Reconstituted as the Joseph Schlitz Brewing Company in 1933, the brewery continued to brew the 'beer that made Milwaukee famous' until 1982 when it was purchased by the smaller Stroh Brewing Company of Detroit. Of the original big four there were now two.

The last of the great Milwaukee breweries was started by Charles Best, son of Jacob Best whose original brewery evolved into the Pabst empire. Charles Best started his brewery in Wauwatosa just west of the Milwaukee city limits in 1850. He named it the Plank Road Brewery, presumably a reference to the practice of putting planks or timbers in a muddy roadway to prevent wagon wheels from getting stuck in the mud. In 1852, the Plank Road Brewery was the first Milwaukee brewery to export beer to New York. Charles

took his brother Lorenz Best into the firm in 1851, and in 1855 (some sources say 1853) it was sold to a young German brewer named Frederic Miller. Miller's Plank Road Brewery officially became the Menomonee Valley Brewery in 1878, though both names had been used since the days when the Best brothers owned the company. The brewery was incorporated under Frederic Miller's name within Milwaukee's city limits in 1888, although his first name was dropped in 1920, and has remained so until the present. Over the years Miller Brewing became the number two brewer in the United States, second only to Anheuser-Busch. Interestingly, in 1985 Miller began to test market an unpasteurized draft-style beer under the old Plank Road name that had been abandoned, like the muddy streets of Wauwatosa, over a century before.

Below: **A Schlitz beer wagon decked out for a parade, possibly the Fourth of July. The driver is dressed like Uncle Sam, but the man tending the horses wears a strange uniform. The old dray wagons are now a part of Milwaukee folklore.**

Immigrants from central Europe's golden triangle — the region including Munich, Vienna and Pilsen (near Prague) — brought with them the art of lager brewing in the 1850s. Terms like 'Bavarian,' 'Bohemian' and 'Pilsner' came to stand for quality in beer. These immigrants also introduced beer gardens to Americans as a place to sit down with friends to enjoy a stein of one's favorite lager.

Far right: Bernard Stroh came to the United States from Germany in the 1840s to settle in Detroit, where he established the Stroh Brewery Company in 1850. *Far right below:* Like other immigrant brewers from Europe, he began producing a beer that was lighter than the ales being brewed up to then and known as Bohemian beer. To distinguish his brand, he adapted the ancient crest of Bohemia, a gold lion on a red background. In 1893 Stroh's Bohemian beer won a blue ribbon at the Columbian exposition and became a regional favorite.

THE LAGER REVOLUTION SPREADS

Lager brewing in America began in Philadelphia and made Milwaukee famous, but it spread throughout the rest of the continent as well. Lager came to New York City, America's original brewing capital, in 1842 upon the arrival of Maximillian and Frederick Schaefer. They had that year acquired the brewery of Sebastian Sommers on Broadway near West Eighteenth Street. In 1849 after a brief four-year stint on Manhattan's West Side, the Schaefers moved the brewery uptown to Fourth Avenue (later Park Avenue) near East Fiftieth Street, where it remained until 1916. During this period the Schaefer Brewery was to become one of the largest and most important breweries in the eastern United States.

Meanwhile, John Huck and John Schneider started Chicago's first lager brewery in 1847, and the windy city was on its way to becoming Milwaukee's major rival in the Midwest.

By the end of the 1850s German immigrants made up a large part of the population in many of America's major cities. Lager breweries and German-style beer gardens both proliferated. The beer gardens, with their bands, dancing, food and garden-like atmosphere, became major entertainment centers for German-Americans of all ages. A Sunday afternoon at the beer garden was a popular form of family entertainment throughout the balance of the nineteenth century and the first decade of the twentieth.

German immigration was by no means limited to New York and the cities of the north and east. San Antonio, Texas had a large enough German population to support several German-language newspapers and several lager breweries. The first of these was William Menger's Western Brewery in 1855, but it also included those of William Esser (1874), J B Behloradsky (1881), Felix Bachrach (1890) and Lorenz Ochs and George Aschbacher (1890).

Between 1857 and 1860 the sales of lager beer in the United States

Above: Bernard Stroh and *(right)* Stroh bottles over the years. This Bohemian-style beer is still brewed over a direct fire.

Below: Frederick Schaefer bought his former employer's brewery in New York and set up F & M Schaefer with his brother Maximillian. They were pioneers of lager beer.

equaled the sales of all other types of beer. By the Civil War, lager had become America's unsurpassed favorite. In 1850 there had been 431 breweries in the United States producing 23 million gallons of beer annually. By 1860 there were 1269 breweries producing over 30 million gallons—most of them lager.

During the Civil War, the Union troops went into the field without the beer ration that had accompanied their grandfathers in 1776. The beer ration, which became a liquor ration after 1893, was eliminated by Secretary of War Lewis Cass in 1832 in deference to the growing temperance movement. Nevertheless, the German brewers, who were located

primarily in the North, were generally pro-Union. In 1861 the Internal Revenue System was established to finance the war, and the following year a one dollar tax was levied on each barrel of beer produced in the United States. In response to government taxation and the temperance movement, 37 breweries in New York City came together in 1862 to form the industry's first trade organization, which became known as the United States Brewers' Association in 1864.

ANHEUSER-BUSCH

As a major brewing center in the 1860s, St Louis, Missouri was certainly eclipsed in importance by Milwaukee, Philadelphia, New York, Chicago and even San Francisco. However, the huge brewery that developed from the little firm originally started on Carondelet Avenue in 1852 by George Schneider has forever earned St Louis a place in the pages of American brewing history. In 1857 Schneider, like so many small brewers throughout history, realized that he could not compete. He sold his little Bavarian Brewery to Adam and Phillip Carl Hammer, who were underwritten by a loan from a wealthy St Louis soap maker named Eberhard Anheuser. By 1860, when the brewery once again verged on collapse, Anheuser realized he needed to take direct control of operations in order to protect his investment. The firm became known as E Anheuser & Company's Bavarian Brewery. Within a year after Anheuser entered the brewing business, his daughter Lily Anheuser married a 22-year-old brewery supply salesman named Adolphus Busch. In 1864 Busch joined his father-in-law's firm as a salesman. In 1875 the Bavarian Brewery name was dropped and the brewery became E Anheuser and Company's Brewing Association. In 1879 it became the Anheuser-Busch Brewing Association. The following year, upon the death of Eberhard Anheuser, Busch became the president, having been a full partner since 1869.

Busch was brewing's first marketing genius. He was not the first to dream of an American national beer, but he was

Left: **The Anheuser-Busch brewery in St Louis, once the largest single brewhouse in North America.** *Right:* **An early advertising sign for the Anheuser-Busch 'Brewing Association' featuring the A & Eagle trademark adopted in 1872.**

Adolphus Busch *(above)* and his empire. An early view *(below)* of the St Louis brewhouse and delivery wagons. Iced 'beer cars' *(far right)* being loaded for long-distance shipment. Busch started Manufacturers Railway Co in 1877 using refrigerator cars to expand his market. Brewmasters *(far right below)* pose proudly.

the first to realize it. Until Busch's time the American brewing scene was composed only of local and regional brewers. A large brewer might have customers in a neighboring state, but for the most part local demand was satisfied by a local brewer. Cities with large beer-consuming populations, such as Milwaukee or Chicago, could, and did, support several sizable breweries.

St Louis was a mid-sized town with a fairly good market for beer, but nothing compared to the above mentioned cities or Philadelphia or New York. Some men would have been content to be the part owner of a successful, medium-sized brewery in such a town, but not Adolphus Busch. Even before becoming president, he launched a vigorous advertising campaign and formed a wide distribution network. He established a network of railside ice houses to keep long distance shipments of beer cool and fresh. In 1877

he was the first brewer to ship his brew in refrigerated rail cars, and later he helped pioneer the pasteurization of beer.

Busch dreamed of a national beer, a brew specially designed to appeal to people of all walks of life throughout the United States. Along with his friend Carl Conrad, Busch created such a beer (a lager, of course), which was introduced in 1876, the centennial of United States independence.

Busch and Conrad considered the recipe and the name of their 'people's beer' carefully. The most popular brews of the day were those brewed in the manner of the lagers of central Europe's golden triangle (Munich-Vienna-Pilsen). Many breweries produced brand names that alluded to that region. Indeed, the Anheuser-Busch Brewery had begun as George Schneider's 'Bavarian' Brewery. Of the golden lagers, the pale ones from the Pilsen corner of the triangle, the Pil-

sens, epitomized for Busch and Conrad the style they wanted, and in 1876 Adolphus Busch's Budweiser brand was born.

It has been suggested that the Budweiser name was inspired specifically by the small Bohemian brewing town of Budweis (now Ceske Budejovice, Czechoslovakia), but no documentation exists to support this supposition. According to an 1894 letter from Adolphus Busch to trademark attorney Rowland Cox, he selected the Budweiser name 'because it was easily pronounceable by Americans and was not the name of any beer then sold in America.'

Budweiser has not only survived as a brand name, it has prospered. Today Budweiser is the biggest-selling single brand in the United States and in the world—the flagship of Anheuser-Busch, the world's biggest brewer. For Adolphus Busch, the master brewer and master marketer who dared to dream the big dreams, two dreams came true.

Left and right: scenes from the original Anheuser-Busch Brewery in St Louis. *Below:* A vintage metal tray.

BREWING IN CHICAGO

The Windy City has had more local breweries (190) than any city west of Philadelphia, but has never seen the rise of a major national brewery. Perhaps because of Chicago's proximity to Milwaukee or because, like New York, it had such a large number of beer drinkers within its environs, its brewers never thought of a broader market.

In 1833 William Lill had been the first to brew beer commercially, while Huck & Schneider's Eagle Brewery brewed Chicago's first commercial lager in 1847. More than 20 breweries opened their doors in Chicago in the 1850s, and while many did not survive the 1860s, there were at least two new breweries opening for every one that closed. In Chicago, as in the other major cities throughout the United States, the quarter century following the end of the Civil War was a golden age for American brewing.

Among the early Chicago brewers was Valentin Busch, who is sometimes incorrectly mistaken for Valentin Blatz or a relative of Adolphus Busch. Busch started his brewery in 1851 and joined forces with Michael Brand in 1858. Brand is best known for his own brewery which he started in 1878, the year before Busch & Brand Brewing was closed. Brand changed the name of his company to the United States Brewing Company of Chicago in 1889, and in 1890, it became part of Milwaukee & Chicago Breweries Ltd, a British syndicate that owned breweries in both cities, including an interest in the brewery of Valentin Blatz.

Michael Brand's United States Brewing continued to operate with that name, even under British ownership, until Prohibition. In 1932, it re-emerged as United States Brewing and survived until 1955.

Frederick Wacker entered the Chicago brewing world in 1857 as a partner in the former Blattner & Seidenschwanz Brewery. Wacker & Seidenschwanz became Wacker & Company the following year. In 1882, Wacker joined forces with Jacob Birk to form Wacker & Birk Brewing & Malting, a firm that survived until 1918.

One of the more colorful Chicago brewing histories tells of the brewery started by Joseph Jerusalem at the foot of Elm Street in 1868. Twenty years later, ownership was shifted to Ms Ulrike Jerusalem. In 1891, the brewery was owned by Gustav Eberlein who operated it until 1903. In that year the name of Gustav Eberlein was replaced by Ulrike Eberlein, who operated the Eberlein Weiss Beer Brewery until 1908. It appears that Ulrike outlived two husbands in the 40-year history of the brewery.

When Prohibition ended in 1933, 15 breweries reopened in Chicago out of the dozens that had been there during turn of the century heyday. For a quarter century, the number remained relatively constant, but by 1963 consolidations had brought the number of Chicago breweries down to only seven. By the 1970s only the Peter Hand Brewery on North Avenue remained. By 1978, it too was gone. Chicago's last remaining brewery, its last reminder of the great brewing days of the 1890s, had closed after 87 years in business.

BREWING IN THE UPPER MIDWEST

Among the states of the upper plains sitting astride the richest grain-growing region on earth there is a distinct paucity of brewing history. The relatively sparse population and an inclination toward stringent local prohibition allowed Iowa, Kansas, Nebraska and the Dakotas a bare handful of brewers. Even the state of Missouri beyond St Louis boasted only Kansas City as a brewing center, and Kansas City, despite its fun-loving reputation, has hosted just 16 breweries in its history compared to 102 in St Louis.

South Dakota, wracked by prohibitionist fervor from time to time (notably from 1889 to 1896), managed to attract immense talent in the person of Moritz Levinger. Bavarian by birth, Levinger learned the brewing art at Munich's great Spaten brewery and immigrated to the United States in 1869 at age 18. Having worked for both Philip Schaefer and Jacob Ruppert in New York City, he came west to South Dakota where he established the Sioux Falls Brewing and Malting Company. One of only 26 breweries established in South Dakota's history, Sioux Falls Brewing (the 'Malting' was dropped in 1912) survived until Prohibition but an attempt to reopen the establish-

ABE KLEE & SON

DEALERS IN

DRIVING, HEAVY DRAFT, FINE COACH and SADDLE

HORSES

OUR SPECIALTY

BREWERY HORSES

From 150 to 200 Head Constantly on Hand

270-274 NORTH CENTER AVENUE

Long Distance
Phone Monroe 1006 **CHICAGO, ILL.** Cable Address "KLEESON"

REFERENCES:

Conrad Seipp Brewing Co.	United States Express Co.
City Brewing Co.	Swift & Co.
K. G. Schmidt Brewing Co.	H. W. Hoyt & Co.
Atlas Brewing Co.	Deering Harvester Co.
West Side Brewing Co.	United States Brewing Co.
Gambrinus Brewing Co.	Monarch Brewing Co.
Citizens Brewing Co.	Wacker & Birk Brewing Co.
National Brewing Co.	Bartholomae & Roesing Brewing Co.
Marshall Field & Co.	
Montgomery Ward & Co.	Pabst Brewing Co.
Carson, Pirie, Scott & Co.	Chicago Brewing Co.
Anheuser-Busch Brewing Co.	Seattle Brewing & Malting Co. of
McAvoy Brewing Co.	Seattle, Wash.
P. Schoenhofen Brewing Co.	American Express Co.
Star Brewing Co.	Libby, McNeil & Libby.
Val. Blatz Brewing Co.	Steele, Wedeles & Co.
Standard Brewing Co.	New York Biscuit Co.
Fred Miller Brewing Co.	Sunset Brg. Co., Wallace, Idaho.
R.H.Graupner Br'y,Harrisburg,Pa.	John Kazmaier Br'y, Altoona, Pa.
Altoona Brewery, Altoona, Pa.	AND MANY OTHERS

Left: **Companies like that of Frank Headen supplied the necessary brewing equipment.**

Above: **Horses, a necessity in the early days, are now used only in promotions.**

ment in 1934 failed. In fact, of five breweries started in South Dakota in 1934, only one survived the first year. Dakota Brewing of Huron (originally established in 1884) survived until 1942. In North Dakota, by comparison, 17 breweries were started between 1874 and 1890, and all of them had gone out of business by the turn of the century. Aside from the East Grand Forks Brewing Company which opened and closed in the town of the same name in 1910, only one brewery operated in the state in the twentieth century. This was Dakota Brewing & Malting which produced its brew in Bismarck from 1961 to 1965.

Among the states of the upper Midwest, Minnesota, with a large German population and ice-cold winters ideal for lager brewing, stands out as the most important to American brewing history. Though overshad-

owed by neighboring Wisconsin with 542 breweries throughout its history, Minnesota has had 210 compared to a total of 102 for Nebraska and the Dakotas combined. Historically, most of Minnesota's brewing activity took place within a triangle between New Ulm, Rochester and the twin cities of Minneapolis/St Paul. The Twin Cities, however, are the true brewing capital of this section of the United States and have traditionally boasted more breweries than any other city between Milwaukee and Seattle. If Minneapolis/ St Paul are the region's premier brewing center, then the establishment started by Theodore Hamm would have to be, along with that of Jacob Schmidt, one of the Twin Cities' premier breweries. Hamm was born in Baden, Germany in 1825 and immigrated to St Paul in 1856. Nine years later he bought the

Above: The premises of the Jacob Schmidt Brewing Company in St Paul Minnesota. *Right:* The Grain Belt Brewery in Minneapolis, Minnesota as it appeared in 1948,

an ideal name for a brewery in the Midwest. The brewery actually started out as John Orth's Brewery in 1850 and went through a series of several name changes over the

years. *Below:* A Stroh Brewing Company wagon photographed at the Detroit brewery in 1885 together with Stroh drivers and their Labrador mascot.

Above: Theodore Hamm created the Theodore Hamm Brewing Co that was eventually bought out by Pabst. *Left:* Hamm's employees c 1910 fill the brew kettle with hops. *Below:* The famous Hamm's bear.

Pittsburgh Brewery of St Paul which had been started by Andrew Keller in 1860. By the turn of the century, the Theodore Hamm Brewing Company was producing a half-million barrels of beer annually. The company survived Prohibition and continued as a major regional brewer in the north . plains and mountain states. Its brands Burgie and Buckhorn were important trademarks, but the Hamm's brand and the Hamm's cartoon bear were veritable icons for several generations of beer drinkers. The Hamm's slogan 'from the land of sky blue waters' conjured up images of Minnesota with its

many sparkling lakes. Starting in 1975, however, the Hamm's bear very nearly became extinct as Hamm's sky blue waters transformed in the rapids of a corporate ownership shuffle. In that year, the Theodore Hamm Brewing company was purchased by Olympia Brewing of Tumwater, Washington, which was in turn taken over by Pabst in 1983. First Olympia, then Pabst, chose to retain the Hamm's brand, and the familiar Hamm's bear had a new lease on life.

BREWING IN THE SOUTH

No region of North America has had fewer breweries in its history than the states of the confederacy. Alabama, Georgia and the Carolinas have had a combined total of only 40 breweries throughout their entire histories, and Mississippi stands as the only American state to have never had a commercial brewery. Florida also fitted this mold until after World War II when large-scale brewing began in the state. Kentucky, Tennessee and the Virginias have all had a relatively larger number of breweries than the other southern states, and indeed it was in Virginia that European-style beer was first brewed in North America.

The South's two major brewing cities are located at opposite ends of the region. Louisville, Kentucky is located across the river from Indiana and a short distance from Ohio, which are both states with a large German population. Its opposite, New Orleans, is located deep in the heart of Dixie. New Orleans, with its rich cosmopolitan history, has always been an exception to any rule drawn about the South. There have been 24 breweries in New Orleans compared to just four in the rest of the state of Louisiana, and two of those four were operated for less than a year without permits.

The first brewery in New Orleans and one of the first in the South was started about 1850 by George Merz at Villere and Toulouse streets. This establishment evolved into the New Orleans Brewing Association's Southern Brewery but it finally closed in 1900. Of the seven New Orleans breweries that survived Prohibition, four were gone by 1965. The Jackson brewery, home of the popular Jax Beer, closed its doors in

Below: An early view showing the old world ambience of the G Heileman office and bottling plant in La Crosse, Wisconsin. Legend has it that Gottlieb Heileman won the brewery in a coin toss with his partner John Gund. As part of the same 1872 transaction, Gund is said to have taken possesion of the bakery that the two had owned.

1974 leaving only the Falstaff Brewery on Gavier Street and the Dixie Brewing Company on Tulane Street. Dixie Beer, the only surviving indigenous Louisiana beer, found increasing popularity as Louisiana's cajun/creole cuisine came into vogue in the 1980s.

BREWING IN THE WEST

Prior to the Civil War the vast majority of the population of the United States was located east of the Mississippi River. With the exception of San Francisco no large cities existed in the West. The major towns such as Denver, Portland, Sacramento and Butte were tiny by eastern standards. Not until the purchase of the Oregon Country from Britain in 1846 and the Mexican cession of California and the Southwest two years later did the present western United States actually became part of the United States.

Founded as a Spanish mission in 1776, San Francisco was populated largely by Americans even before California was given statehood. The gold rush of 1849 turned it into the West's first metropolis as well as the West's major brewing center. Beer may have been brewed in San Francisco as early as 1837, and the city certainly had at least one commercial brewery by 1849.

Outside of San Francisco the first commercial brewery in the West was probably the City Brewery started in 1852 by Henry Saxer in Portland, Oregon Territory. Five years later, a young German brewer named Henry Weinhard arrived in Fort Vancouver, Washington across the Columbia River from Portland where he became involved in the Muench Brewery. In 1859 he became the proprietor of the Muench Brewery, and in 1862 he bought Saxer's City Brewery as well. Two years later he sold his Vancouver interest to Anton Young and moved his entire operation to Portland. Over the years these two breweries would grow to become two of the West's most important brewers. The Vancouver operation grew to become the Lucky Lager Brewery, which became affili-

ated with General Brewing in 1964. It in turn became part of the Falstaff brewing empire (under the General name) in 1975. Henry Weinhard's City Brewery became the Henry Weinhard Brewery in 1904 and the Blitz-Weinhard company in 1928. The Blitz-Weinhard Company was purchased by Pabst Brewing in 1979, which in turn was purchased by Heileman Brewing in 1983. The Blitz-Weinhard name, however, continued as a brand name in regional distribution, and Henry Weinhard's name was revived in the late 1970s for a premium beer called Henry Weinhard's Private Reserve which developed a strong following on the West Coast.

The Oregon-Washington area became the West's second major population center. When the Civil War began, for example, only Oregon and California, amid the territories of the far west, had achieved statehood. It was only natural, then, that this area would begin to develop a brewing industry. From the original center in the Portland-Vancouver area the major interest in breweries spread north toward Seattle, although Emil Meyer began his City Brewery in the eastern Washington city of Walla Walla as early as 1855. Both Anton Mueller and Wolf Shafer started breweries in Steilacoom, Washington in 1874, and Martin Schneig, George Cantierri and Stuart Crichton all started breweries in Seattle the same year, although Steilacoom and Seattle may have had their first breweries in 1858 and 1864, respectively.

The year 1874 was important not just in the Seattle area but in the

Henry Weinhard *(above left)* and Adolph Coors *(above right)* both started major brewing companies in the West that survive today. Henry Weinhard bought into the oldest western brewery outside of San Francisco and made it his own. It became Oregon's major brewery and today produces a private reserve premium beer named for Weinhard *(above)*. The Coors brewery became the largest brewing company in the West and the largest single-site brewery in the world. The first mechanical refrigerating unit *(right)* was installed in the Coor's plant in 1890.

area south of Portland-Vancouver as well. In that year breweries were opened for the first time in an incredibly large number of Oregon cities including Albany, Astoria, Baker, Corvallis, Eugene, Oakland and Salem to name just a few. There were in fact two breweries opened in the state capital of Salem in 1874, as well as three in Portland.

As the discovery of gold in California led to the discovery of mineral wealth elsewhere in the West, mining towns proliferated throughout the Sierra Nevada and soon throughout the Rockies. Colorado evolved as the major territory straddling the spine of the Rockies, and Denver became Colorado's commercial hub and in 1859 the home of its first brewery. This brewery, established by F Z Solomon and Charles Tascher on Seventh Street, was appropriately called the Rocky Mountain Brewery. Acquired by Philip Zang in 1870, it was renamed for Zang 10 years later. The Philip Zang Brewery survived until Prohibition, and was very briefly revived during 1934.

Though bustling Denver was by no means a one-horse town in the 1860s, it did have a One Horse Brew-

ery which was started by Louis Hessner and Henry Graff in 1864 and operated by a succession of owners for eight years. Other early breweries in the area included Moritz Sigl's Colorado Brewery in Denver (1864) and those of Paul Lindstrom in Empire (1862), Conrad Elliot in Chase Gulch (1862), William Lehmkuhl in Central City (1866), Rudolf Koenig in Golden (1868), Henry Weiss in Pueblo (1868), Otto Boche in Silver Plume (1869) and Vincent Albus in Trinidad (1869).

Few of these early breweries started in the 1860s survived the 1870s. Some did not survive the 1860s. In 1873, however, a man arrived who not only survived, but put Colorado permanently on the brewing map of the United States. Adolph Coors was born in 1847 at Barmen, Prussia (now Wuppertal, Germany). At the age of 15 he began his apprenticeship at the brewery of Henry Wenker in Dortmund. In 1868, having worked for three years at breweries in Berlin, Kassel and Velzen, the 21-year-old Coors immigrated to the United States. By the following year he had worked his way to Naperville, Illinois where he got a job as foreman at the Stenger Brewery and where he stayed until the end of 1871. For Coors, as for so many young men of the time, the West represented the promise of a rewarding (or at least adventurous) future, and 1872 found him enroute to Colorado. In Denver, young Adolph invested his savings in a bottling company and within a year he was advertising himself as a dealer in 'bottled beer, ale, porter, cider, imported and domestic wines and seltzer water.'

50

Below: The Coors brewery in 1884, eleven years after it was founded. Eventually huge red brick brewery buildings (as shown in the 1900 lithograph on pages 54-55) replaced the early wood and stone ones. The mountain above the Coors plant became part of the company's early trademark *(far right)*.

Eager to get out of the bottling business and back into the business of brewing the beer to fill the bottles, Coors decided to start a brewery. He persuaded one of his customers, Jacob Schueler, a Denver ice cream and candy tycoon, to invest $18,000 in the idea, and Coors himself added $2000. They purchased an old tannery by a stream in nearby Golden, Colorado and converted it into a brewery. Before the end of 1873, their Golden Brewery was in business, and within a year it had turned a profit. Seven years later Coors bought Schueler's share of the business, which then became the Adolph Coors Golden Brewery. Between 1880 and 1890, the output of Coors' brewery increased from 3500 barrels annually to 17,600. Ten years later output increased to 48,000 barrels per year. The brewery survived Prohibition, becoming the Adolph Coors Company in 1933, and went on to become the largest single-site brewing company in the world.

Texas, for its size, has had relatively fewer breweries in its history than many other states—fewer than Oregon, Washington, Colorado or even Idaho. California has had four times as many, and even Missouri has had more than twice as many. San Antonio, where William Menger started the first brewery in Texas (the Western Brewery, 1855), became the state's original brewing center mainly because of its large German population. It was in San

The Kessler Brewery *(below)* in Helena, Montana was founded by Charles Beehrer in 1864 and purchased by Nick Kessler in 1866. It eventually became Montana's foremost brewery. The Montana Brewing Co *(right)* in Great Falls was established by Andrew Johnson in 1891 and went out of business in 1950.

Antonio that the Lone Star State's two most important and well known breweries were founded. The first, appropriately named Lone Star Brewing Company, was started by none other than Adolphus Busch in 1884. Busch started the brewery as an early effort in multisite diversification that also led him to invest in breweries in Fort Worth, Texas and Shreveport, Louisiana, all of which produced beer under their own labels rather than Busch's Budweiser label. Otto Koehler, the man hired by Busch to manage Lone Star, later moved to the San Antonio Brewing Association, the brewery originally started by J B Behloradsky in 1881. San Antonio Brewing became Pearl Brewing in 1952; its brand became one of Texas's majors and survives today under the ownership of General Brewing.

Lone Star, which was divested by Busch and went through a succession of other names between 1918 and 1940 before becoming Lone Star again, evolved with an image that was almost synonymous with the lifestyle of the Lone Star State. Still known as the 'National Beer of Texas.' Lone Star was bought by Olympia Brewing in 1976 and then sold to Heileman in 1983.

Few states have had more breweries or more brewing centers for the size of their populations than Montana. Thomas Smith established Montana's first brewery at Virginia City in 1863, the year before Montana became a territory. In 1874 Helena replaced Virginia City as the capital and the commercial hub of the new territory, and in 1883 the Northern Pacific Railroad linked the state's rich mining towns with the rest of the world. By that time, breweries had been established at Bannack, Billings Blackfoot, Bozeman, Butte, Deer Lodge, Fort Benton,

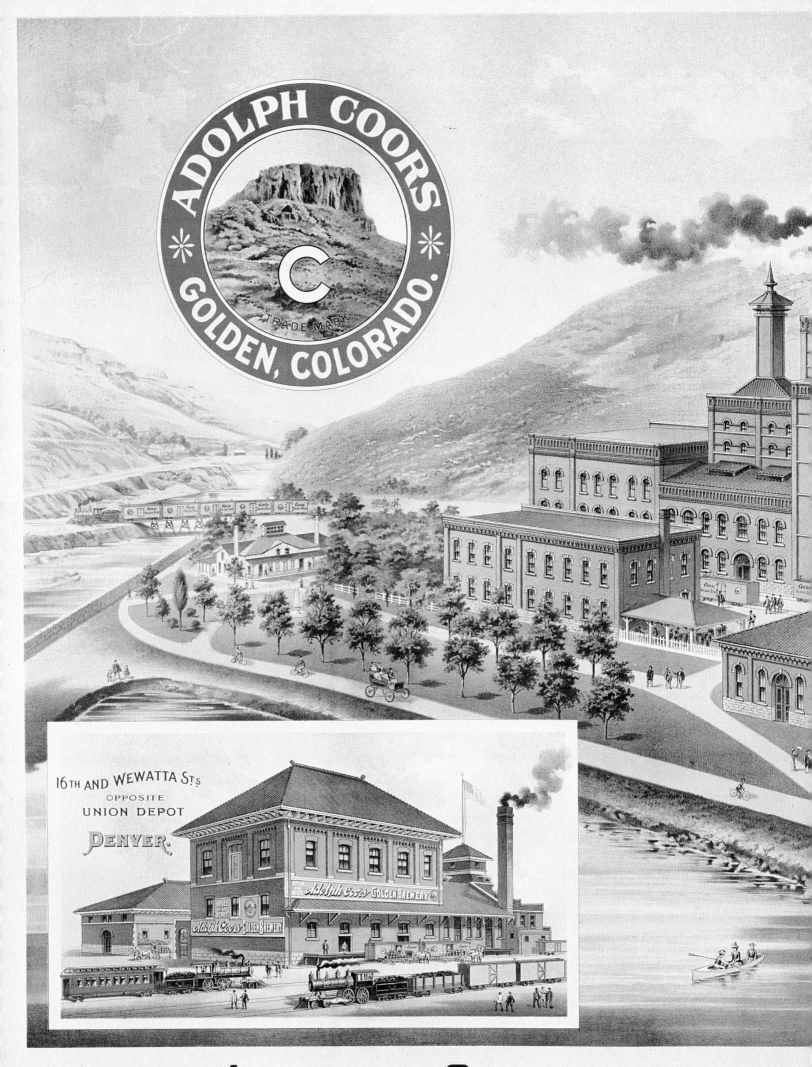

ADOLPH COORS

GOLDEN, COLORADO.

TRADE MARK.

16TH AND WEWATTA STS
OPPOSITE
UNION DEPOT
DENVER.

Adolph Coors Golden Brewery

ADOLPH COORS GOLDEN

BREWERY, GOLDEN, COLO.

56

Nick Kessler *(left)* and his brewery *(below).* The big fermenting tanks on Norfolk & Western and Seaboard flat cars were brought in from the East Coast as part of Kessler's efforts to remodel and upgrade the plant. He also added the first refrigeration unit to be used in Montana. *Overleaf:* A Kessler brewery wagon around 1927. This single barrel must have been very special.

Glendive, Miles City, Missoula, Philipsburg, Radersburg, Silverbow, Sun River, Townsend and, of course, Helena. It was in Helena that one of Montana's most famous breweries was founded. Started by Charles Beehrer in 1864, it was taken over two years later by an immigrant from Luxemburg named Nicholas Kessler. Nick Kessler turned the enterprise into Montana's finest. In 1886 he built a brand new brewery on the site that included the first refrigeration unit ever used in Montana and the first carbonic acid machine to be installed in any United States brewery. Kessler himself died in 1901, but the brewery survived until 1958.

While Kessler may have been a leading name in nineteenth century Montana brewing, another star shone briefly on the scene in Montana and in Washington. Leopold Schmitt arrived in the Montana boomtown of Butte by way of Deer Lodge, a day's ride to the north, in 1876. Butte, with enormous gold and silver mines in the center of town, was a land of opportunity for anyone who cared to become a purveyor to the thirsty miners, and Schmitt determined that he'd be the first local brewer to cater to the taverns that catered to the tastes of the men who dug the treasure of Butte's self-named 'richest hill on earth.' Schmidt's aptly named Centennial Brewery was Butte's first and a success. Over the next quarter of a century Schmitt also became regionally respected by other brewers. He made a trip to Germany to study brewing technique (something few immigrant brewers did), and re-

turned to Montana with a new wife at his side.

By the mid-1890s Schmitt's travels took him to Washington where he discovered the natural artesian water of the little town of Tumwater near the state capital of Olympia, south of Seattle. Here, in 1896, he founded the Capital Brewing Company. Schmitt's Centennial Brewery eventually closed its doors in 1918, never to survive Prohibition and Butte's waning mineral wealth, but the Capital Brewery (remained Olympia Brewing Company in 1902) returned after Prohibition to become one of the West's leading lager brewers.

It may or may not be a coincidence that the only Indian tribe in the United States known to have brewed beer before the arrival of the white man was also the last tribe to finally surrender to the white man. Thanks to Geronimo, the Apaches in Arizona were able to maintain their ancient lifestyle past 1890, the year that Congress declared as the 'end of the frontier.' Against this backdrop it is interesting that commercial brewing arrived in Arizona as early as it did. It is also interesting that aboriginal *tesguino* maize beer brewing may have taken place in Arizona at the same time as relatively modern lager brewing. The first commercial brewery in Arizona was Tucson's Pioneer Brewery which was started by Alex Levin in 1866 and operated by him with a succession of partners until 1872 when it was renamed the Park Brewery. The Park Brewery was operated until 1880 by Alex and Zenona Levin when it was sold. Over the next six years the Park Brewery changed hands six times before finally going out of business.

Other early brewing ventures in the Grand Canyon State were Abe Peeples' Magnolia Brewery in Wickenburg (1868–1871) and two Prescott breweries which, like the Pioneer/Park brewery in Tucson, went through an unusual number of ownership changes. These were the Arizona Brewery started by John Littig in 1868 which changed hands eight times through 1885 and the Pacific Brewery in which founder

Right: **The bottlewashing crew at the Kessler Brewing Co in Helena, Montana in the early 1900s, after electric power became available in the state. Note the filled bottles at the lower left.**

62

Below: Charles Hansen's National Brewery at the corner of Webster and Fulton streets in San Francisco was built in 1865, ten years after the brewery was established.

John Raible changed partners five times between 1867 and 1890.

The story of brewing in Montana or Arizona during the years between the Civil War and Prohibition was typical of brewing throughout the West as a whole. Most small breweries came and went in the space of less than a decade. Of the hundreds of breweries that each had its brief shining (or tarnished) hour on the stage of American brewing history in the nineteenth century west of Texas, only Olympia, Blitz-Weinhard and Coors became major modern breweries. Of the cities in the West that boasted a group of competing breweries in its nineteenth-century heyday, only one became an important twentieth-century American brewing center, and that one was also the first: San Francisco.

BREWING IN SAN FRANCISCO

The City by the Golden Gate has always been a city of hard-working people who thoroughly enjoy the rewards of their hard work. Unlike any American city since perhaps Jamestown, San Francisco grew to maturity isolated from the rest of the world and thus developed its own traditions and its own economic infrastructure independent of any other center. Its nearest neighboring American city was several months and several thousand miles away by ship. By the time the transcontinental railroad was completed in 1869, San Francisco was a major self-sufficient and self-reliant metropolis.

The first beer came to San Francisco in the holds of ships that had carried it from the East around Cape Horn. This beer, which had en route crossed the equator twice and been subjected to freezing temperatures in between, was hardly fresh, and the means of its delivery were hardly reliable. As with other things, San Franciscans decided that local beer demand required a local supplier. The first to answer this demand may have been William 'Billy the Brewer' McGlore, who is said to have been brewing beer in San Francisco as early as 1837. Though records of this first 'Billy' beer are sketchy, the 1849 gold rush provided the catalyst for Adam Schuppert's brewery at Stockton and Jackson streets which

is recorded as being California's, and the West's, first commercial brewery. The choice of this site near Portsmouth Square was ideal because the square was the commercial hub of San Francisco and home to more taverns than existed in some entire western territories. Another brewery which opened its doors in 1849, and perhaps even sooner, was William Bull's Empire Brewery at Mission and Second streets. These were followed in 1850 by John Neep's California Brewery at Powell and Vallejo.

By 1856, when many territories had yet to see the founding of their first brewery, the city of San Francisco had 15 commercial breweries in operation, most of them in the area which today is the site of the city's financial district. Included were those of Ambrose Carner on Sacramento Street and of G F Joseph on California Street. In its history, San Francisco has had roughly 80 breweries, more than most entire states, and more than most American cities including even Milwaukee.

Some of San Francisco's notable early breweries included those started by Charles Wilmot in 1856 on Telegraph Hill and John Wieland's Philadelphia Brewery established on

Second Street during the same year. Called simply the John Wieland Brewing Company after 1887, the firm survived until 1920 and the eve of Prohibition, but an attempted revival in 1934 failed. Farther from the center of the city was the intriguing American Railroad Brewery on Valencia Street near 15th which was started in 1858 by Thomas Pfether and which merged with the Union Brewing and Malting Company in 1902. The latter grew out of the brewery started by Albert Koster in 1854 and which was finally disbanded in 1916.

In 1858, a 30-year-old German immigrant and Second Street grocer named Claus Spreckels started the Albany Brewery at 71–75 Everett Street. It was the first major business venture by the man who later went on to control the Hawaiian sugar trade and much of the Pacific shipping trade. By 1877 when the 'Sugar King' sold his Albany Brewery to F Hagemenn, Spreckels was one of the richest men in the West. Hagemann's Albany Brewery went on to survive at 271 Natoma Street and later at 405–415 Eighth Street until 1920.

In the 1860s, two breweries were started in San Francisco which changed hands a number of times,

Above: The Philadelphia Brewery, founded by John Weiland in 1856, was located at 228-246 Second Street in San Francisco.

but which because of their size evolved into major city landmarks over the next 100 years. The first of these was the National Brewery established by John Glueck and Charles Hansen at Fulton and Webster streets near San Francisco's city hall. The firm operated under its original name until 1916 and under the California Brewing name until it closed in 1958, except during the Prohibition era (1923–1936) when it was known as the Cereal Products Refining Corporation. The brewery was best known, however, for the brand name Acme, kept alive by Blitz-Weinhard until the late 1970s.

The second of San Francisco's really big breweries was started by O Lurman in 1868 as the Bay Brewery at 612–616 Seventh Street. In deference to the city that was making beer famous, Lurmann in 1880 renamed his company the Milwaukee Brewery, a name that it retained until 1920 and for two years after its post-Prohibition revival. It is curious to note here that whereas midwestern and eastern brewers of the era often named their breweries after places in Germany and central

Vintage nineteenth-century brewhouse equipment from San Francisco's Anchor Brewery. The malt mill *(above)* readied the malt for mashing, and the device *(above right)* capped the filled kegs. The gauge told the pressure in the keg, which would increase as the beer continued to ferment. The sturdy oak kegs *(below)* were banded with iron straps. Empty they could weigh 100 pounds.

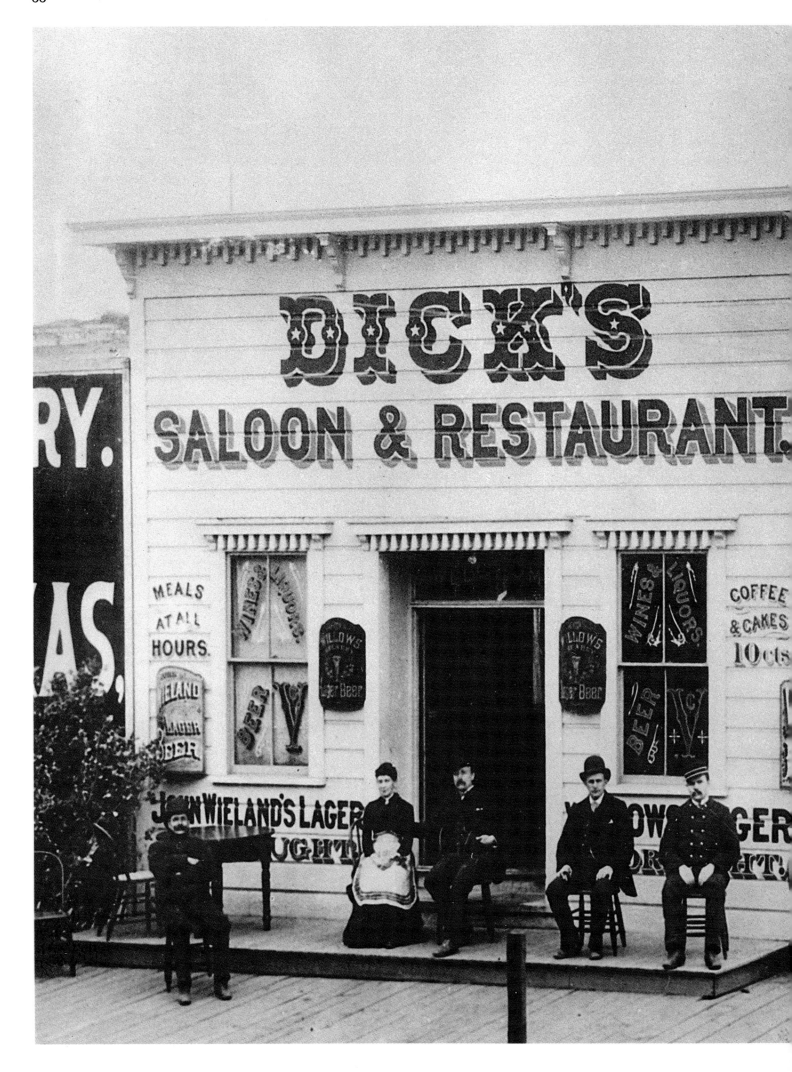

Dick's, at 43rd and Point Lobos, was one of San Francisco's original 24-hour restaurants and it featured the lager of the Willows and Wieland breweries. The Broadway Brewery's steam beer *(right)* was another San Francisco favorite.

Europe, San Francisco brewers often named their firms after places in the East and Midwest. In addition to Philadelphia, Albany and Milwaukee breweries, nineteenth-century San Francisco boasted breweries named after Chicago, Jackson, New York and St Louis.

In 1935 The Milwaukee Brewery finally adopted the city where it was born and the big white building on Tenth Street where the brewery had moved in 1891 became the San Francisco Brewing Corporation. This name was retained until 1956 when it became the Burgermeister Brewing Corporation, which in turn became a division of first the Joseph Schlitz empire (1961–1969) and then of Meister Brau of Chicago (1969–1971). The building then became a Falstaff brewery until the doors were closed in 1978.

When the forty-niners arrived in San Francisco en route to the gold fields they brought with them the ales, porters and lagers they had enjoyed at home. When the first brewers arrived in San Francisco around 1849 they realized that it would be virtually impossible to brew lager. Lager brewing requires fermentation at temperatures very near freezing. Such temperatures were taken for granted in Milwaukee and Chicago where ice could be harvested in the winter and stored through the summer. In San Francisco it can get very cold. Ironically the summer

John Wieland *(above)* established the Philadelphia Brewery in 1856 and renamed it the John Wieland Brewery in 1893. The Wieland drivers *(left)* pose for a photo sometime before Prohibition.

months are the coldest because of ocean fog, but the temperature almost never dips below freezing. Practical artificial ice-making would not be commonplace for nearly 20 years and it was almost that long before a railroad linked the city and the ice fields of the high Sierra Nevada. Ice could be brought in by ship from Alaska, but that was very expensive.

San Francisco's early brewmasters solved the problem in a logical way. They began the brewing process the same way as they would have brewed lager. They even used bottom fermenting lager yeast. Once it was brewed, however, the wort was fermented in large shallow pans at San Francisco's year round median temperature of roughly 60 degrees rather than in tanks and fermented at near-freezing temperatures. The resultant product lacked the sparkling carbonation characteristic of a lager because the open fermentation allowed the carbon dioxide to escape. This flat beer was then pumped into kegs where fermentation was allowed to continue. When the kegs were tapped the carbonation that had built up with the kegs escaped in what appeared to be cloud of steam. This is perhaps what led San Franciscans to call this unique creation 'steam beer.' In the 1850s and 1860s steam beer was extremely popular in San Francisco and throughout the West. A thirsty patron ordered beer simply by asking the bartender for 'glass of

Below: Staff and patrons assembled for a group photograph in front of San Francisco's famous '7 Mile House,' notable for its hot steam clams and cold steam beer. *Far right:* An assortment of vintage keg taps from the Anchor Brewing collection.

steam.' By the late 1870s, however, artificial refrigeration was introduced and lager brewing at last became possible in the West. For a time many brewers brewed both lager and steam since the latter was cheaper to produce. Gradually the steam beer brewing art died, disappearing like the cloud of vapor escaping from a newly tapped keg.

No recipe for steam beer is known to exist, but it was certainly more complicated than just a beer brewed with lager yeast and fermented at any median temperature. When Prohibition ended only one brewery reopened making what it called steam beer. The Anchor Brewery, founded in San Francisco in 1896, reopened to a market that had forgotten steam beer. By that time the precise definition of steam beer, if it had ever existed, was forgotten as well. The Anchor Brewery struggled along for another 30 years until 1965, when it was snatched from the brink of bankruptcy by appliance heir Fritz Maytag. The young Maytag reintroduced quality control and the notion of using only pure barley malt to produce the wort. He took what little was known about the idea of steam beer, refined it and made it his own. Over the next two decades he turned the dilapidated Anchor Brewery into a showplace. He took a beer of inconsistent quality and turned it into a highly prized premium product. In so doing he built a landmark small American brewery and molded the elusive legend of steam beer into his own trademark. Whatever 'steam beer' meant in the days of the California gold rush, after Maytag it meant Anchor Steam Beer.

BREWING IN CALIFORNIA

San Francisco quickly became the brewing capital of the West, but it was not California's only brewing city. Sacramento, the state capital, probably had some brewing activity during the 1849 gold rush, and by 1859 Hilbert & Borchers had established what evolved into the City Brewery in 1865 and survived until 1920. Los Angeles didn't really become a brewing town until after Prohibition, but Joseph Leiber, Henry Lemmert, Louis Schwartz and Ed Preuss are all recorded as active brewers briefly during the 1874 to 1879 period.

While many California towns had breweries by the 1870s, several breweries had come even earlier, such as those of Joseph Hartman in San Jose (1851), Frederick Walter in Weaverville (1852), Gottlieb Lieber in Marysville (1854), Bush and Denlacker in Stockton (1855), Samuel and Frank Daiser in Auburn (1855), Gottfried 'Fred' Krahenberg in San Jose (1856), Gottfried Gamble in Yreka (1858) and John Bauman in the Sierra Nevada gold town of Sonora (1866).

BREWING IN ALASKA

As with California, it took a gold rush to spark economic development in Alaska, but unlike California, Alaska's harsh climate prevented any significant economic growth until late in the twentieth century. The gold rush in Alaska and in Canada's neighboring Yukon

Continued on page 77

A SMALL AMERICAN BREWER

ANCHOR BREWING COMPANY

Right: The Anchor Brewing Company was born on San Francisco's Potrero Hill in 1896, but it moved to the city's South of Market Street industrial district after Prohibition. The brewery was on Eighth Street and also on the verge of collapse when Fritz Maytag bought it in 1965. In 1979, Maytag moved Anchor into new quarters, a former coffee roasting plant, back on Potrero Hill.

Below: The elegant copper vessels in the Anchor brewhouse were built by Ziemann in Germany and once graced a small Karlsruhe brewery. The brewhouse has a 110-barrel daily capacity, double that of Anchor's Eighth Street brewhouse. *Left to right,* in order of use, are the mash tun, the lauter tun and the brew kettle.

Above: The Anchor hop room, chilled to retain the freshness of the hops. Anchor uses only air-dried hops from Germany, Czechoslovakia and Washington's Yakima Valley.

Above: Breweries traditionally have used copper brewing vessels because they provide even heat. In the mash tun crushed barley malt is mixed with warm water and gradually warmed to 170° as starches in the malt turn to fermentable and unfermentable sugars. Anchor prides itself on being an 'all-malt' brewery. Except for the malted German wheat they import for their wheat beer, Anchor uses only malted two-row barley, grown in Washington and malted in California.

BREWERY CLOSE-UP

Above: After being filtered in the lauter tun, the wort trickles through the grant, a trough with adjustable spigots, where it is aerated and checked for clarity.

Right: The lauter tun serves as a gravity filtration system; the husks from the malted barley form a porous filter bed.

Below: After the lauter tun, the wort is placed in the copper brew kettle where it is boiled for 90 minutes. During this time a blend of fresh hops (in yellow barrels, *left*) will be added. The hops are carefully blended to provide the precise mix of aroma and bitterness required for the distinctive taste of each Anchor product.

Above: After cooling, wort that will become Anchor Steam Beer is placed in the unusual, wide, shallow stainless steel fermenting pans. Bottom-fermenting lager yeast is then 'pitched' into the wort and fermentation begins.

Anchor Steam Beer is fermented at between 60°F and 72°F, the typical year-round San Francisco temperature. If it were to get hotter, the automatic refrigeration system would be used. The large surface area of the pans helps to keep the temperature uniform.

Anchor's ales are fermented in much deeper open stainless steel tanks using top-fermenting ale yeasts.

Above: Anchor's copper brewing vessels are cleaned frequently to keep them sparkling clean inside and out.

Left: The initial fermentation process yields a 'big tub of flat beer,' which is placed into large closed stainless steel tanks where the beer is 'krausened,' or naturally carbonated, by the old German method. A few days after it is placed in the tanks, fresh still-fermenting beer is added to the original batch. For the next several weeks the fermentation continues in an environment of gradually increasing pressure, as the yeast continues to produce carbon dioxide.

The krausening of the beer produces a finer bubble and better bonding between beer and carbon dioxide, which gives Anchor Steam Beer its characteristic rich creaminess and longer-lasting head.

Below: During bottling, Anchor uses special techniques and quick handling to avoid exposing the beer to air.

Territory began in the mid-1880s, 35 years after the forty-niners poured into California. Like the forty-niners, the followers of Alaska's gold rush brought a taste for beer, but unlike California's early brewers, the first Alaskan brewers had no trouble finding an adequate supply of ice for lager brewing.

The first brewery in Alaska was established in Juneau by Abraham Cohen about 1870. In 1874, with two partners, he opened a second brewery in Sitka. These two establishments on Alaska's southern panhandle were the territory's only breweries for over a decade, but the gold rush also brought a rush of brewers to the frozen north. Between 1888 and 1906, 32 breweries were started in 15 Alaskan towns, but most were short-lived. Many survived less than a year. By 1919 and the eve of Prohibition, only four Alaskan breweries remained in Fairbanks, Nome, Valdez and Juneau. Both of the original Cohen breweries were gone by 1904.

After Prohibition, none of the earlier breweries reopened, but three new ones started up. The Fairbanks Brewing Association and the Pioneer Brewing company opened their doors in 1934 in Fairbanks and the Pilsener Brewing Company of Alaska began brewing in Ketchikan the following year. Fairbanks Brewing survived for only one year, but the other two continued until 1942 when the shortages of materials that accompanied the Second World War forced them out of business. The only other Alaskan brewery to open since Prohibition was Prinz Brau Alaska, which operated in Anchorage between 1976 and 1979 at the end of the North Slope oil boom.

THE MAKING OF A MAJOR REGIONAL BREWERY

Most of the major brewers who emerged as national powers in the last years of the nineteenth century and went on to dominate American brewing in the twentieth century trace their origins to the era prior to the Civil War. However, a number of breweries started in the late 1800s survived as major regional breweries. A good example is the Hudepohl Brewery in Cincinnati. This city in the fertile Ohio River valley had attracted a large number

Left: Ludwig Hudepohl at the St Aloysius Orphanage festival c 1900. The tent had a sign that read: 'Alive within the rail, Where the head is, Ought to be the tail.' Festivalgoers paid a dime to enter only to find a horse with his tail at the feed trough. Hudepohl gave everyone a stein of beer to soften the joke. *Above:* Ludwig Hudepohl's display ad for the Buckeye Brewery, placed between 1885 and 1900 and believed to be the company's earliest.

of German settlers who by 1850 accounted for 77 percent of the city's population. Their German taste for lager invited German brewers. In 1848, there were 11 brewers in Cincinnati and 12 years later there were 36. During this time, such big names of early Cincinnati brewing as John Hauch, Herman Lackman and Christian Moerlin were just getting started. Moerlin's brewery, in fact, enjoyed a brief national reputation and survived four years after Prohibition as the Old Munich Brewing Company.

Most of Cincinnati's brewers were content to remain regional; because of the area's large German population, they could do so with comfortable success. It was in 1885 that Ludwig Hudepohl and George Kotte acquired the Koehler brothers' Buckeye Brewery (founded in 1852) on Buckeye Street. Their timing was perfect, because by the 1890s the people of Cincinnati were drinking more beer per capita than the people of any other city in the country; when the per capita national average was 16 gallons, the people of Cincinnati were drinking 40. German-style

beer gardens abounded and there were over 1800 saloons in town. George Kotte died in 1893, and in 1900 his widow sold his share to Ludwig 'Louis' Hudepohl II, the son of Kotte's former partner. Louis Hudepohl II promptly renamed the brewery the Hudepohl Brewing Company and introduced his Golden Jubilee brand which became popular throughout Kentucky and Indiana as well as Ohio. Before his death in 1902 at the age of 59, the enterprising younger Hudepohl gained a reputation as quite a character. His regional marketing success aside, his notoriety as a practical joker rivaled that of P T Barnum. At the St Aloysius Orphanage Festival in 1900, for example, he set up a tent marked with a sign reading 'Alive within the rail, where the head is, ought to be a tail.' Expecting to see some bizarre freak of nature, many people paid 10 cents to peek into the tent only to find a horse standing with its tail over a feeding trough. Once duped, the embarrassed or irate Cincinnatians were each treated to a cold mug of Hudepohl by the brewery's proprietor.

Like many German-American institutions, the Hudepohl Brewery suffered in the anti-German backlash of the First World War era besides the disaster of Prohibition and the depression. Unlike most of its contemporaries, the Hudepohl firm not only survived but flourished and remains today a major American regional brewer.

BREWING AT THE TURN OF THE CENTURY

The history of American brewing in the nineteenth century can be broken into five 20-year periods. The first two periods (1800–1840) saw the general decline of brewing, followed by a period of very little brewing activity, the establishment of Yuengling in 1829 notwithstanding. The third period (1840–1860) saw the rise of German-style lager brewing and an increase in the number of breweries. The fourth period (1860–1880) saw a tremendous brewing boom from coast to coast, with more new breweries established throughout the United States than at any other period in history. Between 1860 and 1873 the United States went from 1269 to 4131 breweries.

The final two decades of the nineteenth century and the first decade of the twentieth was a period of consolidation and merging. This era saw fewer and fewer breweries producing more and more beer. The record number of 4131 breweries in 1873 produced 9 million barrels of beer. In 1910, 1568 breweries produced 53 million barrels. This meant that the average brewer of 1910 produced 15 times as much beer as his counterpart of 37 years before.

The last decades of the nineteenth century saw both the collapse of

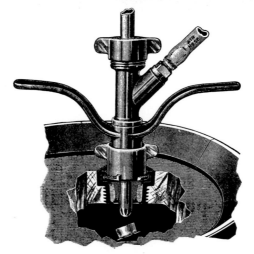

MAGIC BEER TAP IN USE

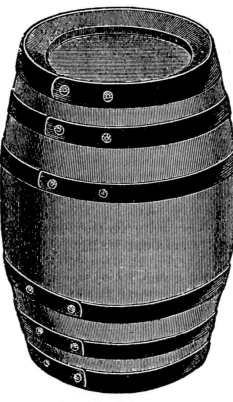

many small breweries and for the first time the rise of major national brands. Making this possible were such innovations as salt brine artificial ice-making and a network of railroads that had spread across both the United States and Canada in the years following the American Civil War. Between 1865 and 1890 railroad mileage in the United States increased from 35,085 to 163,597, a fivefold increase in just 25 years. Railroads and ice-making paved the way for the emergence of truly national brewers. Some of the emerging giants even established their own railroads. Joseph Schlitz owned Union Refrigerated Transit Corporation, and Anheuser-Busch set up the Manufacturers Railway Company, a subsidiary which is still going strong 100 years later.

In many other ways, the major brewers became increasingly sophisticated as they discovered the finer points of the art of 'marketing.' Two of the finer points exploited to their fullest potential prior to the last quarter of the nineteenth century were bottling and brand names. Bottling produced a convenient consumer item that permitted a higher retail price than could be asked for an equivalent volume of draft beer. The large-scale adoption of the bottling process was delayed and made difficult for smaller brewers by a federal government law that prohibited brewing and bottling to take place on the same premises. Until the law was repealed in 1890, brewers had to move their product across town to off-site bottling plants, a process that kept many small brewers from competing for the bottled beer market.

While bottling produced a convenient consumer item, brand names helped produce an identity for the item, and an identity helped to generate loyalty to a particular product. Adolphus Busch's Budweiser brand, adopted in 1876, exemplifies a successful brand name. Another is Pabst's Blue Ribbon brand derived from the gold medals won by the brewery at Philadelphia's 1876 Centennial Exposition and the 1893

Top, both: Charles Stolper's cooperage made and repaired wooden casks like the one above. The cutaway drawing shows how the beer tap fits into the keg. Anheuser-Busch's Clydesdale team *(left)* and Pabst's pin-up girl *(right)*. These companies were North America's largest brewers in 1900.

Paris World's Fair, as well as its first place showing at Chicago's 1893 Columbian Exposition.

Throughout the American brewing industry, the trend pointed to fewer brewers brewing less beer. Through mergers smaller brewers could pool their resources. In 1889 eighteen St Louis breweries merged in a single firm, and in 1890 six brewers in New Orleans followed suit. In 1901 mergers brought 10 brewers in Boston and 16 in Baltimore into two regional conglomerates. A merger in Pittsburgh is particularly illustrative of the trend: in 1899 and 1905, no fewer than 36 brewers funneled themselves into just two brewing companies—Pittsburgh Brewing and Independent Brewing.

The size of the breweries that survived this era was staggering compared to their predecessors. In 1880, a brewer was considered large if he produced 150,000 barrels annually. By the turn of the century, three brewers (Pabst, Anheuser-Busch and Schlitz) were each brewing a million barrels each year!

By the turn of the century, the United States had surpassed England as the world's second largest brewing nation. Germany was still brewing twice as much beer as the

Continued on page 84

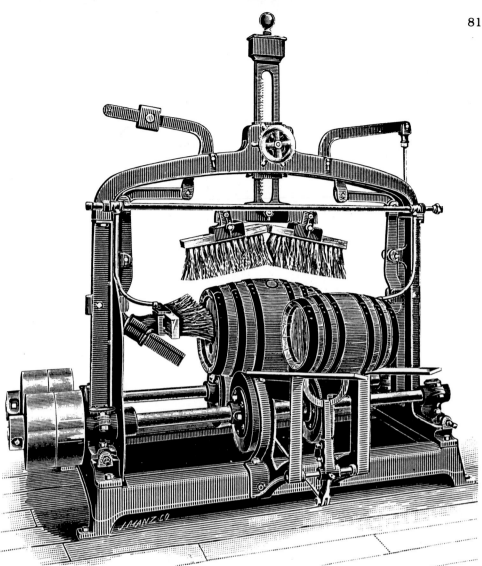

Left: Pabst was the world's largest brewer by 1900. Its 'dreadnaughts' were brew kettles named after the battleships of the day.

The malt extract was boiled in the kettles with the hops. The belt-driven keg scrubber *(above)* cleaned the kegs for reuse.

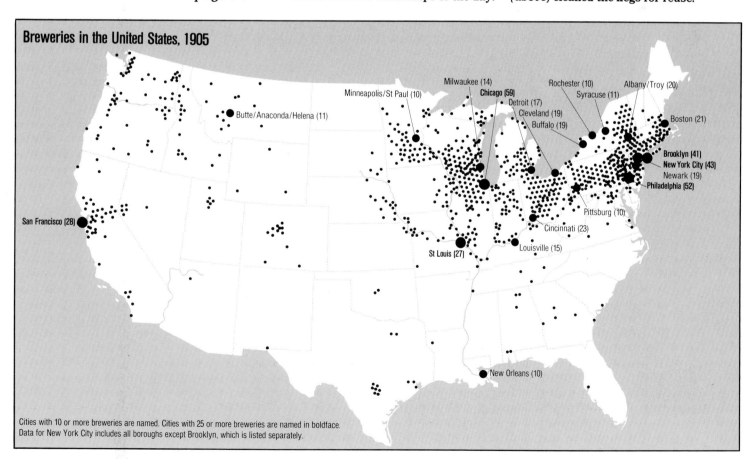

Breweries in the United States, 1905

Butte/Anaconda/Helena (11) · Minneapolis/St Paul (10) · Milwaukee (14) · Chicago (59) · Detroit (17) · Cleveland (19) · Buffalo (19) · Rochester (10) · Syracuse (11) · Albany/Troy (20) · Boston (21) · Brooklyn (41) · New York City (43) · Newark (19) · Philadelphia (52) · Pittsburg (10) · Cincinnati (23) · Louisville (15) · St Louis (27) · San Francisco (28) · New Orleans (10)

Cities with 10 or more breweries are named. Cities with 25 or more breweries are named in boldface. Data for New York City includes all boroughs except Brooklyn, which is listed separately.

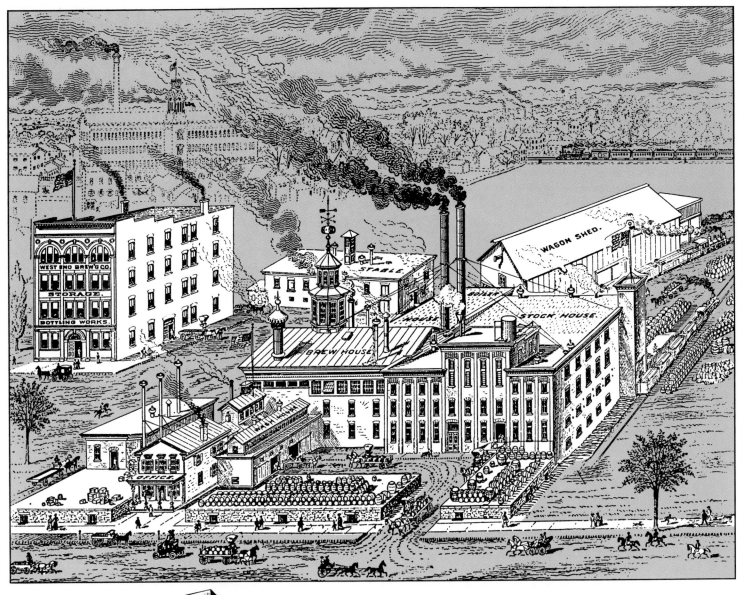

Above: Overall layout of the West End Brewing Company of Utica, New York, a typical North American brewery of 1800s.

Above right: This cutaway shows the layout of that section of a typical brewhouse devoted to the processes that follow mashing and brewing. The vats and casks were still constructed of oak.

Below: Turn-of-the-century brewery equipment includes *(from left)* an improved grader and separator, oak fermeting tanks, a copper brew kettle designed for a smaller-scale brewery than the dreadnaught kettles and a stationary mash machine.

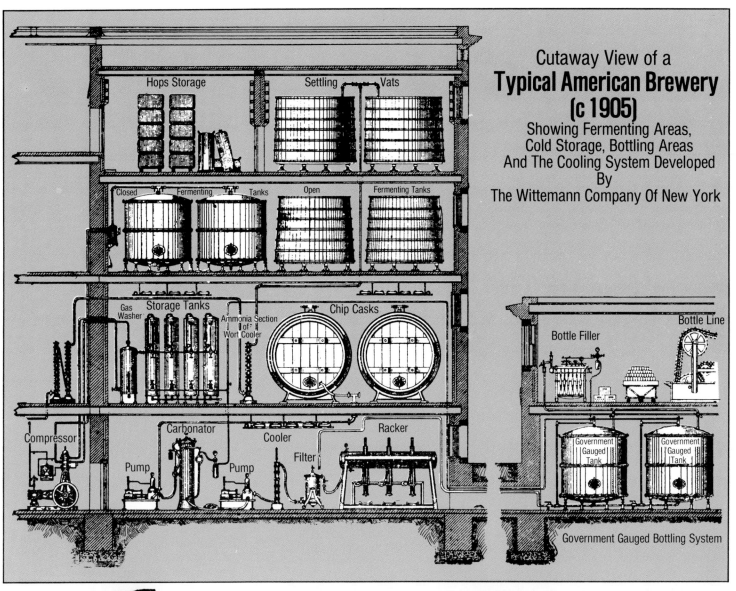

Cutaway View of a
**Typical American Brewery
(c 1905)**
Showing Fermenting Areas,
Cold Storage, Bottling Areas
And The Cooling System Developed
By
The Wittemann Company Of New York

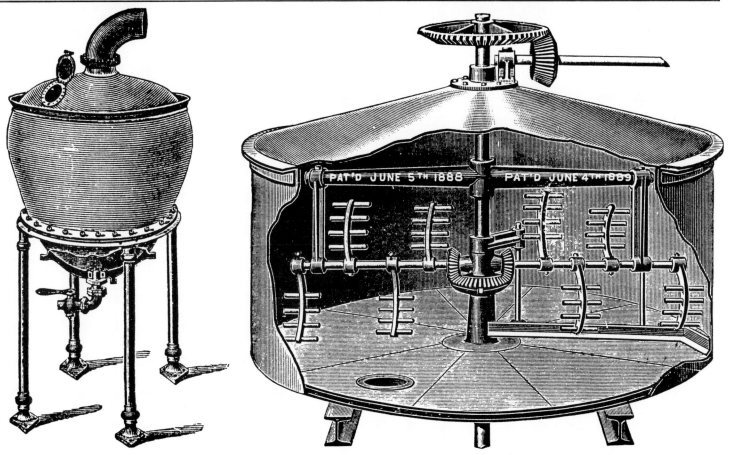

84

United States, but only one of its brewers, Schultheiss in Berlin, was in the million-barrel class of America's big three. At that time, Spaten, the largest of the Munich brewers, was brewing 600,000 barrels and Burgerliches Brauhaus at Pilsen in Bohemia was brewing 842,000 barrels of the original Pilsner (Pilsner Urquell). In 1900 Brauberechtigte Burger at Budweis in Bohemia was brewing 121,000 barrels of the original Budweiser while, notably, Anheuser-Busch was brewing eight times that much of the American Budweiser.

BREWING IN MEXICO

North American brewing began in Mexico, first with the Indians and then with the first Spanish brewery or *cerveceria* established there in the 1500s. In the ensuing three centuries, however, Mexican tastes paralleled those of Spain just as American tastes paralleled those of England, and this meant an inclination toward wine and distilled spirits such as *mescal* and *tequila* rather than beer (cerveza). There was also *pulque,* a fermented beverage favored in the nineteenth century by Mexican peasants. Even through an influx of German immigrants in the mid-nineteenth century, the tropical nature of much of Mexico prevented the brewing of lager until the latter part of the century when artificial ice-making technology became widely available.

By the turn of the century Mexico had 29 breweries, over half of them brewing lager. The remaining rela-

Above: **Santiago Graf introduced lager brewing to Mexico.** *Right:* **A technician checks the storage tanks at the Moctezuma brewery in Guadalajara. Here, beer is aged and readied for bottling.**

tively small breweries brewed *sencilla* or *corriente* beer which was similar to lager but fermented for a shorter period of time. Unlike the United States and Canada, most beer sold in Mexico around the turn of the century was bottled rather than put into kegs. A good deal of beer was imported from the United States which probably helps explain the rapid conversion from brown beer to lager in the 1890s. With the exception of the Toluca Brewery near Mexico City and La Perla Brewery in Guadalajara, the major Mexican breweries themselves imported their malt from north of the border.

The first Mexican breweries of modern times were founded in Mexico City prior to 1845—the Pila Seca founded by Bernhard Bolgard of

Switzerland and the Candelaria started by the Bavarian immigrant Frederick Herzog. These breweries survived until the 1880s brewing beer with sun-dried Mexican barley and brown sugar. The quality of these products was unable to measure up to that of lager, which was being brewed in substantial quantities by that time. The arrival of lager brewing in Mexico can be traced to the winter of 1884–85 when the first rail line was opened between Mexico City and El Paso, Texas. One of the first consignments brought south over the new steel was an ice-making machine bound for the Toluca Brewery of Santiago Graf, who had imported the first ice-making machine to Mexico just two years before. The Toluca Brewery, 20 miles from Mexico City, had been started by Augustin Marendaz, late of Switzerland, in 1865 and was acquired by Graf in 1875. Santiago Graf had already established a reputation for brewing a high-quality ale and his new ice machines helped him branch into the field of lager brewing. Lager brewing, in turn, helped Graf to become one of Mexico's largest and most successful brewers. By the turn of the century, he had a glass factory in Toluca, branches in several other cities and a second brewery in Oaxaca. The second Mexican brewer to convert his production from ale to lager was Juan Ohrner, proprietor of the Cerveceria La Perla in Guadalajara.

In 1891, the first Mexican cerveceria to be built as a lager brewery was opened in Monterey. The Cerveceria Cuauhtemoc, which was

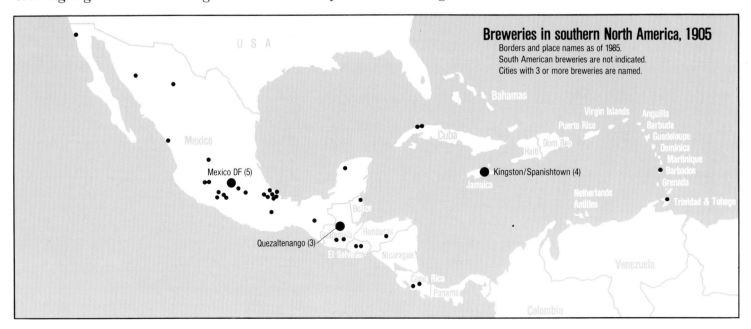

Breweries in southern North America, 1905
Borders and place names as of 1985.
South American breweries are not indicated.
Cities with 3 or more breweries are named.

Mexico DF (5)
Quezaltenango (3)
Kingston/Spanishtown (4)

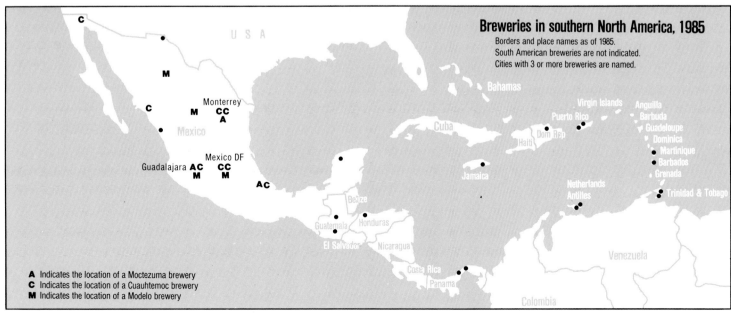

Breweries in southern North America, 1985

Borders and place names as of 1985.
South American breweries are not indicated.
Cities with 3 or more breweries are named.

USA

Bahamas

Cuba

Virgin Islands · Anguilla
Puerto Rico · Barbuda
· Guadeloupe
Haiti · Dom Rep · Dominica
· Martinique
· Barbados
Jamaica · Grenada
Netherlands
Antilles · Trinidad & Tobago

C

M

C
Monterrey
M   CC
A

Mexico

Mexico DF
Guadalajara **AC** **CC**
M **M**

AC

Belize

Guatemala   Honduras

El Salvador   Nicaragua

Costa Rica
Panama

Venezuela

Colombia

A Indicates the location of a Moctezuma brewery
C Indicates the location of a Cuauhtemoc brewery
M Indicates the location of a Modelo brewery

founded by Joseph Schnaider, an immigrant from St Louis, Missouri and his partner Isaac Garza, had by 1897 become the largest brewery in Mexico, producing more than 100,000 barrels annually. Though Schnaider left Cuauhtemoc to purchase La Perla later that year, the brewery prospered and today continues to be one of Mexico's three major breweries.

After Mexico City, the state of Veracruz surrounding the great port city of the same name, became the country's second major brewing center. By 1905, six breweries operated in the state of Veracruz and among them was the Cerveceria Moctezuma, which would eventually become another of Mexico's three largest. Started in 1894 by Henry Manthy and Adolf Brukhardt along with German brewmaster Wilhelm Hasse, Moctezuma began brewing lager in 1896.

Another relatively early Mexican brewery surviving today is the Cerveceria del Pacifico in Mazatlan. Built with American equipment, this brewery was founded in 1900 by Jacob Schuehle who had four years earlier helped to found the now-defunct Cerveceria de Sonora in Hermosillo along with the Clifton, Arizona entrepreneur George Grunig.

Unlike the United States and Canada, Mexico did not experience a prohibition in the 1920s. Understandably, those breweries located in the northern part of the country did rather well during the period, and in 1930 the Mexican brewing industry produced 838,000 barrels. Though this was a far cry from the 66 million barrels the United States industry had produced in 1914, it was 838,000 barrels more than were produced in the United States in 1930. The worldwide depression soon took its toll and by 1932 Mexican production had sunk to just 489,000 barrels even though Prohibition was still in effect in the United States.

By 1936, however, the Mexican industry was back on its feet and had just surpassed the million-barrel mark. Four years later Mexican beer production had doubled to two million barrels, although this represented an output only four percent of that of the United States brewing industry. By 1960 Mexican production was up to 10 million barrels and

was nine percent of the size of the American industry. In 1975, Mexico reached 23 million barrels and just barely surpassed Canada as the second largest brewing nation in North America. The Mexican brewing industry reached a 32.8-million-barrel peak in 1981, but declined to 27.6 million in 1983 in the midst of its national economic crisis.

NORTH AMERICAN BREWING SOUTH OF MEXICO

Though the Indians brewed beer in the region centuries ago and British ships sailing there certainly carried beer, the brewing tradition in Central America and the Caribbean simply never developed to the extent that it did in the north. A West Indies porter however existed in the early nineteenth century. By the latter nineteenth century there were fewer breweries thoughout the region than in Mexico; imported beer was a ma-

jor factor. Most of the beer imported to Central America came from Germany and the United States, although British beer was an understandably important import in British Honduras (now Belize). Lager, however, was generally more popular than British-style beers. For example, 75 percent of the beer brought into Costa Rica in 1900 originated in Bavaria. Prosperous Costa Rica was in fact by this time an important early brewing center, with three breweries in San Jose and one at Cartago. By 1905, however, only the Traube Brewery in Cartago and G Richmond's Cerveceria Costaricense in San Jose remained. After Costa Rica, Guatemala was the next most important brewing center in the area. By 1905, there were six breweries in the country, half of

Brewing in the Caribbean: Desnoes & Geddes Red Stripe lager on the bottling line (below), and the picturesque Antillian Brewery in Curacao (right), which has won many gold medals for its Amstel beer.

Above: Cerveceria Hondurena, in San Pedro Sula, is the major brewery of Honduras.

them located in Quezaltenango. The latter three included the rival Cerveceria Republicana of Molina Hermanos and the Heussler Brothers' Cerveceria Alemana (German Brewery).

In the Caribbean at the turn of the century breweries existed on just four of the islands. Trinidad and Barbados had one each and Jamaica had four including the West India Brewing Company in Kingston. The others were the smaller proprietorships of C M Lindo and J Harris Carr in Kingston and Edwin Charley in Spanishtown. Cuba, prior to its independence from Spain in 1898, had a single brewery, La Tropical, in Havana. Following the American victory in the Spanish-American War, the New York firm of David Obermeyer and Joseph Liebmann (they operated a brewery in Brooklyn) went south to set up a modern American-style brewery in the Cuban capital. Their establishment, the Havana Brewery, was noted for its Cerveza Aguila (Eagle Beer) which was brewed in Cuba until 1924, well into the era of Prohibition in the United States.

In 1918 Eugene Desnoes and Thomas Geddes of Kingston, Jamaica merged their competing soft drink businesses to form a company whose products one day joined the most sought-after beers in the Caribbean. In 1920 Desnoes & Geddes Ltd added their first beer to an otherwise soft drink line. Though Dragon Stout was a short-lived experiment, Desnoes & Geddes were not entirely discouraged. When Prohibition in the United States dried up a major supplier of beer for the Caribbean, the firm returned to the brewing business permanently. Utilizing the talents of brewmasters recruited in England and Germany, Desnoes & Geddes Ltd first brewed their famous Red Stripe beer in 1927. In 1934 one of the original English brewmasters, Bill Martindale, along with Paul Geddes (descendant of the co-founder and the first Jamaican brewmaster), teamed up to alter the Red Stripe formula. The resultant pale lager has been brewed by the company ever since. Red Stripe lager was joined in the Desnoes & Geddes repertoire by another beer product when the company revived Dragon Stout in 1961. Since that time, both products have become available thoughout the Caribbean and have been exported to the United States, and Red Stripe is brewed under license in England.

WINDS OF CHANGE

Even as the American brewing industry was growing and evolving through the period from 1880 to 1910, a dark cloud was growing on the horizon. It was the harbinger of an ill wind that would still forever the happy sounds of many of America's beer gardens.

The idea of temperance is as old as brewing. The Congregational Church formed a temperance society as early as 1808 and the American Temperance Society (formed in Boston in 1826) had 100,000 members by 1829. The objective of temperance was prohibition and, beginning in New England, entire states began to prohibit brewing and selling beer. Between 1846 and 1855 thirteen states followed Maine's lead and experimented with prohibition, but many of these laws were repealed in the years after the Civil War.

By 1910 the boom years for brewing had come to a close, and the pendulum began to swing the other way. By 1912 nine states had gone 'dry' and four years later the number of dry states had increased to 23. Despite the efforts of the temperance societies and the Anti-Saloon League, it took the anti-German hysteria of World War I to push the idea of national prohibition into law. The United States was neutral when the war began in 1914, but by 1917 the tide of sentiment was clearly against Germany on the issue of the latter's barbarous U-boat attacks. The sinking of the liner *Lusitania* was the last straw; the United States declared war on Germany on 6 April 1917. On 10 April the Food Control Act was passed with the stated intention of conserving grain for the war effort. Under the new law the production of distilled spirits was forbidden and severe restrictions were placed on brewers and vintners. President Woodrow Wilson, under powers granted to him under the Food Control Act, moved in December 1917 to restrict brewing and to limit alcohol content in beer to 2.75 percent by weight. Anti-German feelings fueled the prohibitionist fire, and the vast majority of pro-American German-American brewers were signed along with the handful of German nationals who had interests in American breweries. The Sheppard resolution calling for a constitutional amendment for national prohibition was submitted to the state legislatures in December 1917. Caught up in the mood of a nation at war with Germany, legislators across the nation succumbed to the prohibitionist flames.

By 16 January 1919, the 18th Amendment to the Constitution of the United States was ratified. One year later, Prohibition was a reality.

PROHIBITION

Effective on 19 January 1920, 'the manufacture, sale, or transportation of intoxicating liquors within, the importation thereof into, or the exportation thereof from the United States and all territory subject to the jurisdiction thereof for beverage purposes is hereby prohibited.'

With a single poorly worded sentence, the brewing history of the United States changed forever. The Volstead Enforcement Act, passed over President Wilson's veto in October 1919, stood ready to go into force at midnight on 18 January 1920. Some states like California waited until the last minute to submit, but many were already dry when the nightfall of Prohibition descended upon the land. Many small family-owned businesses from the brewers of Milwaukee to the vinters of California's Napa Valley went out of business overnight. What had been normal commercial activity one day was a criminal act the next. Given a year's warning, many breweries attempted to get into other related businesses such as cereal production or industrial alcohol, but many simply closed their doors forever.

Many of the industry's leaders stayed in business, diversifying into other fields and brewing nonalcoholic or 'near' beer. Auheuser-Busch brought out a near beer with the brand name Bevo, while Miller marketed its near beer under the name Vivo. Schlitz, which had brewed the beer that had 'made Milwaukee famous,' now hoped to perpetuate its own fame through a near beer appropriately called Famo. Coors, one of the few brewers left in Colorado,

Above: Anheuser-Busch diversified into the commercial yeast field during Prohibition to stay in business.

chose the auspicious name Mannah, while industry leader Pabst registered three near beer brand names: Hoppy, Pablo and Yip. In an apparent industry marketing trend toward ending brand names with the letter 'O,' some names got used twice. The Stroh Brewery in Michigan and the Blitz-Weinhard Brewery in Oregon each used the brand name Luxo. In 1921 there were about 10 million barrels of near beer produced versus 23 million barrels of real beer in 1918 and twice that amount four years before.

In addition to near beer, some former breweries kept their plants and bottling lines humming with other types of beverages. Anheuser-Busch produced chocolate-flavored Carcho, coffee-flavored Kafo, tea-leaf-flavored Buschtee, grape-flavored Grape Bouquet and Busch Ginger Ale. Hudepohl produced root beer, and Coors became a giant in the malted milk industry. Prohibition was a golden age for soft drinks and like Anheuser-Busch some brewers were able to make the transition, although it was a field that few would stay in after Prohibition.

For some companies, the forced diversification turned out to be to their long-term benefit. Anheuser-Busch began producing baker's yeast during Prohibition, continued after repeal and eventually became

the industry leader. Coors developed its Coors Porcelain Company into what became one of the world's leading producers of scientific and industrial ceramics.

The food conservation and anti-German hysteria that had helped create Prohibition subsided in the early 1920s, and thoughts of repeal soon followed, but it was over 10 years before the national mistake would be rectified. During the Roaring Twenties, while breweries made near beer and malted mild, bootleggers brewed beer and bathtub gin. An industry once controlled by serious businessmen was now the playground and the battleground of organized crime. Attempts to enforce the Volstead Act were expensive and far from effective. Large numbers. of otherwise respectable citizens were openly co-operating with criminals in the evasion of the Volstead amendment, and the gang rule created by the entry of organized crime into the alcoholic beverage industry made law and order hard to maintain. With the arrival of the depression in 1929 the problem reached crisis proportions. Public sentiment was clearly against Prohibition throughout the country. The people wanted to see unemployed brewers and bottlers back to work and paying taxes, and they wanted to see the brewing industry out of the hands of mobsters.

Every Canadian province except Quebec had adopted Prohibition during World War I, but had re-

Breweries in the United States, May 1933

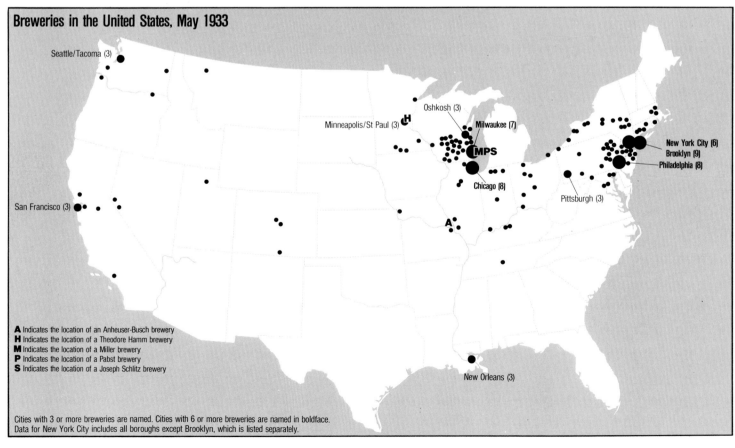

Seattle/Tacoma (3)

Oshkosh (3)

Minneapolis/St Paul (3)   H

Milwaukee (7)

MPS

Chicago (8)

New York City (6)
Brooklyn (9)
Philadelphia (8)

Pittsburgh (3)

San Francisco (3)

A

New Orleans (3)

A Indicates the location of an Anheuser-Busch brewery
H Indicates the location of a Theodore Hamm brewery
M Indicates the location of a Miller brewery
P Indicates the location of a Pabst brewery
S Indicates the location of a Joseph Schlitz brewery

Cities with 3 or more breweries are named. Cities with 6 or more breweries are named in boldface.
Data for New York City includes all boroughs except Brooklyn, which is listed separately.

pealed the laws soon after. The people of the United States wanted their government to follow suit. Congressman Volstead of Minnesota, who had authored the 18th Amendment's implementing act, was defeated for re-election in 1922, and in 1926 Montana became the first of many states to repeal its state prohibition enforcement law. Finally, in 1932, Franklin D Roosevelt ran for president on a Democratic Party platform that called for absolute repeal of the 18th Amendment. Roosevelt was elected by a landslide in November and inaugurated the following March. In February 1933 Congress submitted a repeal resolution to the states, and a month later they passed the Cullen Act redefining the phrase 'intoxicating beverage,' thereby permitting the sale of beer with 3.2 percent alcohol before the official repeal of the 18th Amendment.

REPEAL

On 7 April 1933 the headline on the front page of the New York Times read 'Beer Flows in 19 States at Midnight as City Awaits Legal Brew Today.' Within three weeks of President Roosevelt's inauguration the American brewing industry was back in business with temporary permits issued in time to ferment

Left: General superintendent and brewmaster William Figge of Theodore Hamm Brewing Co draws the first stein of legal beer in St Paul, Minnesota in 1933. *Above:* The finishing touches are applied to a 14-foot-high brew kettle in March 1933.

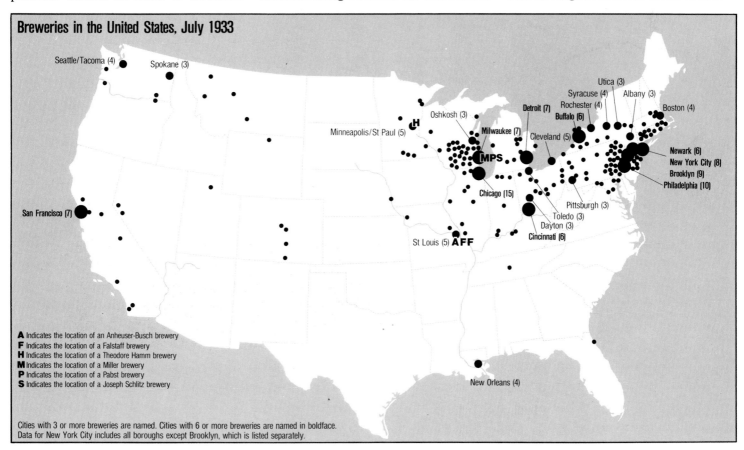

Breweries in the United States, July 1933

Seattle/Tacoma (4)   Spokane (3)

Oshkosh (3)   Detroit (7)   Utica (3)

Minneapolis/St Paul (5)   Milwaukee (7)   Syracuse (4)   Albany (3)

Rochester (4)   Buffalo (6)   Boston (4)

MPS   Cleveland (5)

Chicago (15)   Newark (6)
New York City (8)
Brooklyn (9)
Philadelphia (10)

San Francisco (7)   Pittsburgh (3)

St Louis (5) AFF   Toledo (3)
Dayton (3)   Cincinnati (6)

New Orleans (4)

A Indicates the location of an Anheuser-Busch brewery
F Indicates the location of a Falstaff brewery
H Indicates the location of a Theodore Hamm brewery
M Indicates the location of a Miller brewery
P Indicates the location of a Pabst brewery
S Indicates the location of a Joseph Schlitz brewery

Cities with 3 or more breweries are named. Cities with 6 or more breweries are named in boldface.
Data for New York City includes all boroughs except Brooklyn, which is listed separately.

A Fauerbach Beer Co display *(left)* in 1933. The company ceased operations between 1920 and 1933. *Above:* The General Brewing Co of San Francisco still found a use for horse teams in 1934, but just for show.

JUST LIKE RIP VAN WINKLE

When the American brewing industry awoke in 1933–34 from its long slumber, it faced a nation and marketplace much different from those of more than a decade before. The soft drink industry was now firmly established, and consumers were more sophisticated. Consumers could, for example, enjoy Coca-Cola at the soda fountain or take it home in those familiar pale green 'Coke-bottle-shaped' bottles. Perhaps because of Prohibition, a trend grew for packaged beer that could be taken home. At the turn of the century and indeed up to the eve of Prohibition, bottled beer accounted for just a tiny fraction of beer sales. By 1934 a quarter of the beer sold in the United States was in bottles, and by 1941 packaged beer had surpassed draft beer by a 52 to 48 percent margin.

Packaged beer in the context of 1934 referred only to bottles, but after 1935 bottled beer was joined on the shelves by a new phenomenon— canned beer. The first canned beer was introduced on 24 June 1935 by the American Can Company and the Krueger Brewing Company of Newark, New Jersey. Schlitz quickly joined forces with the Continental

their first brew by 7 April. By June 1933 there were 31 brewers brewing beer in the United States out of the 1568 that had existed before Prohibition. A year later the number had risen to 756, but many of these failed in the depression.

In December 1933, when Utah became the thirty-sixth state to ratify the 21st Amendment repealing the 18th Amendment, the production and sale of all alcoholic beverages became legal in the United States for the first time in nearly 14 years. Some states, however, retained prohibition; as late as 1948, Kansas, Oklahoma and Mississippi still prohibited the sale of alcoholic beverages. In 1935 the Federal Alcohol Administration was established by the US Government to control and supervise the American liquor industry—a function absorbed by the Alcohol Tax Unit of the Internal Revenue Service in 1940. Of the states permitting the sale of liquor, 17 adopted laws prescribing a state-controlled sales monopoly. These laws were gradually amended to exclude beer, which then became available at grocery stores.

Can Company, introducing a 'cone top' can the same year. The cone top can was just that: a can topped by a cone topped by a bottle cap. It looked something like a metal bottle. Cans were made of first tin, then steel and finally, in 1959, Coors introduced the lightweight aluminum cans that were quickly adopted by the entire

Continued on page 96

BREWERY CLOSE-UP

AMERICAN BREWING IN THE 1940s

ACME BREWING

Above: Acme Brewing began in the nine-teenth century in San Francisco and branched out to Los Angeles in 1935. The centerpiece of the company's big expansion of the 1940s was a glass-walled building in San Francisco that Acme called the 'most modern bottle shop in the world' and one that architects and designers described as 'one of the world's most beautiful industrial buildings.'

Below: Sampling the Acme brew on the San Francisco production line.

Above and below: As late as the 1940s, California's central valley was one of North America's leading hop-producing regions. The Acme hop ranch near Yuba City won first place at the California State Fair for two consecutive years. Shirley Kimball, the State Fair's Queen of Hops, was invited to Yuba City for a tour of the Acme ranch.

The vines on the Acme ranch's Hop Avenue *(above left)* reached 18 feet in height. Hops are picked at the peak of ripeness, then cleaned *(above center)*, kiln-dried and bailed in burlap to retain their pungent aroma and flavor. It was not unusual in the 1940s for a brewery to operate its own hop ranch, but today's brewers buy their hops from independent growers. After mashing and straining, the wort that would become Acme beer went into the 450-barrel brew kettle. As the wort was cooked in the big copper kettle, hops from Acme's ranch were added to season it *(above right)*.

Above: After brewing in the brew kettle, Acme's wort was cooled, then fermented in open fermenting tanks to add 'life and sparkle.'

Above: Prior to packaging, Acme beer, like all beer brewed in the 1930s and 1940s, went through a government tax meter.

Above: Based on its faith in the fast-growing West, Acme almost doubled its capacity after World War II. The breweries were sold in 1954, however. The San Francisco plant finally ceased brewing in 1958, and the Los Angeles brewery survived until 1972, spending its last 14 years as a Theodore Hamm brewery.

Above: Acme president Carl Schuster invited Queen of Hops Shirley Kimball to his San Francisco office to view the Acme stein collection. Kimball appeared in the film *What's Brewing* (c 1946) which featured Acme Brewing.

Above: The Sequoia Lodge adjacent to Acme's Los Angeles brewery on East 49th Street was used to entertain dealers, and it could also be rented for civic meetings. Taste tests, some of which were held at the Sequoia Lodge prior to World War II, had determined Acme beer to be 'the West's favorite, ever since repeal.'

industry. Except for the World War II era of tin rationing, sales of beer in nonreturnable cans gained against sales of bottled beer until 1969 when canned beer finally outsold bottled beer for the first time.

Despite the postrepeal resurgence of the industry, growth was slow during the 1930s because of the depression. Annual production went from zero to 53 million barrels between 1933 and 1940, but the 1940 figures were the same as the 1910 figures and well below the 1914 pre-Prohibition peak of 66 million barrels.

WORLD WAR II

Just as the American brewing industry was getting back to its pre-World War I levels, the United States once again found itself at war. In 1941 little of the anti-German sentiment that had been seen at the beginning of World War I existed. This time American brewers, regardless of the spelling of their last names, were thought of as American brewers. Another big change in World War II was that the military establishment had come to realize that the men they were drafting for service liked to drink beer. As a result, the military leadership from Army Chief of Staff George Marshall on down stood by the decision to permit beer sales on military bases.

During the massive mobilization that accompanied World War II, the American brewing industry set aside 15 percent of its output for the troops. Also resulting from the mobilization, young men with long-standing loyalties to hometown brews were exposed to national brands. Their resultant taste for and loyalty to the national brands carried over into the huge expansion of the national brands that followed the war.

The Second World War produced an unprecedented expansion in the American economy, and the brewing industry was certainly part of it. Between 1940 and 1945, the output of beer increased 51 percent to 80 million barrels annually. By comparison, the 26 years before 1940

Right: Lucille Knutson stands in front of the glassed-walled million-dollar Acme bottle plant, once dubbed 'one of the world's most beautiful industrial buildings,' for a photograph in March 1942.

saw a 20 percent decline, and the years from 1945 to 1960 saw just a moderate 11 percent increase. At the turn of the century there were three million-barrel breweries: Pabst, Schlitz and Anheuser-Busch. By World War II these national brands were joined by three more: Ballantine, Ruppert and Schaefer, all in the New York City metropolitan area, and therein lies a tale.

NEW YORK'S BIG THREE

New York City had been the New World's first major brewing center when it was still New Amsterdam, but by World War II it had become the capital of the world. With all of the world's other major cities either under seige or occupied by foreign armies, the world's power and wealth gravitated toward the bustling colossus on the Hudson that was edging past London to become the world's *largest* city as well. In the era before street crime and urban decay, New York represented the hopes and dreams of a war-weary world yearning for a postwar future of peace and prosperity. Manhattan's gleaming skyscrapers, then

unmatched anywhere, were like a beacon for the best and brightest from every field whether arts, science or industry. They came not just from America's cities and towns but from throughout the world. Then, as if to crown this great city and confirm its place as the capital of the world, the United Nations established its world headquarters in New York.

It was little wonder then that the world's largest and greatest city should have three of the nation's biggest breweries. They were Ballantine, Ruppert (doing business as Rheingold) and Schaefer, all household words among the households of North America's most populous region.

Ballantine was the first of the big three although Peter Ballantine was one of the last of the English-tradition brewers to set up shop in North America. Ballantine established his shop in Albany in 1833, but moved to Newark, New Jersey across the Hudson River from New York City in 1840. In Newark he joined forces with Erastus Patterson and together they acquired a brewery that had been started in 1805 by General

Below left: Schaefer was one of the household words in New York City brewing. Frederick and Maximillian Schaefer, founders of the company, were pioneers in lager beer brewing. *Below:* The Schaefer Brewery in Brooklyn before Prohibition. In 1916 it moved from Park Avenue to the riverfront of Brooklyn and stayed in business during Prohibition by making near beers, dyes and ice.

John Cumming. In 1847 Peter Ballantine became sole proprietor of the firm, which operated from the location on Front Street until 1920 when Prohibition permanently closed the doors. In 1879, however, Ballantine acquired a second brewery on Freeman Street from the Schalk brothers who had started there in 1852. Also in 1879, Ballantine adopted the legendary three rings logo, its trademark of quality for the next century. When Prohibition ended in 1933, Ballantine reopened at Freeman Street, and in 1943 as wartime demand began to skyrocket, a Plant 2 was opened nearby and it remained in service until 1948. These years were a golden age for Ballantine, whose three rings were omnipresent in the New York area and whose sales placed it among the top brewers in the United States even though it was a regional or, more precisely, a hometown brewery. Ballantine was particularly notable because it brewed top-fermenting ale in an era dominated by lager brewers. In 1960 Ballantine was still the sixth biggest brewer in the nation, but by 1970 it was out of the top 10 and in 1972 the company was sold to Falstaff.

The second of New York's big three breweries was the empire of Jacob Ruppert, Inc, known by its ever-popular Rheingold brand name. Ruppert began operations in 1867 at 1639 Third Avenue on Manhattan's Upper East Side. Over the years the Rheingold brand developed a very loyal following throughout the New York area. Between 1915 and 1939 Ruppert owned the remarkable New York Yankees baseball team. During World War II, with many New Yorkers in the service, Ruppert even set up a Rheingold brewery near the big US Navy yard in Norfolk, Virginia. Originally started in 1896 as Consumers Brewing, the Norfolk brewery was purchased from Southern Breweries, Inc in 1942 and operated as Jacob Ruppert-Virginia, Inc until 1953 when it was sold to the Century Brewery Corp.

The Rheingold flagship remained on Third Avenue through the golden years of the 1940s and 1950s, but the changing nature of the urban landscape in the 1960s cost New York City a good many of its long-established companies. In 1943 New York City (excluding Brooklyn) had eight breweries. In 1953 four re-

Above: Jacob Ruppert, whose Rheingold beer was one of New York City's big three brands. *Left:* R J Schaefer in 1965, grandson of Maximillian Schaefer, at the height of his kingdom's glory. *Below:* An ad announcing 1936 Bock Beer Day in New York.

mained, and by 1963 only one. In 1964 Ruppert established new satellite breweries in Brooklyn and in Orange, New Jersey. The following year the Third Avenue plant was closed forever. In Brooklyn, Ruppert bought the Liebman Brewery that had been established by Samuel Liebman in 1854 and in Orange the old Orange Brewery (established in 1901) that had been owned by Leibman since 1950. In 1967 Ruppert bought Dawson's Brewery in New Bedford, Massachusetts. By 1976 the changing conditions that led to

the demise of the old Third Avenue flag-ship had reached Brooklyn, and in 1977 the Orange and New Bedford breweries closed their doors as well.

Frederick and Maximillian Schaefer had arrived in New York on the crest of the lager revolution and established one of Manhattan's first lager brew-eries in 1842. After 67 years in their huge, red brick brewery on Park Ave-nue and East 51st Street, Schaefer was one of the first big Manhattan brewers to move operations entirely to Brooklyn. Schaefer survived Prohibi-tion by brewing near beer and emerged from those dark days with the motto 'Our hand has never lost its skill.'

Within five years the company had reached the million-barrel mark. In the expansive decades after World War II, Schaefer operated satellite breweries in Albany, New York (1950-1972), Cleve-land, Ohio (1961-1963) and Baltimore, Maryland (1963-1978) to help meet the demand for his popular brew. In 1972, when the Albany facility was closed, its production was transferred to a new, ultramodern brewery near Allentown in Pennsylvania's Lehigh Valley. In 1976 Schaefer's 60-year-old Brooklyn brewery, no longer economically viable, was closed. The closing of Schaefer's Brooklyn operation in 1976 brought an end to over three centuries of brewing history. It was the last brewery in New York City (until the microbrewery revo-lution a decade later), North America's original brewing center.

MAKE WAY FOR THE NATIONALS

New York's big three brewers would probably have survived as independent brewers had they decided to go national after World War II. They were certainly big enough and had the power, but it was probably for the rea-son of size that they did not. Why should they expend their energy on national expansion when they were sit-ting on top of the hemisphere's largest beer market, where they could remain hometown brewers and still be part of America's top six, which included the nationals, Anheuser-Busch, Schlitz and Pabst? For nearly a quarter cen-tury, this theory worked. Though each would attempt briefly to expand as regional brewing companies, they remained essentially hometown New York brewers. However, as the popula-tion center of the United States shifted westward and California overtook New

America's Largest Selling Ale

York as the most populous state, the once powerful New Yorkers, who had themselves abandoned Manhattan, were ironically swallowed by out-of-state national brands.

A new chapter in American brewing history began to unfold in the years immediately after World War II, but while the strategy was bold and new, the players were familiar. The Joseph Schlitz Company had been early in rec-ognizing the importance of distribu-tion and multisite brewing, and in fact the company had built a satellite brew-ery in Cleveland, Ohio from scratch in 1908 and had operated there for two years. Anheuser-Busch, an innovator in mass distribution for over half a cen-tury, was also ready to play for a large slice of the national pie. Both com-

panies began to look beyond national distribution and toward a truly national system of satellite breweries unheard of prior to World War II.

When the war ended, neither Schlitz nor Anheuser-Busch was based in a major, growing market. The major market at the time was, of course, New York, which was dominated by Ballan-tine, Rheingold and Schaefer, whose breweries were located there. The first step toward cracking the market was simply to build breweries in that area. Schlitz was the first by two years, when it bought the George Ahret Brewery in Brooklyn in 1949. Anheuser-Busch opted to build a brand new plant in Newark, New Jersey, which opened in 1951.

Three years later, in 1954, the two

Above: **To celebrate the end of Prohibition in 1933, August A Busch presented his father with a team of Clydesdales, the rebirth of a tradition dating back to 1876, when Budweiser was delivered by wagons drawn by draft horses.** *Left:* **An ad for Ballantine's Ale. Note the legendary three rings logo.**

competitors became the first brewers with a coast-to-coast network of breweries, as they both opened new facilities in the Los Angeles area. Schlitz, the postwar industry leader, made its next move in 1956 by acquiring the former Muehleback Brewery in Kansas City, Missouri, Anheuser-Busch's back yard. In 1959 both of the national giants opened facilities in Tampa, Florida, but by the following year, Anheuser-Busch had replaced Schlitz as America's leading brewer.

Over the course of the next 16 years, Anheuser-Busch began brewing at six additional locations: Houston, Texas (1966); Columbus, Ohio (1968); Jacksonville, Florida (1969); Merrimack, New Hampshire (1970); Williamsburg, Virginia (1972); and Fairfield, near San Francisco, California (1976).

During the same period Schlitz expanded into the South with new breweries in Longview, Texas (1966); Winston-Salem, North Carolina (1970); and Memphis, Tennessee (1971). Schlitz also operated the old Milwaukee Brewery in San Francisco as a Schlitz brewery between 1964 and 1969. In 1973 Schlitz consolidated its map of the United States by closing the Brooklyn and Kansas City breweries.

In the mid-1970s Schlitz was still the nation's number two brewer, (with a 15 percent market share compared to 23 percent for Anheuser-Busch) but by 1980 the once-powerful Milwaukee giant had fallen to number four. An event symbolic of the times for Schlitz came in 1979, with the sale of its two-year-old Baldwinsville, New York brewery to Anheuser-Busch. The final blow came in 1982, when the brewer that brewed the beer that made Milwaukee famous was sold to the Stroh Brewing Company of Detroit, who would close the Schlitz plant in Milwaukee.

When World War II ended, Schlitz and Anheuser-Busch represented the top rung in the market, but it was a market with fewer and fewer brewers

serving a growing market, opening the door for other national brands.

Pabst was another important contender, and it remained in the top three through the 1970s. The continent's industry leader at the turn of the century, Pabst emerged from Prohibition to pioneer multisite brewing by reopening in Milwaukee and starting a new brewery at Peoria Heights near Chicago in 1934. After World War II Pabst had actually gotten into the New York market before either Schlitz or Anheuser-Busch, through the purchase of the Hoffman Beverage Company of Newark in 1946. From then on Pabst's expansion was much slower than its two major rivals. In 1958 Pabst bought the Blatz Brewery, one of its original Milwaukee rivals. From its small number of sites, Pabst continued among the top five national brewers without further expansion until 1972, when a new brewery was opened at Perry, Georgia, and 1979, when the company acquired the Blitz-Weinhard Brewery in Portland, Oregon. Three years later, in 1983, Pabst sold both of its later acquisitions to Heileman and bought the former Schlitz plant in Tampa, Florida (which became a Pabst brewery) and the Olympia Brewing Company in Tumwater, Washington, which continued to operate under the Olympia name.

FALSTAFF

A fourth brewer to emerge as a national power around the time of World War II was Falstaff. The company was started by 'Papa Joe' Griesdieck, who purchased two breweries in St Louis between 1911 and 1917. These two breweries, the Independent/Consumers on Shenandoah Avenue and the Forest Park on the boulevard of the same name, were both renamed after their new owner; together they formed the basis for a small empire of breweries formed along the banks of the Mississippi and Missouri rivers. During Prohibition, the company was renamed Falstaff after the Shakespeare character, and it whiled away those years brewing near beer and smoking hams.

After Prohibition, Falstaff acquired the former Union Brewery in St Louis in 1933, then went upriver to acquire the former Fred Krug Brewery in Omaha in 1935, and down river to New Orleans, where it purchased the former National Brewery in 1937. Falstaff emerged from World War II with more

Right: The Burgermeister building at 470 Tenth Street in San Francisco as it appeared in 1951. The largest single brewery west of St Louis when it was built, it cost $1.5 million and had a 900,000 bbl capacity. The site was once occupied by the Milwaukee Brewery. established in 1880 *(see pages 4-5),* and was a Falstaff brewery from 1975 to 1978, when it closed permanently. The building is still standing.

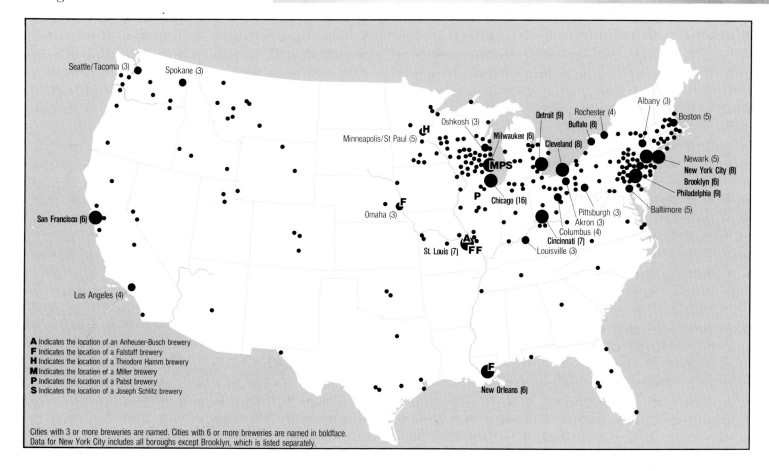

A Indicates the location of an Anheuser-Busch brewery
F Indicates the location of a Falstaff brewery
H Indicates the location of a Theodore Hamm brewery
M Indicates the location of a Miller brewery
P Indicates the location of a Pabst brewery
S Indicates the location of a Joseph Schlitz brewery

Cities with 3 or more breweries are named. Cities with 6 or more breweries are named in boldface.
Data for New York City includes all boroughs except Brooklyn, which is listed separately.

Breweries in the United States, July 1953

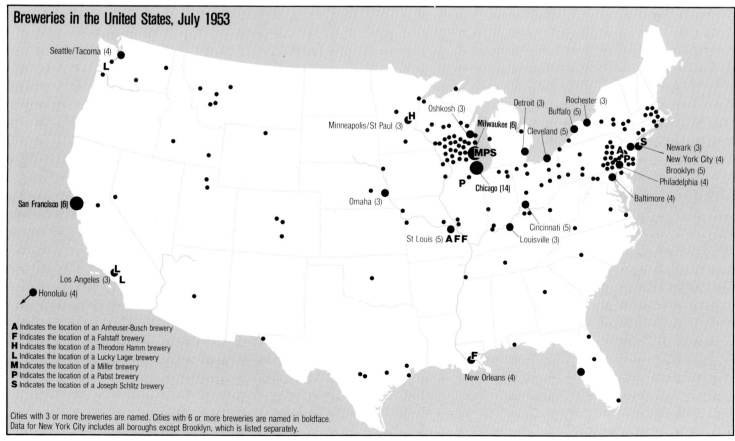

Seattle/Tacoma (4)
L

Oshkosh (3)
H
Minneapolis/St Paul (3)
Milwaukee [6]
Detroit (3)
Rochester (3)
Buffalo (5)
Cleveland (5)
MPS
P
Chicago [14]
Omaha (3)
St Louis (5) AFF
Cincinnati (5)
Louisville (3)
San Francisco [6]
A
P
S
Newark (3)
New York City (4)
Brooklyn (5)
Philadelphia (4)
Baltimore (4)

Los Angeles (3)
L
L
Honolulu (4)

F
New Orleans (4)

A Indicates the location of an Anheuser-Busch brewery
F Indicates the location of a Falstaff brewery
H Indicates the location of a Theodore Hamm brewery
L Indicates the location of a Lucky Lager brewery
M Indicates the location of a Miller brewery
P Indicates the location of a Pabst brewery
S Indicates the location of a Joseph Schlitz brewery

Cities with 3 or more breweries are named. Cities with 6 or more breweries are named in boldface.
Data for New York City includes all boroughs except Brooklyn, which is listed separately.

(albeit smaller) breweries in St Louis than Anheuser-Busch, but while the latter moved forward to a truly national market, Falstaff continued to concentrate on the Mississippi/Missouri River country. In 1948 Falstaff purchased two breweries from Columbia Brewing, one in East St Louis, Illinois and another in St Louis, which gave Falstaff five breweries in the St Louis metropolitan area. Within three years, however, two of these had been closed.

In 1952 Falstaff reached toward the rapidly expanding California market by acquiring Wieland's Brewery in San Jose, which had originally been Gottfried Krahenberg's Fredericksburg Brewery (established in 1856), one of the first breweries in California. In doing so, Falstaff was the first major eastern brewer to expand into the Golden State, beating both Schlitz and Anheuser-Busch (who were then concentrating on the New York area) by two years.

In 1954 Falstaff purchased the former Berghoff Brewing Company in Fort Wayne, Indiana, which today serves as the company's flagship brewery, while Berghoff Beer—beer packaged for the famous Berghoff Restaurant in Chicago—went on to be produced by Huber in Wisconsin, until 1989, when Berghoff *bought* Huber.

The next few years saw Falstaff moving into Texas, again ahead of Anheuser-Busch and Schlitz. Falstaff breweries were opened in El Paso in 1955 and Galveston in 1956, but they were closed in 1976 and 1981 respectively. Falstaff also moved deeper into California, and briefly operated two breweries in San Francisco: the former Milwaukee (later Joseph Schlitz) Brewery on Tenth Street (between 1971 and 1978), and the former Lucky Lager Brewery on Newhall Street (between 1975 and 1978).

Falstaff closed all of its California plants by 1978 (the San Jose brewery was closed in 1973), and all of its St Louis plants by 1977, leaving the New Orleans, Omaha and Ft Wayne plants as the only ones brewing beer under the Falstaff name. In the meantime, however, Falstaff had acquired Ballantine in 1972 and Narragansett in 1965. The Narragansett Brewing Company in Cranston, Rhode Island had been established in 1890 and had become a popular brand name in New England. For this reason, Falstaff for a time continued operations under the Narragansett name.

Above: Falstaff drivers in Austin, Texas, one year after Prohibition. *Below:* Naragansett is still featured in this Boston shop. *Right:* At the end of the evening, the butler could finally have one himself.

Though it slipped from third place nationally in 1960 to sixth place in 1970, Falstaff, through its 1975 affiliation with General Brewing, remained the ninth largest brewer in the United States in 1985. For details of their long, intertwined relationship, one is referred in turn to the listings for Falstaff and General in Part II of this work.

THE WESTERN REGIONALS

When it was acquired by Pabst in 1983, Olympia was the last of a breed of independent western brewers that had emerged from Prohibition and survived for many years after the postwar arrival in the West of the major national brands. These western brewers included Olympia at Tumwater, Blitz-Weinhard at Portland, the Sick's Empire that was centered in Seattle and Lucky Lager with locations throughout the West.

Both Olympia and Blitz-Weinhard were essentially single-site brewers that passed to their new owners (Pabst and Heileman, respectively) with their identities intact. Largely *because* they remained single-site breweries, they had developed strong regional identities. Unlike their two neighbors, Sick's and Lucky Lager represented postwar attempts at creating multisite regional empires that paralleled in geographic scope those being created in the East at the same time by the major national brands. Excluding their California and Texas operations, neither Schlitz, Pabst nor Anheuser-Busch had breweries spread over a larger area than Lucky Lager at its peak had in the West.

The story of Lucky Lager is thoroughly intertwined with that of the General Brewing Company of Vancouver, Washington, which has owned the Lucky trademark since 1971. The first Lucky Lager brewery is a case in point. Located on Newhall Street in San Francisco, it was started by General in 1934 and became a Lucky Lager brewery in 1948. It passed from Lucky back to General in 1963 and back again to Lucky in 1969. It was closed in 1978, seven years after Lucky Lager became a General brand.

The second Lucky brewery, at Azuza in Southern California, was started in 1949, sold to General in 1963, and then to Miller in 1966. The third Lucky brewery was located in Vancouver, Washington and actually traced its heritage back to the brewery that Henry

Weinhard had owned between 1859 and 1864. Restarted after Prohibition as the Interstate Brewery, it was sold to Lucky in 1950, to General in 1964 and back to Lucky in 1969. After General's 1971 purchase of Lucky, the Vancouver brewery served as the flagship brewery until its closure in October 1985.

Throughout their long courtship both Lucky and General established other widely dispersed satellite breweries in the West, including Los Angeles (General, 1971-1974), Pueblo, Colorado (General, 1971-1975) and in Salt Lake City, Utah (Lucky, 1960-1964 and General, 1964-1967). In the case of Lucky Lager, this move helped establish it as one of the West's most important and widely recognized brand names in the 1960s. Even today, the Lucky Lager name is General Brewing's most prominent brand, even if both are now mere shadows of their former selves.

The Emil Sick empire of Seattle had many similarities to the Jacob Ruppert empire in New York. Both produced a very popular beer under a brand name other than their own: Ruppert brewed Rheingold and Sick brewed Rainier. Both were associated with a baseball team: Ruppert with the New York Yankees of the American League and Sick with the Seattle Rainiers of the Pacific Coast League. Both made serious bids toward regional expansion during and after World War II: Ruppert in New York, New Jersey, Virginia and Massachusetts and Sick in Washington, Oregon, Montana and the Canadian province of Alberta.

Above: **The Spoetzel Brewery, in Shiner, Texas.** *Right, above:* **Sick's Lethbridge Brewery in Alberta as it appeared between 1955 and 1960. Today, Sick's Lethbridge still brews Lethbridge Beer, known as 'bridge beer,' but it is owned by Molson of Montreal.** *Right:* **General Brewing's Lucky Lager plant in Vancouver, Washington in 1970.**

Like many founders of North American breweries, Emil Sick was not American-born. His father, Fritz Sick, had started the Lethbridge Brewing & Malting Company Ltd in Lethbridge, Alberta, Canada in 1901. Emil took over from his father and used the Lethbridge brewery as a springboard for his American empire.

The Sick empire in World War II traces its ancestry to the post-Prohibition Century Brewing Association, which operated breweries on Westlake Avenue and on Airport Way, and which became Seattle Brewing & Malting in the 1930s. There was, however, an earlier Seattle Brewing & Malting, located on Duwamish Avenue, which operated between 1892 and 1915, that brewed the Rainier brand between 1906 and 1915.

The Westlake and Airport Way breweries became Sick's Century and Sick's Seattle, respectively, in 1944. The two Seattle plants were just the beginning. By the time the Americans had defeated the Germans in the Battle of the Bulge on Christmas Day 1944, Sick had staked out a brewing empire that spanned the Northwest. He had acquired the Spokane Brewery (started by Galland-Burke in 1892) in Spokane; the Salem Brewery (started by Samuel

Adolph in 1874) in Salem, Oregon; Missoula Brewing (started by George Gerber in 1874) in Missoula, Montana; and the Great Falls Brewery (started in 1895 as American Brewing) in Great Falls, Montana.

New brand names like Highlander (brewed in Seattle and Missoula) and Rheinlander were added to the program, but gradually the breweries slipped away. The two Montana breweries left the Sick fold in 1949. The brewery in Salem was closed in 1953, the Century in Seattle closed in 1957, and the one in Spokane closed in 1962.

Above: **The offices of the Seattle Brewing & Malting. The company brewed the famous Rainier brand from 1906 until it closed in 1915.**

In 1970 only the Airport Way brewery remained, and by then a majority interest was owned by Molson, the Canadian giant. Molson took over Sick's Lethbridge in 1958, and Emil Sick, then chairman of Sick's Breweries Ltd, joined Molson's board of directors. In 1977 Molson sold the Seattle brewery to Heileman of LaCrosse, Wisconsin, which continued to brew Rainier lager and Rainier ale in Seattle.

BREWING IN HAWAII

While it is geographically not part of North America, much of Hawaii's recent economic and cultural history is intertwined with North America because of its long association with the United States. A territory of the United States since 1900 (it was annexed in 1898), Hawaii has been a state since 1959. The first commercial brewery in the Hawaiian Islands, the Honolulu Brewing Company established in 1898, was also the only commercial brewery to be located there prior to Prohibition. With the repeal of the 18th Amendment, which had applied to US territories as well as states, a number of breweries opened in Hawaii. The former Honolulu Brewing reopened as American Brewing in 1933, and another corporation, Hawaii Brewing, opened on Honolulu's Kapiolani Boulevard in 1934.

By the 1930s a sizable portion of Hawaii's population was of Japanese ancestry, and many of them favored the traditional Japanese beverage, sake, which is brewed and fermented like beer. The major differences are that sake is made with rice rather than malted barley; it is not hopped; it is drunk warm rather than chilled or at room temperature; and it has an alcohol content roughly four times that of most beer.

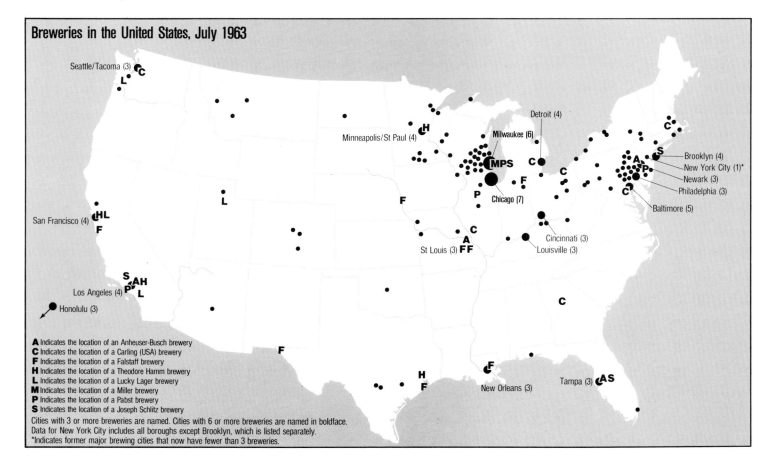

Breweries in the United States, July 1963

A Indicates the location of an Anheuser-Busch brewery
C Indicates the location of a Carling (USA) brewery
F Indicates the location of a Falstaff brewery
H Indicates the location of a Theodore Hamm brewery
L Indicates the location of a Lucky Lager brewery
M Indicates the location of a Miller brewery
P Indicates the location of a Pabst brewery
S Indicates the location of a Joseph Schlitz brewery

Cities with 3 or more breweries are named. Cities with 6 or more breweries are named in boldface.
Data for New York City includes all boroughs except Brooklyn, which is listed separately.
*Indicates former major brewing cities that now have fewer than 3 breweries.

All but two of the breweries in Hawaii's history brewed sake rather than beer. The first had been a short-lived experiment in 1915, but after Prohibition five sake breweries appeared in Hawaii, two in Honolulu, two in Hilo on the island of Hawaii and one in Kula on Maui. With the Japanese air attack on Honolulu's Pearl Harbor in December 1941, the United States government moved to close down Japanese businesses on the islands, including all the sake breweries, because many of them had ties to parent companies in Japan. After the war, Fuji Sake in Honolulu and the Kokusui Company in Hilo reopened, but by the time of statehood only Fuji remained, and it closed in 1965.

American Brewing, Hawaii's original beer brewer, closed in 1962, and Hawaii Brewing was sold to the Joseph Schlitz Brewing Company in 1964. Schlitz went to great lengths to promote the Primo brand, which by this time was the only beer still brewed in Hawaii. The Primo label celebrated the fact that beer had been brewed in the islands since 1897 and noted that 'pure Hawaiian water, naturally filtered through thousands of layers of lava rock, was combined with the finest quality brewing ingredients to give Primo beer a distinctive light golden taste!'

Though it was a typical American-style lager, Primo became a cult classic, and every beer drinker who ventured to the islands during this period sampled the brew, and many returned home with blue-labeled Primo bottles in suitcases. By 1979 the financial woes of the Joseph Schlitz Brewing Company became such that the parent company had to choose between the survival of the Joseph Schlitz Brewing Company and the survival of the last vestige of Hawaiian brewing history. They chose the former and the Hawaii Brewing subsidiary was closed. Schlitz did, however, continue to brew Primo 'on the mainland,' making what was once Hawaii's proudest brand an import.

In 1986, however, brewing of beer in Hawaii resumed, as Aloysius Klink, a German immigrant, started Pacific Brewing on the island of Maui with the help of Robert Kritzer, a globe-trotting German brewer with experience at breweries in Bangkok, Santiago and Damascus, as well as a long-term consulting agreement with six breweries in China. In 1988 the Koolau Brewery (Honolulu Brewing after 1989) was founded, giving America's island state two native beer breweries for the first time in a quarter century.

Right, above: Primo Beer was brewed in Hawaii until 1979, when brewing was moved to the mainland. In 1986, however, beer brewing resumed in Hawaii, with the advent of Maui Beer *(right)*.

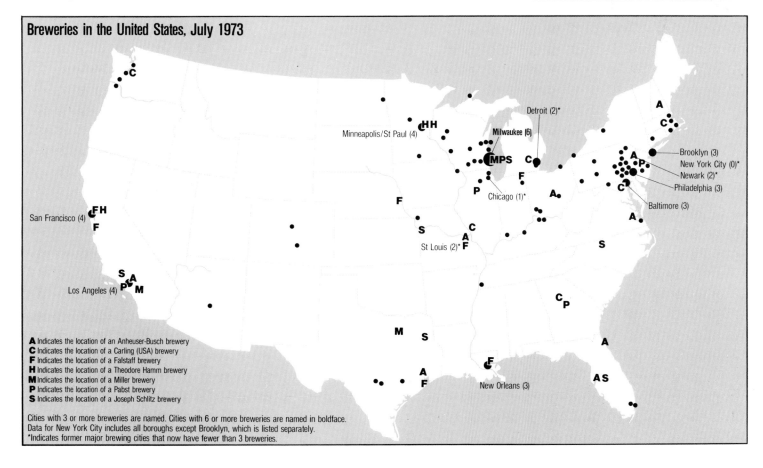

Breweries in the United States, July 1973

A Indicates the location of an Anheuser-Busch brewery
C Indicates the location of a Carling (USA) brewery
F Indicates the location of a Falstaff brewery
H Indicates the location of a Theodore Hamm brewery
M Indicates the location of a Miller brewery
P Indicates the location of a Pabst brewery
S Indicates the location of a Joseph Schlitz brewery

Cities with 3 or more breweries are named. Cities with 6 or more breweries are named in boldface.
Data for New York City includes all boroughs except Brooklyn, which is listed separately.
*Indicates former major brewing cities that now have fewer than 3 breweries.

Images from Molson's long brewing history—*(above)* a case of Molson's fine brew coming down the bottling line at the Montreal plant in the 1930s, and a sleigh of the type used by Molson to deliver their beer in Quebec's harsh and snowy north country *(below)*. Molson is one of Canada's Big Three.

CANADA'S BIG THREE

Just as the 'big three' United States brewers at the turn of the century remained near the top of the heap through most of the century, so it was in Canada. However, these breweries—Molson, Labatt's and Carling O'Keefe—faced marketing conditions quite different from those in the United States. Canada has a larger area but a much smaller population. Its population remained concentrated in the east long after the United States' population began to disperse westward. For this reason the big breweries of Quebec and Ontario faced no competition from national brands because outside of these two provinces, there could be no national brand. Even though they constitute just 25 percent of Canada's total land area, they contained 75 percent of her population in 1896, and were still home to 60 percent of Canadians in 1980.

By 1900 Canada's 132 breweries were producing 27.6 million gallons of beer, of which 54 percent were produced in Ontario, 31 percent in Quebec and five percent in British Columbia. Ninety years later the percentages would be 52 percent, 35 percent and 10 percent. British Columbia in 1900—as in 1990—had an unusually large number of smaller breweries,

whose output was then 96 percent lager. By contrast, eastern breweries, especially those in the maritime provinces, were more apt to produce ale or porter. Today lager accounts for the majority of Canada's beer consumption, although per capita ale consumption is higher than in the United States.

Meanwhile, on the vast plains of central Canada, marketing anything meant creating a demand where none previously existed. Konrad Witteman, who established a brewery at Prince Albert, Saskatchewan in 1896 (when it was still part of the Northwest Territories), wrote in 1902: 'When we came here there was hardly any demand for beer, everybody drinking whiskey; but since we started the brewery, the sale of beer has increased right along and the taste here will be cultivated.'

Aside from Canada's vastness and the cultural and economic domination of Ontario and Quebec, Canada's lag in developing national brands as early as the United States resulted from the autonomous nature of her provincial governments.

Many types of governmental regulations concerning brewing that are written by the federal government in the United States are written by the provincial governments in Canada, and even today, a brewer must operate

Labatt and Carling O'Keefe, along with Molson, were Canada's great Big Three Brewers. *Above:* A turn-of-the-century poster showing two gentlemen enjoying Labatt's at their club. *Below:* The big Carling O'Keefe plant in Ontario.

a brewery *within* a province in order to sell his beer there.

In 1916, as the United States was beginning to toy with the idea of a national Prohibition, Canada's provinces had already begun to adopt provincial Prohibition as a wartime measure. By 1919 Prohibition was complete except for Quebec, which exempted beer and wine. During 1920-21, Quebec was the only place north of the Mexican border where beer could legally be brewed. The other provinces gradually began to repeal their Prohibition in 1921, and by 1930 Prince Edward Island, the only province to adopt Prohibition before 1916, was the only province to still retain it.

During the years between Prohibition and World War II, Canada's big three, like their counterparts in the United States, began to improve their distribution system in order to capture larger segments of the market. The most colorful stories belong to Labatt's and begin in 1919. Prior to Prohibition in Ontario, the brewery of John Labatt, like that of John Molson, had transported its beer by rail or by horse-drawn wagons by summer and by sleds the rest of the year. In 1919 the United States government blocked the sale of some White Motor Company trucks to

Introduced in 1932, Labatt's red streamliner trucks (*above*) were designed by a Russian count who once designed coaches for the Tsar. The streamliners were more distinctive, but no more reliable than vehicles of today, such as the Molson's truck seen below,

winding its way through Montreal bringing the brew to friendly and congenial neighborhood taverns such as the one above.

the revolution-ridden Mexican government. As a result, White found another international customer and Labatt's had its first motor-driven distribution vehicles.

By 1932 trucks had become commonplace and Labatt's was ready to try the uncommon. In that year the company introduced its bright red Streamliner truck. Designed by the Russian expatriate coach designer Count Alexis de Sakhnoffsky, these striking, aerodynamic vehicles won 'Best Design' at the 1939 New York World's Fair and earned a place as the most innovative beer truck in the history of North America. Although they were withdrawn from service in 1942, one of the trucks was preserved and today remains as a major company showpiece.

After World War II, Canadian brewers, like American brewers, began to set their sights on multisite operations. Labatt's purchased its second brewery, the former Copland Brewing Company of Toronto, in 1946, and Molson, Canada's oldest brewer, opened its second site in 1955, just 169 years after its first. Though it would not take Molson as long to open its third, the leader in Canadian multisite expansion was Carling O'Keefe.

Behind its flagship brand, Carling Black Label, the company was spreading its empire beyond Ontario, where breweries were in operation at Toronto, Waterloo, Sudbury and Thunder Bay. The Carling O'Keefe group included Golden West and Calgary Export in Alberta, Standard in Manitoba and Four-X Special, a stout brewed in Vancouver, British Columbia.

Carling was not content to remain solely a Canadian brewer either. Through international licensing agreements, Carling Black Label was appearing throughout the world, and the company was plying that huge beer market south of Canada's borders. Carling made its first inroads in the United States in Cleveland, Ohio, through the Brewing Corporation of America, before World War II. However, it was after the war that Carling moved south in a big way. The Brewing Corporation of America's brewery on Quincy Avenue in Cleveland became the Carling Brewing Company in 1953. The following year Carling acquired the former Griesedieck Western breweries in Belleville, Illinois and St Louis. In 1956 Carling added breweries in Natick, Massachusetts and Frankenmuth, near Detroit, in Michigan. Two years later the Canadian-based brewer put

Right: **A 1930 photo of the headquarters for Prince Albert Breweries Ltd, in Prince Albert, Saskatchewan.** *Far right:* **The main offices of Pelisser's Brewery in Fort Garry, Alberta in 1919.**

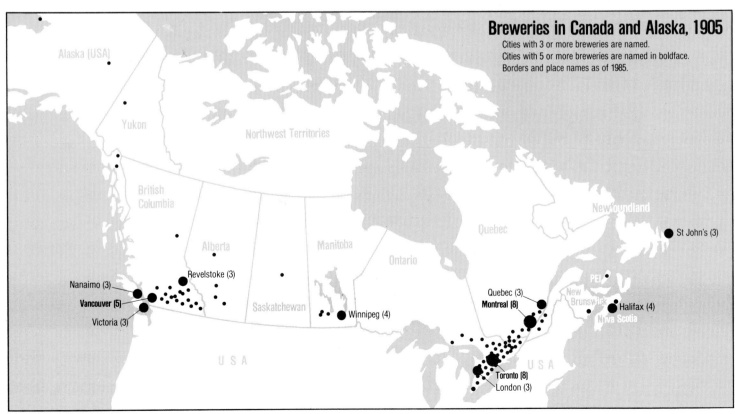

Breweries in Canada and Alaska, 1905
Cities with 3 or more breweries are named.
Cities with 5 or more breweries are named in boldface.
Borders and place names as of 1985.

117

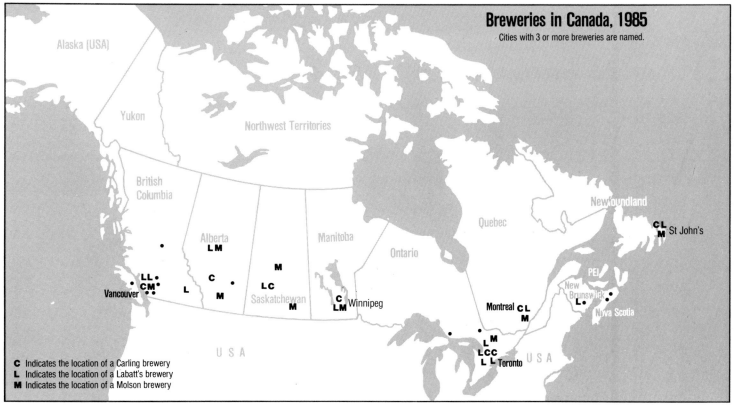

Breweries in Canada, 1985
Cities with 3 or more breweries are named.

Alaska (USA)

Yukon

Northwest Territories

British Columbia

Newfoundland

C L
M St John's

Alberta
L M

Manitoba

Quebec

Ontario

PEI

New Brunswick

L L
C M
Vancouver

C
L

M

L C

M

C
L M Winnipeg

Montreal C L
M

Nova Scotia

L .

M
L
L C C
L L Toronto

U S A

U S A

C Indicates the location of a Carling brewery
L Indicates the location of a Labatt's brewery
M Indicates the location of a Molson brewery

out its shingle in Atlanta, Georgia and Tacoma, Washington, creating an archipelago of breweries that was the envy of many American brewers.

During the early 1960s Carling opened breweries in Baltimore, Fort Worth and Phoenix, but the latter part of the decade was marked by the company's gradual decline in the market. In 1960 Carling had been the fourth largest brewer in the United States. By 1970 its position had slipped to eighth, and by 1975 it wasn't even in the top 10.

In the meantime, Carling closed or sold its breweries in Cleveland, Atlanta and Natick. In March 1979 Carling left the United States market, selling its holdings to Heileman, which acquired the Carling breweries in Phoenix, Baltimore, Frankenmuth, Tacoma and Belleville, Illinois. Stag Beer was but one of the many brand names that came along with the breweries. Carling also sold two important international brewing licenses to Heileman. The first was for Carling's products, which Heileman continued to brew in the United States; the second was for Tuborg, a Danish beer for which Carling had acquired the license in 1973, and which had been introduced in the United States market amid much fanfare in the mid-1970s.

In 1989 the financially troubled Carling O'Keefe group became part of Molson, with the net result that Canada's big three became a big two. With the addition of Carling, Molson moved ahead of Labatt's as Canada's largest brewer.

Canada by the mid-1970s had ceased to be North America's second largest brewing country, and by 1986

Above: A century after Carling was founded in Canada, it moved into the United States via its Brewing Corporation of America (later Carling National). *Below:* Antique labels from Labatt and *(right)* a sampling of the today's products.

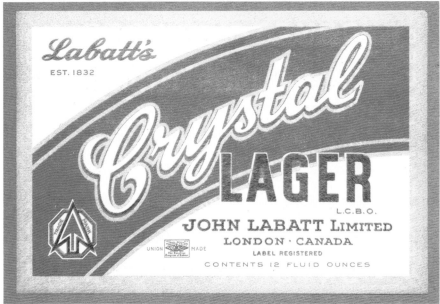

Left: An ad for Moosehead with CEO and Chairman of the Board Philip W Oland himself proclaiming the beer's worldwide fame. Oland knows of where he speaks—he is part of the same family of Canadian brewers that has in the past, and continues to play, a major role in the operations of Labatt's.

The cutaway *below* provides an insider's look at the brewing process, which begins with the mashing of barley malt in a temperature controlled 'mash-tun.' (1) The result is 'sweet wort,' which is then filtered (2) to take out the solids. It is then boiled in the copper and hops are added to stabilize and add flavor (3). After the wort is cooled, (4) fermenting begins with the addition of yeast. The young beer is then moved to aging vessels where it will cold age (5). Beer flows from aging vessels into bottles (6), which are pasteurized

was brewing 18 million barrels, compared to 20 million in Mexico. Foreign acquisition of Hamilton Breweries of Hamilton, Ontario by Heineken NV of the Netherlands brought an infusion of license-brewed beer to Canada. These include not only Heineken's own Amstel brand, but Henninger from Germany and Peroni from Italy as well.

Moosehead Breweries was a small Canadian regional company indigenous to New Brunswick until it started a major export drive into the United States in the early 1980s. Moosehead cannot by law be distributed in Canada outside New Brunswick and Nova Scotia because these are the only provinces where its beer is brewed. Ironically, Moosehead is virtually unknown throughout most of Canada, but it is one of the most—perhaps *the* most—widely recognized Canadian brand in the United States, where it is the number five imported brand. As a result of this marketing and the Molson-Carling merger, Moosehead is Cana-

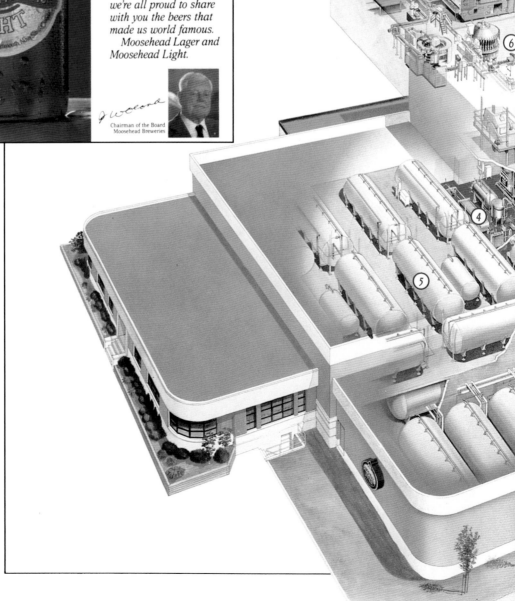

to preserve freshness, inspected, la-
belled, and crowned.

(7) Draft beer, which is unpasteurized,
goes from aging directly to the draft area.
Finally, bottles and cans are placed into
an assortment of packages for distribution to consumers (8).

This plant, located in Hamilton,
Ontario, was built in 1981 as the Hamilton Brewery but is now owned by Heineken and operated as an Amstel
Brewery. It is typical of a modern large-
scale brewery.

Above: A bottle inspector at work at the
Upper Canada Brewery. This activity
would occur at number six in the Amstel/
Hamilton cutaway *at left.*

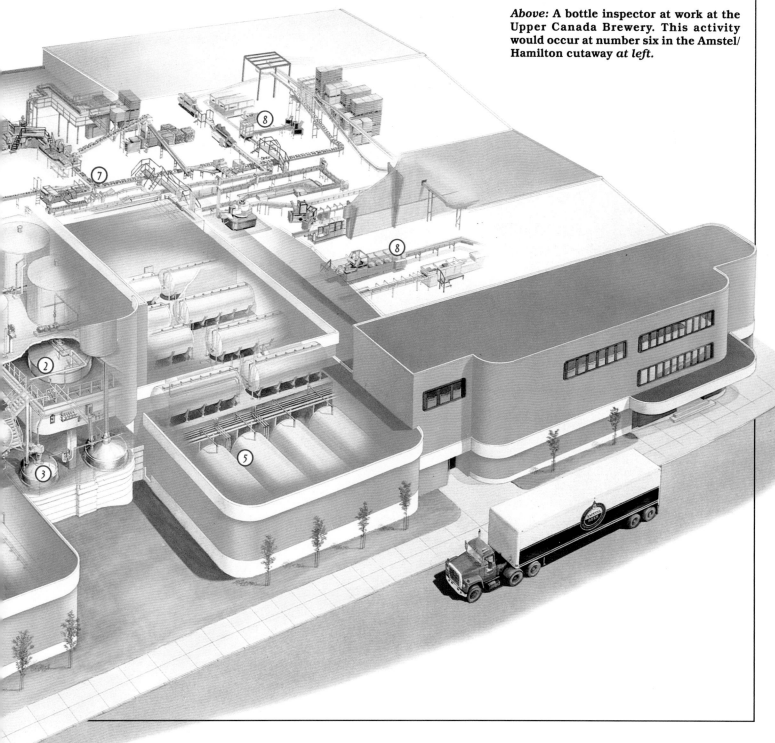

da's third largest brewer, and its 1.4-million barrel plant in St John is the largest brewery in Canada outside Quebec or Ontario.

Another major change in the Canadian market in the 1980s was the rise of a number of smaller regional brewers. These included Brick Brewing, founded in 1984 in Waterloo, Ontario; the Big Rock Brewery, founded in 1985 in Calgary, Alberta; and Upper Canada Brewing, founded in 1985 in Toronto. Brewpubs have also appeared in Canada, although they are not nearly so widespread as in the United States, and many of them seem to be concentrated near Vancouver and Toronto. These include Island Pacific in Victoria, Horseshoe Bay in Horseshoe Bay and Spinnakers in Victoria. The Granite Brewery (serving Ginger's Tavern) was previously the first Canadian brewpub outside of British Columbia when it opened in 1985.

The Brick Brewery *(above)* in Waterloo, and Upper Canada *(below)* in Toronto are part of a generation of Canadian breweries that have grown up in the shadow of Molson, whose Montreal plant *(right)* has been on the same site for two centuries.

BREWERY CLOSE-UP
NORTH AMERICA'S OLDEST BREWERY

MOLSON LTD

Above: The present day Molson brewery (Brasserie Molson) in Montreal, Quebec is located on the same site as the brewery John Molson established in 1786. Today, there are eight Molson breweries located in seven Canadian provinces from British Columbia to Newfoundland.

Above: Unlike most smaller brewers, Molson malts and mills its own barley.

Above: Putting the Molson signature on the back of a Molson delivery truck.

Above and right: The first step in the brewing process is to mix and heat malted barley and water in the mash tun. After mashing, the thick mash mixture is piped to a large lauter tun. Here the mash is carefully filtered through the natural grain bed and the resultant golden amber wort is piped to the brew kettle.

Above: The technicians at Molson's brewery laboratories run continuous tests for shelf stability, clarity, foaming and carbonation. Spectrophotometer tests are used to check color.

In big stainless steel *(above)* or copper *(below)* brew kettles, the wort is cooked and the hops are added which will season the brew and give each Molson product its characteristic flavor. The quantities, varieties and even the times that hops are added vary with the type of beer being brewed. The older breweries use copper, the newer ones, stainless steel.

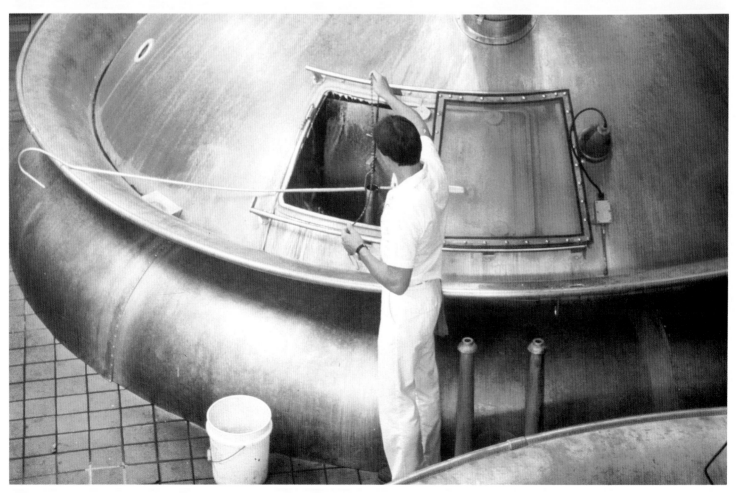

Above: Cooled wort goes into fermentation tanks where Molson brewmasters use both laboratory tests and their own practical experience to monitor the fermentation process. Visual inspections are made at regular intervals, and only when all of the brewmaster's requirements are met is the fermentation deemed complete and cooling started. After leaving the fermentation tanks, the beer passes through coolers, bringing the temperature down almost to freezing. It is then allowed to rest in the primary aging tanks where the yeast will settle out. The beer is then filtered and carbonated using the carbon dioxide produced earlier during fermentation. The beer is then transferred to aging tanks.

Above left: After secondary aging and final filtration, Molson beer is ready for packaging, pasteurization and labeling.

Left: Deposit-returned bottles are carefully inspected prior to filling.

Above: Filled bottles are inspected at random as a final quality check.

MAJOR TRENDS IN MASS MARKET BREWING

The story of American brewing in the third quarter of the twentieth century closely paralleled that of the last quarter of the nineteenth, which can be characterized simply as fewer breweries brewing more beer. At the end of World War II over 450 brewing companies existed in the United States alone, but by 1980 there were fewer than 60. Many—indeed most—small regional brewing companies felt compelled to abandon their unique styles of beer in order to emulate the giants, and in turn found themselves unable to compete. In 1965 America's top three (Anheuser-Busch, Schlitz and Pabst) controlled 27 percent of the domestic market, while in 1990 the top three (Anheuser-Busch, Miller and Stroh) controlled 71 percent.

At the end of World War II, multisite brewers, or even brewers with two plants, were a rarity, but in 1980 companies such as Anheuser-Busch and Heileman were operating 10 or more plants in the United States. Canadian

Right and far right: **Anheuser-Busch and Miller, North America's two largest brewers, both suggest enjoying their lagers ice cold.** *Below:* **Miller's 8.5-million-barrel plant is Milwaukee's largest brewery.**

PURE AS THE DRIVEN SNOW.

Pure. Genuine. A beer that's made unlike any other.

Cold-Filtered™ Miller Genuine Draft.

It contains no additives. No preservatives. And best of all, it hasn't been heat-pasteurized like most other beers.

That's because Miller Genuine Draft is the one that's Cold-Filtered™ to give you the rich, smooth taste of real draft beer in a bottle. Heat-pasteurized beers just can't do that.

Cold-Filtered™ Miller Genuine Draft. It's as real as it gets. Pure and simple.

COLD-FILTERED™ MILLER GENUINE DRAFT
IT'S AS REAL AS IT GETS.

giants like Molson and Labatt's had operations in practically every province.

A major sign of the times during the 1960s and 1970s was that many of the great brand names in the United States ceased to exist as independent entities. Miller was acquired by Philip Morris, while the once great Schlitz was acquired by the much smaller Stroh. Hamm's was acquired by Olympia, which was acquired by Pabst, which was in turn acquired by Paul Kalmanovitz, whose holdings already included Ballantine, Falstaff, General, Lucky Lager, Narragansett and Pearl. In that period Heileman, once a small brewer from La Crosse, Wisconsin, worked its way from thirty-first to fourth among American brewers by collecting an extensive roster of formerly independent regional brewers from around the country, which included Blitz-Weinhard, Blatz, Heidelberg, Lone Star, Schmidt and Rainier.

As fewer brewers each brewed more beer, they were actually brewing it for a market that was growing. During the post-Prohibition 1930s, Americans averaged 11 gallons of beer per capita annually, but by the end of World War II,

Right: **When Detroit's Stroh Brewery changed its label in 1989, it compared itself to another Detroit landmark.** *Facing page:* **A regional favorite turned national brand, Coors nearly bought Stroh in 1989.**

What's So Odd About Us Changing Our Package? Other Companies Do It Every Year.

We've never been one to seek change just for the sake of change, but in our two centuries of brewing, we've had our share of classic packages.

And now we're pleased to introduce you to our latest. One that we believe reflects even more of the 214 years of our Stroh family heritage and brewing tradition.

We hope you like it, since we don't plan on making another change for at least the next century.

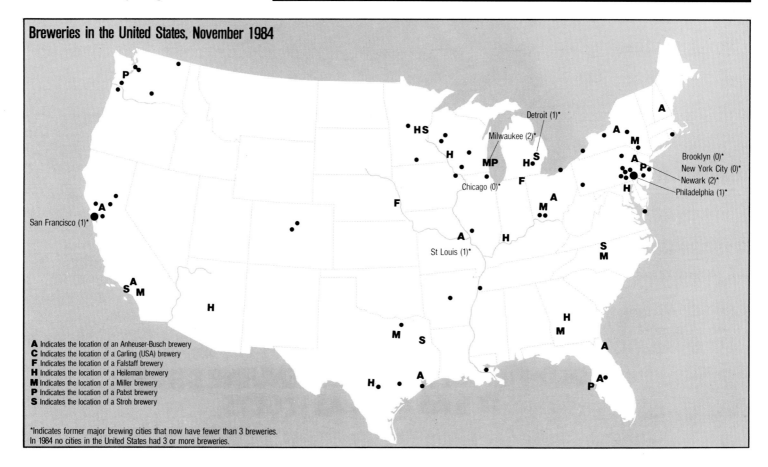

Breweries in the United States, November 1984

A Indicates the location of an Anheuser-Busch brewery
C Indicates the location of a Carling (USA) brewery
F Indicates the location of a Falstaff brewery
H Indicates the location of a Heileman brewery
M Indicates the location of a Miller brewery
P Indicates the location of a Pabst brewery
S Indicates the location of a Stroh brewery

*Indicates former major brewing cities that now have fewer than 3 breweries. In 1984 no cities in the United States had 3 or more breweries.

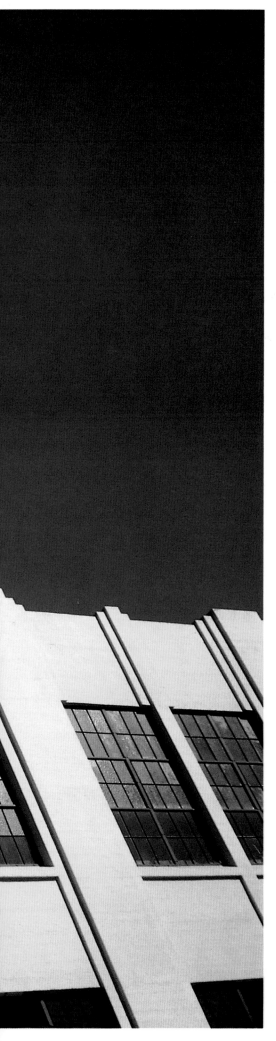

they were drinking 18.6 gallons of beer per capita. This decreased to an average of 16 gallons per capita during the 1950s and 1960s, but during the early 1970s it grew again to over 19 gallons per capita. The introduction of light beer in 1975 (see below) helped to push per capita consumption to over 22 gallons by 1980. Although it remained relatively constant throughout the 1980s, per capita consumption stayed above 22 gallons, well above the former peak decade, the 1940s, when it averaged 18.2 gallons.

Because per capita consumption changed very little between 1945 and 1973, market share reflected a major part of the story as the big brewers got even bigger. Miller expanded its market share from eight percent to 22 percent as part of Philip Morris, and Stroh grew from three percent to 12 percent after it acquired the assets of Schlitz in 1981. Simultaneously, Anheuser-Busch, the world's largest brewer, increased steadily from a one-quarter share of the domestic market to over 40 percent.

Still, there was room for smaller breweries which had maintained their local character and their local followings. An example of this is the Stevens Point Brewery of Stevens Point, Wisconsin, which dates from the brewery established prior to 1857 by Frank Wahle and George Ruder. The success of the Stevens Point Brewery and its Point Special Beer is due, at least in part, to its decision to limit distribution to a very narrow geographical area, permitting demand to exceed

Two small long-established brewers whose products enjoyed renewed popularity in the 1980s were Stevens Point *(above)* in Stevens Point, Wisconsin and Anchor *(left)* in San Francisco, California.

supply. The popularity of the brewery was further ensured in 1973, when *Chicago Sun-Times* columnist Mike Royko held a taste test in which Point Special was judged to be the best beer in the United States and second best in the world. Since then, the company's willingness to sell its beer no more than 100 miles away has been tested many times. Although it became a cult favorite in Chicago, the brewery refused to distribute Point Special that far afield. A distributor from Colorado once sent a semitrailer truck but was given only a couple of cases because the brewery didn't want to disrupt regular shipments to nearby Hatley and Polonia. Trans World Airlines wanted to serve Point Special aboard its flights, but its order for 200 cases was politely declined. Even distributors from as far away as Hong Kong have been rebuffed in their attempts to obtain international distribution rights because Stevens Point doesn't want to distribute its product outside of Wisconsin.

The brewery in the little, white, hop-covered building at the corner of Beer and Water streets has only a 55,000-barrel annual capacity for its Point Special and Seasonal Point Bock Beers, and it continues to cling tenaciously to the image and reality of a successful, small-town American brewery. As the slogan goes: 'When you're out of Point, you're out of town!'

A MEXICAN CERVECERIA

CERVECERIA MOCTEZUMA

Above: Surrounded by a moat like a medieval castle, the powerplant of Moctezuma's Guadalajara Cervecería is described as the 'heart of the factory.' It provides steam power for the cervecería as well as carbon dioxide to carbonate the cerveza.

Left: Malta (barley malt) is brought in from Central de Malta in Pueblo for milling at the Moctezuma Cervecería. Dark carmel *malta* is used in the brewing of the Dos Equis brand, while lighter *maltas* are used in lighter brands such as Sol.

Top right: The *malta* is heated in the *cocedor* (mash tun) to transform starches into fermentable sugars.

Right: From the *cocedor*, the sweet *mosto* (wort) is piped into the *filtro lauter* (lauter tun) for filtering prior to brewing.

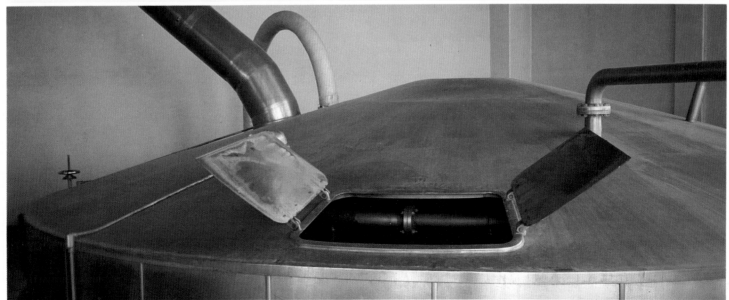

BREWERY CLOSE-UP

Above: After filtering in the *filtro lauter,* the sweet *mosto* goes into the *paila de cocinientos* (brew kettle) where the brewing takes place. The *lupulo* (hops) will be added at this stage in the form of pellets or oil rather than as whole hops. The hops will transform the *mosto* from sweet to hopped *mosto.* Moctezuma imports its hops from Yakima Valley, USA.

Above: Moctezuma's Guadalajara brewmaster, José Paz Aguirre, confers with American beer columnist Fred Eckhardt in the cervecería's laboratory.

Right: The laboratory at Moctezuma's Guadalajara Cervecería provides a constant quality control check.

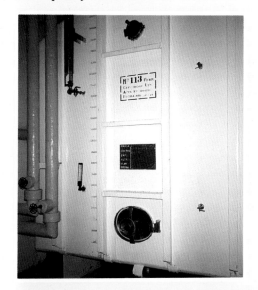

Left: After brewing in the *paila de cocinientos,* yeast is added to the *mosto* and it is placed in large closed tanks for seven days of fermentation at 12°C. As is the case with Anheuser-Busch, the yeast is recycled three times before it is discarded. It is then sold for use in animal food and medical products because of its high Vitamin B concentration.

Right: Used Moctezuma bottles are sterilized prior to refilling. The 60-peso bottle deposit, which is higher even than that in Oregon, has contributed to a high rate of recycling.

Below: Bottles used on the bottle lines at all three of Moctezuma's Cervecerías come from the Moctezuma glass factory at Orizaba.

LIGHT AND DRY

In the spirit of intense competition for a non-growth market that prevailed in the 1960s and early 1970s, American brewing companies sought to expand the overall market for beer by developing a wider product line with new types of beers that would appeal to people who otherwise would have been less inclined to drink beer. Demographically, beer drinkers were more likely to be men, so in an effort to attract more women, major brewers introduced reduced-calorie, or 'light,' beers in 1975. Miller's product, known simply as Lite, or Miller Lite, was the first and today remains the world's leading reduced-calorie beer, outselling both Anheuser-Busch's Michelob Light and Bud Light.

In 1976-1977 the light beer phenomenon helped to fuel a 7.5 percent increase in overall beer consumption, the largest increase in the United States since World War II. By the mid-1980s, light beers had secured a per-

manent niche in the North American market, which accounted for 22 percent of all beer being sold.

A light beer typically has between 70 and 100 calories per 12-ounce serving, compared to 150 or more for standard, mass market lagers. This is achieved by using less malt and allowing the sugars to ferment more completely. The resulting beer is low on malt and hop

flavor, but if served cold, it is 'clean' and refreshing, and this is very much to the American taste in mass market beers. Miller also notes in its advertising that its Lite—like other lights—is 'less filling.'

It is interesting to note that once the concept of a light beer was introduced, light beers became part of every major brewer's repertoire almost imme-

Facing page: **Women became important as consumers of beer during the 1970s with the advent of light beer.** *Above and below:* **Miller's Lite helped launch the light beer phenomenon in 1975 and is now the world leader.**

Above: Between 1986 and 1989, Anheuser-Busch used a bull terrier as a mascot to help direct its Bud Light brand to the young female market. *Below:* Reduced alcohol beer, such as Anheuser-Busch's LA, has been less widely accepted than light beers.

Above: **Because of the aluminum can, Coors calls its Coors' Light 'The Silver Bullet,' a name that has been adopted for a Coors-owned ultralight aircraft.** *Right:* **Michelob was America's first 'dry.'**

diately. There was virtually no major flagship brand anywhere in the United States or Canada that did not also market a companion 'light' variant. Stroh introduced a Stroh Light, Coor's a Coor's Light, Olympia an Olympia Light, and so on. Anheuser-Busch produced two: a Bud Light to complement Budweiser and a Michelob Light for calorie-conscious Michelob devotees. Using an already recognizable brand name seemed preferable to the idea of producing an all new product with an all new name, such as Miller had done. Miller, after all, had been first, and had taken the most obvious new brand name.

The immense success and market acceptance of reduced-calorie beers prompted some interest among major brewers to attempt to market reduced-alcohol beers. Anheuser-Busch unveiled its LA (Low Alcohol) beer at the same time as the 1984 Los Angeles Olympics, of which they were a sponsor, but the phenomenal success of light beers eight years earlier was not repeated. LA remains in the Anheuser-Busch product line, but it has few imitators.

In the summer of 1989 Anheuser-Busch launched a third wave of new products designed to reach a wider slice of the market with the introduction of their Michelob Dry. By definition, 'dry beer' is beer in which all of the fermentable sugars from the original malt have been converted to alcohol. In order to conclude the process

STARTS BOLD FINISHES CLEAN REFRESHES COMPLETELY™

ONE TASTE AND YOU'LL DRINK IT DRY.™

with a beer of acceptable alcohol content (roughly 3.2 percent by weight), a brewer must start with less malt. Hence, dry beer has a low original gravity and will have very little flavor unless it is more heavily hopped than typical beers. The process is similar to that used by brewers to produce light beer, and the results are very similar. In fact, most American mass market lagers, including light and dry beers, are very similar in taste.

Beer in which all fermentable sugars are fermented was developed in Germany and Switzerland in the 1970s as Diat (*not* diet) beer, a beer designed originally for diabetics. The concept

caught on in Japan, where Asahi and Kirin began producing it in 1987, and where dry beers eventually attained a 30 percent market share. This fact, and the introduction of Japanese dry beer into the United States in 1988, undoubtedly played a major role in the decision of American brewers to begin producing dry beer in the United States in 1989. Anheuser-Busch's Michelob Dry was first, but it was quickly followed by a number of Heileman 'Dry' products, including Lone Star, Rainier and Old Style. Molson, which was already producing Kirin under license in Canada, introduced a Molson Dry in 1989.

THE MICROBREWERY REVOLUTION

The advent of microbreweries and brewpubs in the United States and certain parts of Canada during the 1980s was probably the most exciting event in the history of North American brewing since Prohibition was repealed in 1933. For the first time in over a century, the number of brewing companies in North America began to increase. In the United States the number of breweries went from 53 in 1983 to 190 in 1988. The microbrewery revolution has given North Americans a vastly wider selection of styles and varieties of fresh, domestically produced beers than has been available since the nineteenth century. It also signaled a return to the concept of regional, and even neighborhood, breweries, an idea that was thought to have perished at the end of World War II.

Unlike regional breweries which attempted, and failed, to compete with the national brands in the 1950s and 1960s, today's smaller breweries brew specialty beers with unique characters and much richer flavors than any of the national brands. While these styles do not appeal to the same millions that buy Budweiser and Miller Lite, many have attracted large and enthusiastic followings.

By definition, a *microbrewery* was originally considered to be a brewery with a capacity of less than 3000 barrels, but by the end of the 1980s this threshold increased to 15,000 barrels as the demand for microbrewed beer doubled and then *tripled*. A *brewpub* is, by definition, a pub or tavern that brews its own beer on the premises. Until the 1980s, as a holdover from Prohibition laws, it was illegal in most states and Canadian provinces to both brew beer and sell it directly to the public on the same site. Subsequent changes in local laws have rescinded these outdated restrictions and have made it possible for brewpubs to become more widespread. Ironically, brewpubs were once very much a part of American history. During the seventeenth century many of the original establishments in places such as New Amsterdam were, in fact, brewpubs.

A brewpub differs from a microbrewery in that its primary market is under its own roof. Some brewpubs bottle their beers for sale to patrons and for wholesale to retailers, while some microbreweries also operate brew-

pubs, so the distinction between the two is somewhat blurred. Both, however, share a commitment to their own unique beers, and most brew-publicans entered their trade out of a love for brewing and an interest in distinctive beer styles.

The specialty beers of the new microbreweries arrived on the scene just as consumers were tiring of the white wine vogue that had taken hold of the market in the early 1970s. The richness, freshness and unusual variety of the new brews appealed to a generation of consumers who had just begun to experiment with imported specialty beers. This same generation had also come of age after the heyday of local and regional brands, most of which had become defunct prior to the 1970s. The microbreweries were starting up in a market which was, with few exceptions—like Anchor in California and Stevens Point in Wisconsin—almost devoid of small, regional specialty brewers. American brewing history

Above: **Buffalo Bill Owens, one of America's first microbrewers.** *Right:* **The Gordon-Biersch Brewery in Palo Alto is typical of modern, upscale 'brewery restaurants.'**

was repeating itself. A new generation began to discover and take pride in local brews, just as their grandparents had.

The microbrewery revolution started with the now extinct New Albion Brewing of Sonoma, California, which was founded by Jack McAuliffe in 1976. The patron saint of the revolution, however, was certainly Fritz Maytag, who purchased 70-year-old Anchor Brewing in San Francisco in 1965 with the expressed purpose of developing specific and unique specialty beers. Maytag was probably the last person to wish such a mantle upon himself, yet he is almost universally cited by those who followed McAuliffe's lead.

At the same time that McAuliffe was starting New Albion, there was a growing public awareness of beer styles,

Above, from top: **Sierra Nevada's new brewhouse opened in 1988. Kurt Widmer's brewery was one of Portland, Oregon's first micros. Brewmaster Bert Grant and his daughter at his Scotland-themed pub in Yakima.**

such as ales, wheat beers and stouts, that were rare or even unknown in the United States, and imports were becoming increasingly popular, particularly in major cities such as Seattle, Portland, San Francisco and New York. Indeed, it was this interest in European beer styles, nurtured in the 1970s, that was a catalyst for the microbreweries of the 1980s. It also became common to see as many as one dozen draft handles in a tavern.

After New Albion it would be several years before the microbrewery revolution began to spread. In 1980 River City Brewing opened in Sacramento, California and Sierra Nevada Brewing opened in nearby Chico. While River City survived only a few years, Sierra Nevada is now one of the largest of North America's new generation of microbreweries.

A particularly notable Portland bar owner of the era was Mike McMenamin, who, along with his brother Brian, would later found the Hillsdale Brewery, Oregon's first brewpub, and who would use the Hillsdale to anchor the largest chain of brewpubs on the continent. Thanks to the McMenamin brothers and to the spirit of adventure at the western terminus of the old Oregon Trail, Portland once again established itself as a major brewing center.

Portland was the city where Henry Saxer had started the first western brewery outside of San Francisco in 1852, which in turn had become Henry Weinhard's brewery, and later the flagship of Blitz-Weinhard. Eleven breweries had flourished here prior to 1905, but when Prohibition was repealed only Blitz-Weinhard returned. Aside from the Cartwright Brewery, which came and went between 1980 and 1982, Blitz-Weinhard had been the only brewery in Portland in the 50 years that followed repeal. Then suddenly between 1984 and 1985 Portland became a multi-brewery town for the first time in a century, with four breweries located within a one-half mile area on the city's northwest side. Blitz-Weinhard (now flying the Heileman flag) was joined by the Columbia River Brewery, the Portland Brewery (not related to Portland Brewing, which operated between 1905 and 1928) and the Widmer Brewing Company. Kurt Widmer was the second American brewer to make altbier (German style ale) since Prohibition. Stanislaus Brewing in California had been the first.

The microbrewery movement spread to Colorado in 1980 with the opening of the Boulder Brewing Company, and to New York state as William Newman began brewing in Albany the following year. Two microbreweries opened in Washington state during 1982: the Red Hook Ale Brewery in Seattle and Yakima Brewing & Malting, which is coincidentally located in the heart of the best hop-growing region in North America.

Brewpubs began to follow the microbreweries as the laws prohibiting them were repealed. Mendocino Brewing, which was established in the appropriately-named village of Hopland, about two hours north of San Francisco, opened in 1982, and was followed two years later by Buffalo Bill Owens' brewpub in Hayward, across the Bay from San Francisco. By the time that Allen Paul opened San Francisco Brewing—the city's first brewpub since Prohibition—in the old Albatross Saloon in 1986, there was a rush of new brewpubs opening throughout the United States. Mike and Brian

Above: **Small, homey brewpubs like Pacific Coast Brewing in Oakland, CA are typical but in contrast to the huge Oldenberg Brewery & Entertainment Complex *(below)* in Fort Mitchell, KY.**

McMenamin led the brewpub revolution into the Northwest in 1985 with the Hillsdale in Portland, and within four years they had opened six brewpubs in western Oregon.

The style and ambience of brewpubs varies greatly. In a sense, San Francisco Brewing is the definitive American pub. It is small and compact, with a carved mahogany bar and antique Indian 'Oompah' palm fans on the ceiling. Located in a neighborhood that has been a beer drinkers' gathering place since the Gold Rush era, it has the comfortable, well-worn feel that makes it easy to believe that it was one of the first bars to reopen after the 1906 Earthquake, which it was. It is home to both local characters and visitors from hundreds of miles away who are following the brewpub trail through the West.

On the other end of the brewpub spectrum there is the Oldenberg Brewery and entertainment complex on Buttermilk Pike in Ft Mitchell, Kentucky, across the Ohio River from Cincinnati. The name 'entertainment complex'

Left and below: **The 10,000-barrel Boulder Brewery in the picturesque Colorado Rocky Mountain town of the same name was opened in 1984.**

truly tells the story. With perhaps fifty times the square footage of San Francisco Brewing or most typically modest brewpubs, Oldenberg is really a beer drinkers' amusement park. The centerpiece is an immense beer hall with a 65-foot ceiling that seats 650 people and offers live entertainment. There is also a smaller brewpub and an outdoor beer garden. Tours are offered of both the brewery and what Oldenberg characterizes as 'the largest brewing memorabilia collection in the world.'

While most brewpubs specialize in what Allen Paul of San Francisco Brewing describes as 'pub food'—sandwiches, burgers and snacks—the brewpub is no longer necessarily a 'pub' in the traditional sense. The definition of brewpub has now been stretched to include full service restaurants that brew beer. This trend is indicative of the recognition that beer is just as important a complement to fine cuisine as wine. This is particularly true now that American brewers are producing a much wider variety of beer styles, each of which has a character that complements a particular type of food. These may include more familiar ales, porters and lagers, but can also range from the cherry beer pro-

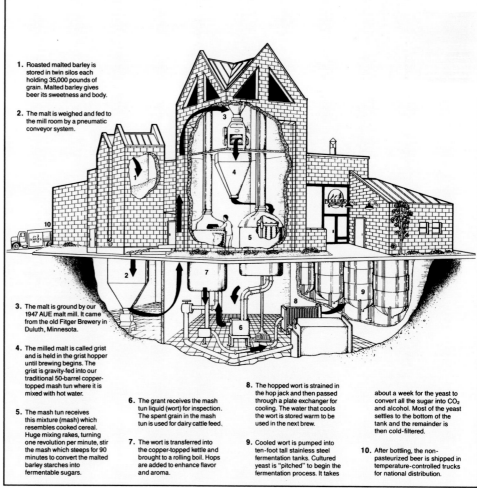

1. Roasted malted barley is stored in twin silos each holding 35,000 pounds of grain. Malted barley gives beer its sweetness and body.

2. The malt is weighed and fed to the mill room by a pneumatic conveyor system.

3. The malt is ground by our 1947 AUE malt mill. It came from the old Fitger Brewery in Duluth, Minnesota.

4. The milled malt is called grist and is held in the grist hopper until brewing begins. The grist is gravity-fed into our traditional 50-barrel copper-topped mash tun where it is mixed with hot water.

5. The mash tun receives this mixture (mash) which resembles cooked cereal. Huge mixing rakes, turning one revolution per minute, stir the mash which steeps for 90 minutes to convert the malted barley starches into fermentable sugars.

6. The grant receives the mash tun liquid (wort) for inspection. The spent grain in the mash tun is used for dairy cattle feed.

7. The wort is transferred into the copper-topped kettle and brought to a rolling boil. Hops are added to enhance flavor and aroma.

8. The hopped wort is strained in the hop jack and then passed through a plate exchanger for cooling. The water that cools the wort is stored warm to be used in the next brew.

9. Cooled wort is pumped into ten-foot tall stainless steel fermentation tanks. Cultured yeast is "pitched" to begin the fermentation process. It takes about a week for the yeast to convert all the sugar into CO_2 and alcohol. Most of the yeast settles to the bottom of the tank and the remainder is then cold-filtered.

10. After bottling, the non-pasteurized beer is shipped in temperature-controlled trucks for national distribution.

duced by the Lakefront Brewery in Milwaukee, which is delightful with deserts or game, to the porter that the Alaskan Brewing brews using barley roasted over an alder wood fire, which is perfect with smoked sausages or any type of barbeque.

The Gordon-Biersch Brewery/Restaurant in Palo Alto, California is a good example of a full service restaurant that also brews beer. Opened in 1988, it not only features the beer of Dan Gordon, who spent five years in the brewing engineering program at the Technical University of Munich, but also the kitchen expertise of noted chef Jamie Carpenter, a graduate of the California Culinary Academy, an apprentice of Jean Luc Chassearu of Maxim's and previously an executive chef at two four-star restaurants.

Although today the area stretching south from western Oregon and Washington to the San Francisco Bay Area contains the largest concentration of brewpubs and microbreweries in

The 1980s saw brewpubs evolve to include full-scale restaurants such as Tampa Bay Brewing in Florida *(top left)*, **SLO** *(left)* **in San Luis Obispo, CA and Gordon-Biersch** *(below)* **in Palo Alto, CA.**

North America, the revolution has spread to every corner of the continent—from Florida Brewing in Miami, to the Granite Brewery in Halifax, Nova Scotia; to Schirf Brewing in Park City, Utah, to Alaskan Brewing (formerly Chinook) in Douglas, Alaska. Milwaukee, once the proud capital of American brewing, experienced the demise of both Schlitz and Blatz, but now has the Lakefront and Sprecher microbreweries, both of which are new since the first edition of this book in 1986.

As microbreweries were beginning to flourish, the public's heightened awareness of distinctive specialty beers created an expanded market for smaller regional brewers whose existence predated the microbrewery revolution. This is certainly true of Anchor Brewing of San Francisco, which was founded in 1896 and 'rescued' by Fritz Maytag in 1965, whose distinctive beers are now available in most states and are considered the yardstick by which many specialty beers are measured. Another good case in point is August Schell Brewing of New Ulm, Minnesota, which was founded in 1860 and which survived the 1862

Sioux uprising because of August Schell's excellent rapport with the tribe. For the first 125 years Schell weathered the ups and downs of the market as a traditional regional brew-

ery until it was discovered by Charles Finkel. The founder of Merchant du Vin of Seattle, Finkel is not only one of America's leading importers of fine European beers, but he is probably *the*

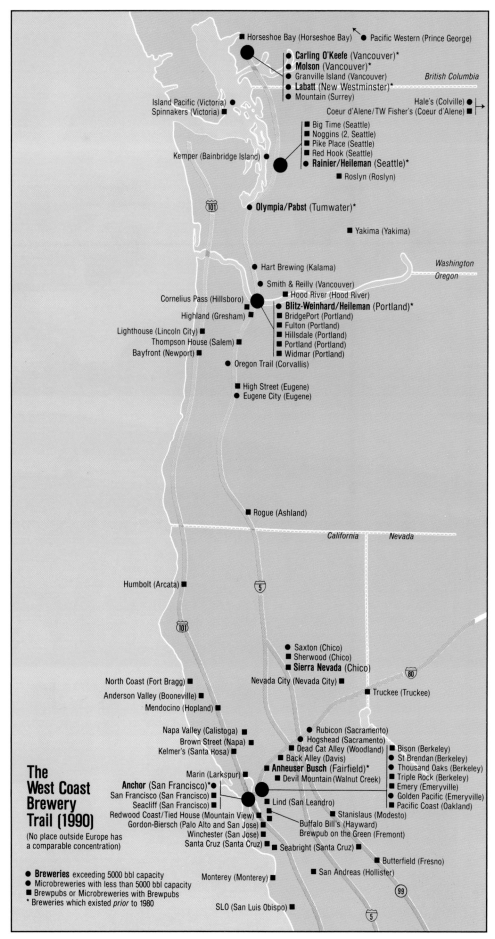

The
**West Coast
Brewery
Trail (1990)**
(No place outside Europe has
a comparable concentration)

● **Breweries** exceeding 5000 bbl capacity
● Microbreweries with less than 5000 bbl capacity
■ Brewpubs or Microbreweries with Brewpubs
* Breweries which existed *prior* to 1980

most outspoken advocate of specialty beers in the United States today. Finkel convinced Schell that there was a national market for their weiss and Pilsner beers and proceeded to tap that market. Thanks to Finkel's efforts, Schell's beers not only enjoyed wider sales but critical success as well. In 1988 the Great American Beer Festival called August Schell Pilsner 'unquestionably America's finest Pilsner beer.'

In the major markets of the Northeast, unlike those of the West, the trend in the mid-1980s was toward *contract* brewing rather than toward microbreweries. Philadelphia, New York and Boston each saw the development of a major local brand that was actually brewed *under contract* somewhere else. Contract brewing typically involves off-site production using a recipe developed by the brewing company's owner, usually with the help of a brewing consultant such as Dr Joseph Owades of the Center for Brewing Studies in San Francisco, who has helped many small brewing companies to get their start.

One of the first and best known contract brewers was Jim Koch, a Boston entrepreneur whose family was involved in the Fred Koch Brewery, which was established in Dunkirk, New York in 1888. Wanting to create a beer which could compete with the best German beers and pass the Reinheitsgebot (German Purity Law), Koch formed his Boston Beer Company in 1985 to produce Samuel Adams Lager. Named for the eighteenth century Boston patriot and home brewer, 'Sam Adams' passed the Reinheitsgebot test and was actually sold in West Germany before Koch expanded his marketing in the United States beyond the Boston area. Brewed under contract by Pittsburgh Brewing until Koch opened his own brewery near Boston in 1987, Sam Adams is now available throughout the United States and is the best-selling beer made by any of the new North American brewing companies that have started since 1980.

Both of Philadlephia's initial 'house' brands—Jeff Ware's Dock Street and Tom Pastorius' Pennsylvania Pilsen— were originally contract brewed, but Pastorius opened his own brewery in

Left, from top: **Importer and distributor Charles Finkel with Ted Marti, president of August Schell; Catamont Brewing in Vermont; and the bar and brew kettles at Manhattan Brewing on Thompson Street in the Soho district of New York City.**

Pittsburgh in 1989. Two other major contract brewing companies in leading eastern markets are the Brooklyn Brewery, which was founded in 1988, and Olde Heurich Brewing in Washington, DC, which was founded by Gary Heurich, grandson of Christian Heurich, who built his brewery in 1873 on the site where the Kennedy Center now stands.

In New York City the first new brewing companies in town after the microbrewery revolution began were Old New York, whose Amsterdam Amber is brewed under contract by FX Matt in Utica, New York, and Manhattan Brewing, a brewpub. Robert D'Addona started Manhattan Brewing in 1984 in a former Consolidated Edison substation on Thompson Street in the city's Soho district. The brewery has suffered some hard times over the years but still stands as the first brewery to operate in Manhattan in the nearly 20 years since the Jacob Ruppert Brewery on Third Avenue closed in 1965. With its elegant all-copper brewhouse, Man-

hattan Brewing not only gave America's original brewing capital a working brewery once again, but it gave the city a place to enjoy local brew in the centuries-old New Amsterdam tradition, combined with a modern brewpub tradition. Brewing in New York had come full circle.

This trend toward contract brewing has proven to be beneficial to older, regional breweries as well because of the new business they have experienced and from the fresh ideas they have obtained through contact with enthusiastic entrepreneurs.

Perhaps the largest of the contract brewers in the East has been the FX Matt Brewing Company of Utica, New York. Originally founded in 1853, the company that had long been famous for its own Utica Club brand now contract brews for Dock Street of Philadelphia, Long Island Brewing of Montauk, New York, Old New York, Maine Coast Brewing, Brooklyn Brewery and Monarch Brewing of Brooklyn, as well as William S Newman Brewing

The Utica, NY brewery presided over by FX Matt II *(above)* produces more 'microbrews' under contract than anyone else in the US. *Below, from left to right:* Rich Doyle, George Ligeti and Dan Kenary of Mass Bay Brewing Company.

of nearby Albany, which opened as a microbrewery in 1981 but found the demand for its beer outstripped its on-site capacity.

The initial trend toward contract brewing in the East, which was looked down upon by western microbrewers, has been changing as brewers such as Koch and Pastorius open their own facilities. At the same time, a good many important microbreweries, with in-house brewing present at start-up, have opened in the Northeast. These include Catamount Brewing in White River Junction, Vermont; DL Geary Brewing in Portland, Maine; Mass Bay Brewing in Boston, Massachusetts; and Virginia Brewing (formerly Chesapeake Bay or Chesbay) in Chesapeake, Virginia.

Contract brewing is not, however, confined to the Northeast. Montana Beverages of Helena, a microbrewery founded in 1982, brews not only its own Kessler brand, but also produces

Above: **Dr Michael Lewis (left) trains brewmasters, while Al Geitner (right) of Pub Brewing, designs, builds and installs brewing systems for microbreweries.**

products for brewing companies in Santa Barbara, California; Eugene, Oregon; and Jackson Hole, Wyoming.

The success of the microbreweries, and certainly the quality of the beers they are producing, is due in part to the establishment in 1975 of a brewing course in the Food Sciences Department at the University of California's Davis campus, which is located half-way between San Francisco and Sacramento. Under the able direction of Dr Michael Lewis, the department has graduated brewmasters who have become employed not only by many of the microbreweries, but by large, established breweries as well. For example, several of the people brewing beer at the Anheuser-Busch facility in nearby Fairfield are graduates of Dr Lewis's courses.

NORTH AMERICAN BREWING AT THE END OF THE CENTURY

As the twentieth century draws to a close, North American brewing is enjoying a renaissance. Total consumption remains relatively constant, but per capita consumption is the highest that it has been since before Prohibition, and, after four decades of decline, the number of brewers multiplied threefold in less than a decade, and the demand for noteworthy specialty beers is on the rise. The North American brewing industry in the late 1980s is in much the same place that the American wine industry was two decades before. It is producing truly world class beers and finally receiving the recognition that it deserves. Many

The past and the future. *Left:* Yuengling, the USA's oldest brewer, made its first beer 160 years before New Haven Brewing *(bottom left)* opened. *Below:* Seattle's Pike Place Brewery opened in 1989.

of the finest restaurants now have *beer* lists prepared with the care and consideration once reserved for their *wine* lists. When New York's Plaza Hotel offers a beer list, it is profoundly clear that beer is getting its due!

While the microbreweries brew far less beer than the megabreweries, by the end of the 1980s they had started to make serious inroads in the North American market against European specialty beers, because they are true world-class beers and because they are much *fresher* than any imported beer.

The major national brands in the United States, Canada and Mexico all produce more beer in a week than microbreweries do in a year, but the microbreweries have had the effect of enriching the overall brewing scene and have prompted the majors to rethink their notions about super premium beers. Certainly this will be part of the legacy of the microbrewery revolution that will be carried forward into the final years of the century.

BREWERY CLOSE-UP

NORTH AMERICA'S LARGEST BREWER

ANHEUSER-BUSCH

Right: All the hardware and procedures in every Anheuser-Busch brewhouse, like the recipes for every Anheuser-Busch beer, conform to carefully prepared corporate specifications to ensure absolute uniformity. A bottle of Budweiser brewed in Fairfield, California should taste exactly the same as a bottle of Budweiser brewed in St Louis, Missouri.

Anheuser-Busch's beers, especially Budweiser, are the most popular in North America. Every year the company's plants fill millions of bottles, cans and draft kegs. In 1984, it produced enough beer to fill 23 billion 11-ounce bottles.

Below: A state-of-the-art laboratory is an important part of every Anheuser-Busch brewery. The lab monitors the characteristics of the beer from brewing to bottling. With modern 'automated beer analysis' it is possible to monitor the fermentation going on in every tank rather than simply relying on spot checks.

Anheuser-Busch brews over 60 million barrels of beer each year at 11 breweries throughout the United States. Even though they are widely separated geographically, the company takes pains to ensure that the products are of uniform high quality.

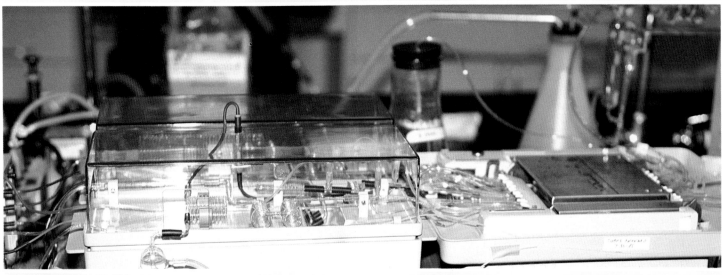

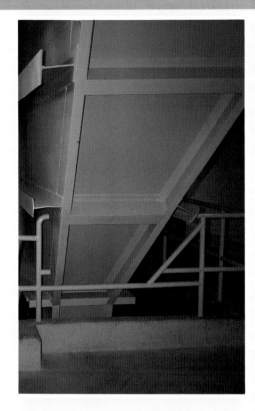

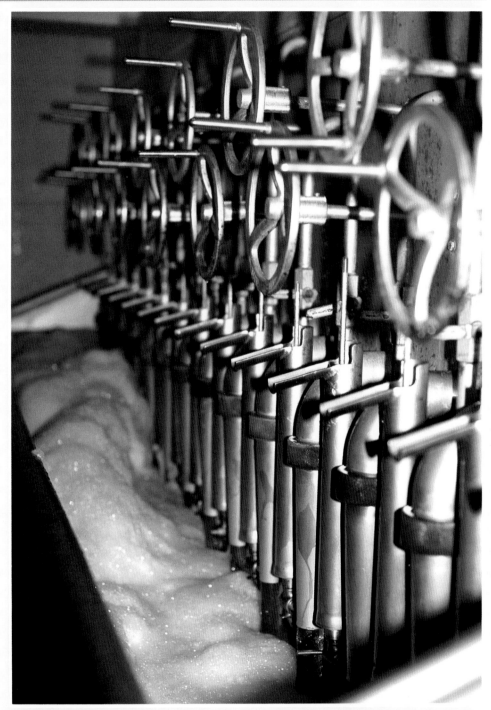

Above: After malted barley and rice are milled the barley is mashed and the rice cooked to change their starches into fermentable sugars. Barley and rice are mixed according to very specific recipes for each Anheuser-Busch product.

The sweet wort, a mixture of cooked rice and mashed barley, is strained in the strainmaster before being placed in the brew kettle. The strainmaster performs the same function as the traditional lauter tun.

Right: After it is strained, the sweet wort moves through the grant, which controls the rate of flow into the brew kettle.

Below: An Anheuser-Busch hop room. A variety of domestic and European hops are used, depending on the particular recipe for each specific Anheuser-Busch beer. Michelob, for example, is made with only European hops.

BREWERY CLOSE-UP

Above: Anheuser-Busch hops, ready to be added to the brew kettle.

Right: After the sweet wort is brought to a boil in the stainless steel brew kettle, hops are added, and the resulting hopped wort is boiled for over three hours. In the nineteenth century, brew kettles such as those at the original Anheuser-Busch brewery in St Louis *(below)* were made of copper for even heat conduction, but most modern large-scale brewers now use stainless steel for easier cleaning.

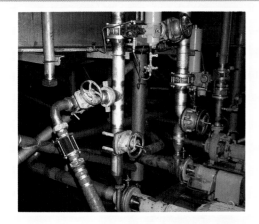

Far left: Anheuser-Busch adds yeast to the hopped wort as it moves through the lines to the fermenting tanks rather than adding it after the wort is in the tanks. To ensure quality and uniformity, the yeast is shipped weekly from St Louis to each Anheuser-Busch Brewery.

Left: The cold wort is placed in Alpha tanks for five to seven days. During this time the yeast converts the fermentable sugars to carbon dioxide and alcohol, and the wort becomes beer.

Far left: Beechwood chips are placed in the second fermentation tanks for the krausening of all Anheuser-Busch beers. The sterilized beechwood is chemically inert, but it serves to help extract the yeast. The beechwood chips themselves are extracted by hand.

Left: After roughly a month in the two fermentation tanks, Anheuser-Busch beers go into the Schone tanks to be clarified. Natural tannin is added, which picks up protein particles and settles them out.

Below: Sophisticated control centers help brewmasters at every Anheuser-Busch brewery carefully monitor every step of the month-long beer-making process, from brewing to finishing.

THE BREWERS OF NORTH AMERICA

A FAMILY PORTRAIT

As was noted in the 1986 edition of *Beers of North America*, any attempt to catalogue and summarize all the breweries on the North American continent is a bit like photographing a moving object. Even though only one frozen moment in time is captured, that snapshot can tell a good deal about the object being photographed— its structure, its past evolution and its present direction. The present portrait attempts to capture the brewers of North America for a family photograph circa the beginning of the twentieth century's last decade. Most of the major family members have held leading positions for many years. Anheuser-Busch has been the number one brewery for more than a quarter century and

has been in the top three since the turn of the century. Canada's 'big three' in 1986 were in similar positions at the end of the nineteenth century, but now they have become a 'big two' through a 1989 merger. Some of the great old regional brewers have disappeared, replaced by vibrant new micro-breweries.

Not only have North America's major brewers become the world's major brewers, but the microbrewery movement has pumped new life into the industry—a development that could not have been predicted even as late as the 1970s. American consumers have begun to take beer seriously. They are supporting the majors as well as the micros who can deliver a quality product. Contained herein are North American brewers from Juneau to Jamaica,

and from the largest multisite breweries to the microbreweries.

Just as the 1986 edition of *Beers of North America* included some breweries which are now no longer in operation and omitted several that came on the scene as that edition went to press, so is this a snapshot of a dynamic and evolving industry. We have made every effort to be complete, and as the industry evolves, we will continue to update our data base for future editions. Anyone wishing to contribute to an update or seeking further information, is invited to telephone Bill Yenne directly at (415) 989-2450 or (415) 826-6749.

Below: **The big copper brew kettles at the 18-million-barrel Coors plant in Golden, CO represent the power of a great tradition born in the old world, but which has become a vital part of new world culture.**

The Top Ten of
North American Brewing

Below and left: With ranking by millions of barrels produced annually, this chart represents North America's top ten brewing companies in 1990 after Moctezuma and Cuauhtemoc joined to form Valores and after Carling O'Keefe became part of Molson.

While the top two are likely to retain their positions through the end of the century, charting the relative positions of the others is like photographing a horse race and change is probable.

Indeed, the merger of Stroh and Coors, which almost occurred in 1989, would have created a rival for the number two position. It is interesting to note that Pabst was the largest brewer in the world at the start of the twentieth century.

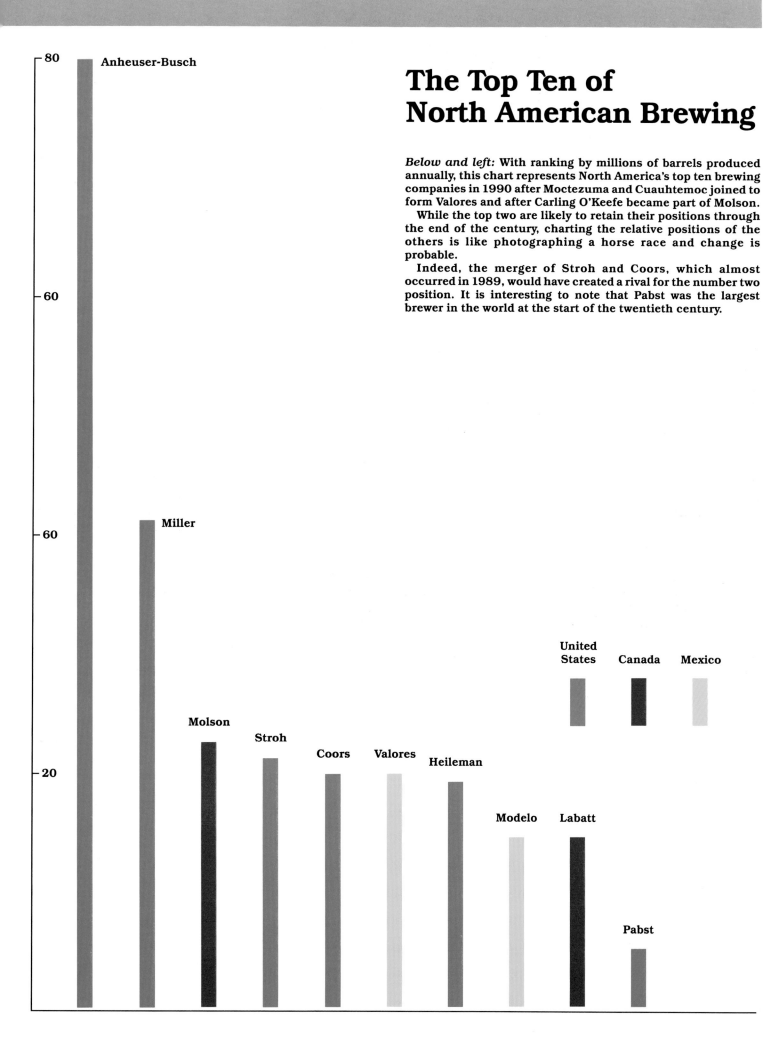

THE UNITED STATES

North America's most populous country is also the world's biggest brewing nation, with an annual output of over 180 million barrels, double that of second-place West Germany and triple that of third-place Great Britain. In 1990 the largest American brewing *companies* by market share were Anheuser-Busch (42 percent), Miller (22 percent), Stroh/Schlitz (10 percent), Coors (9 percent) and Heileman (8 percent). The leading *brands* by market share were Anheuser-Busch's Budweiser (28 percent), Miller Lite (11 percent), Bud Light (6 percent) and Coors Light (5 percent).

The portraits below describe the brewing companies of the United States in alphabetical order. All of the United States brewers—from the largest multisite conglomerate to the smallest brewpub—were contacted during 1989 and asked to supply the labels and the data that we have included here. The breweries and brewpubs marked with a ■ have been added since the 1986 edition of *Beers of North America*. The preponderance of such new establishments is a testimony to the fantastic resurgence of interest in brewing and specialty beers in the late 1980s and early 1990s.

Abita Brewing was founded in the town of Abita Springs, Louisiana in 1986, and in 1988 the brewery's total capacity was 3000 barrels. Brewing is under the direction of brewers Jim Patton and Rush Cumming, who designed their beer to complement Cajun cuisine, which was undergoing a national revival in the mid-1980s. The

principal brands brewed here are Amber Lager, Golden Lager (which are both bottled) and six to eight draft seasonal beers, such as a Oktoberfest, Christmas Dark and, of course, a popular Mardis Gras Bock. ■

Alabama Brewing (see **Jones**)

Alaskan Brewing & Bottling (formerly **Chinook Alaskan**) is located in the town of Douglas, near Juneau, Alaska. Established in 1986, it is the first brewery to be built in Alaska since Prinzbrau folded in 1979. In 1988 the brewery's total capacity was 3600 barrels, with brewing under the direction of brewmaster Geoffrey Larson. The princi-

pal brand brewed here is Alaskan Amber Beer. Alaskan also produces a Smoked Porter, which is reminiscent of the rauchbiers of Bamberg, Germany. In the case of Alaskan Smoked Porter, alder wood fires are used to roast, and impart flavor to, the barley prior to brewing. ■

Albuquerque Brewing & Bottling is a brewpub in Albuquerque, New Mexico. In 1989 its total capacity was 1200 barrels, to

be expanded to 7000 barrels, with brewing under the direction of brewmaster Michael Buckner. The principal brand brewed here is Michael's Golden Ale. ■

Allegheny Brewing & Pub of Pittsburgh, Pennsylvania opened in 1989 as the first microbrewery in the state with on-site production capability. ■

All Saints Brewery opened in 1990 in Phoenix as the first microbrewery in Arizona, and was the first brewery, other than the former Carling/Arizona plant, to operate in the state since prohibition. ■

Alpine Village Hofbrau, a brewpub which opened during 1988 in the city of Torrence, California, is partly owned by the Hofbrauhaus Traunstein of Bavaria. In 1989 the brewery's total capacity was 10,000 barrels, with brewing under the direction of master brewer Thomas Rapp.

The principal brands brewed here are Alpine Village Hofbrau Lager Beer, Alpine Village Hofbrau Pilsner and Alpine Village Hofbrau Light Beer. ■

Ambier Brewing, originally named Vienna Brewing, was founded in July 1985 by Gary and Faye Bauer in Milwaukee, Wisconsin. The company had its first product, Vienna All Malt Lager beer, produced under contract by a small brewery in northwestern Wisconsin, and sales were limited to five Midwestern states. In June 1986 the company switched to brewing facilities at Joseph Huber Brewing in Monroe, Wisconsin. The introduction of the newly repackaged

Vienna Style Lager was made in September 1986. During the course of 1987, 8Vienna Style Lager was the recipient of numerous regional and national awards, including the Gold Medal for Vienna-, Märzen- and Oktoberfest-style beers at the 1987 Great American Beer Festival.

In late 1986 the market expansion of Vienna Style lager brought it into areas where Old Vienna Beer, a conventional light-bodied adjunct beer from the Canadian Carling O'Keefe Brewing Group, was being distributed. Brand confusion among wholesalers and retailers led to a decision by the Vienna Brewing Company in mid-1986 to rename Vienna Lager Beer.

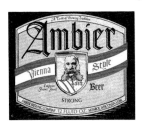

Vienna Brewing Company was officially renamed Ambier Brewing Company in September 1987. The newly rechristened Ambier Vienna Style Amber Beer was first shipped in November 1987. ■

Anchor Brewing Company was originally established in San Francisco in 1896. Appliance heir Fritz Maytag bought the company in 1965 when it was on the verge of collapse and turned it into the very model of an efficient, smaller regional brewery. Despite Maytag's relentless quality control and insistence on high-quality ingredients, such as expensive, pure malted, two-row barley instead of a mix of cheaper cereal grains, the brewery turned a profit by 1975. Over the years Maytag increased the brewery's output from 600 barrels to 45,000 barrels annually.

The company's flagship product is Anchor Steam Beer, one of the West's most prized premium beers, which was developed by master brewer Maytag himself, and is loosely based on what is known of the legendary 'steam' beers produced in Gold Rush days. Other Anchor products include Anchor Porter, Anchor Liberty Ale, Old Foghorn Barley Wine-style Ale, which was first produced in 1975, and on a regular basis after 1985. Old Foghorn has been a consistent award winner in its category. Also in 1985 the brewery became one of the first American brewers to produce a German-style wheat beer. Known the world over for its Steam Beer, Anchor is renowned locally for its annual Christmas beer, which has been specially brewed since 1975, with a different recipe each year, and is available from the day after Thanksgiving until early January. Liberty Ale had its start as one of the original Christmas beers. In 1989 Anchor's Christmas beer was the first beer to receive a gold medal in the Herb Beer category at the Great American Beer Festival. It is worth noting that the first

batch of Anchor's 1989 Christmas beer was in the brew kettle during the great earthquake of that year, and as such, was brewed several hours longer than planned because it couldn't be pumped out until electricity was restored.

In August 1989 Anchor amazed and delighted its many fans by brewing a beer which was based on a 4000-year-old recipe which Fritz Maytag and his consulting historians and archaeologists felt would 'duplicate mankind's earliest professionally brewed beer.' Named Ninkasi after the Sumerian goddess of brewing, the beer was produced from an ancient recipe for barley bread called *bappir*, which is flavored with dates and honey. It was baked by Anchor's brewing team in a bakery hired for the day. It was unveiled at the 1989 National Microbrewers Conference and released privately in 11 ounce bottles for a short time thereafter.

Anderson Valley Brewing of Booneville, California operates a brewpub called The Buckhorn Saloon, a successor to the original Buckhorn Saloon that was established in 1873. With brewing under the direction of brewmaster David Norfleet, the principal brands brewed here are Boont Amber Ale,

High Rollers Wheat Beer, Deep Enders Dark Port and Poleeko Gold Light Ale, each of which is named for the inhabitants of a different region of Anderson Valley. ■

Anheuser-Busch of St Louis is not only the largest brewer in the United States, but the largest brewer in the world, with no close rivals. In 1988 the company brewed 78.5 million barrels of beer—more than the 1988 sales of the Miller, Coors and Stroh breweries combined—accounting for 41.1 percent of total brewing industry sales in the United States. While Anheuser-Busch has many popular brands of beer, its most successful are Budweiser and Bud Light, which together account for one-third of the United States' beer sales.

The world's biggest brewing company traces its roots to a small brewery started in St Louis, Missouri in 1852 by George Schneider and taken over in 1860 by Eberhard Anheuser. Four years later Anheuser's son-in-law Adolphus Busch (1839-1913) joined the firm. A far-sighted marketing genius, Busch turned the small city brewery into a national giant. He launched the extraordinarily successful Budweiser brand as a mass-market beer in 1876, and in 1896 he introduced the still-popular Michelob brand as the company's premium beer. Originally a draft beer, Michelob was not marketed as a bottled beer until 1961.

Today Anheuser-Busch's flagship brewery is still located in St Louis, but beginning in 1951 other breweries were established at Newark, New Jersey (1951): Los Angeles (1954); Tampa, Florida (1959); Houston, Texas (1966); Columbus, Ohio (1968); Jacksonville, Florida (1969); Merrimack, New Hampshire (1970); Williamsburg, Virginia (1972); Fairfield, California (1976); Baldwinsville, New York (1980); and Fort Collins, Colorado (1988). The company's 13th brewery will open in Cartersville, Georgia in 1992. The largest of these are St Louis, with a 12.4-million-barrel annual capacity, Los Angeles (12.1 million), Williamsburg (9.1 million) and Houston (9.5 million).

In addition to 'Bud' and Michelob, Anheuser-Busch brews a variety of other beers. Busch, introduced in 1955, is marketed regionally east of the Rocky Mountains. In 1988 and 1989 Busch received gold medals in the American Pilsner category at the Great American Beer Festival. In the late 1970s and early 1980s the company introduced a family of low-calorie or 'light' beers. These included Natural Light (1977), Michelob Light (1978) and Bud Light (1982). In 1981 Anheuser-Busch introduced its third Michelob product, Michelob Classic Dark, which has been a consistent award winner at such events as the Great American Beer Festival, where it competes alongside some of the nation's best specialty beers. In 1984 the company not only added a malt liquor called King Cobra to its family of products, but also became the first major brewer to mass market a reduced-alcohol beer, which they call 'LA.'

One year later Anheuser-Busch reached an agreement with United Breweries Ltd of Copenhagen, Denmark to be the exclusive American distributor of Danish-brewed Carlsberg, Carlsberg Light and Elephant Malt Liquor.

In 1989 Anheuser-Busch introduced Michelob Dry, America's first super-premium dry beer, to very positive reviews from consumers and retailers. The company also launched its first ultra-premium beer, called Anheuser-Märzen, in the St

162

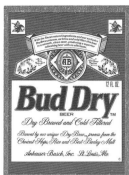

Louis area, and early in 1989, the company introduced Bud Dry and Busch Light. Also during 1989 Anheuser-Busch began test marketing O'Doul's, a no-alcohol beer, a product that was scheduled for national distribution in 1990.

Since 1980 the Anheuser-Busch brands have been brewed under license abroad as well. Budweiser is brewed in Ireland by Guinness Ireland Ltd; in Denmark with United Breweries Ltd; in Canada by Labatt's; in South Korea by Oriental Brewery Co Ltd; in Japan by Suntory; and in the United Kingdom by Grand Metropolitan Brewing Ltd.

The industrial side of Anheuser-Busch does more than just brew beer, however. Subsidiaries of the company process barley into brewer's malt; manufacture metal cans, lids and metalized labels for internal use and for sale to other firms; transport beer by truck and by rail; wholesale beer and wine; and recycle aluminum cans. The company's Eagle Snacks subsidiary produces Honey Roast Nuts, potato chips and other snacks. First widely distributed on airlines, Eagle Snacks are now available in supermarkets from coast to coast. Eagle Snacks also distributes Cape Cod brand potato chips and popcorn. In response to the disastrous San Francisco earthquake in October 1989, Anheuser-Busch's Fairfield plant immediately began canning drinking water for distribution to the hardest hit areas.

The Anheuser-Busch Campbell Taggart subsidiary is the second largest commercial baker in the United States. Its products are marketed under such well-known brand names as Colonial, Grant's Farm, Family Recipes, Rainbo and Earth Grains.

The nonindustrial side of Anheuser-Busch includes interests in sports. The company was a major sponsor of the 1988 Summer Olympic Games in Seoul, South Korea. Anheuser-Busch also owns the St Louis National Baseball Club Inc, better known as the St Louis Cardinals. Purchased by the company in 1953, the Cardinals have won the World Series three times since, in 1964, 1967 and 1982.

Other Anheuser-Busch sports-related activities include speedboat racing, in which the company sponsors the Miss Budweiser Unlimited Hydroplane Racing Team and Bill and Mike Seebold's Bud Light Racing Team. On land the company sponsors auto racing teams and auto races such as the Budweiser Cleveland Grand Prix, the Budweiser 500 at Dover, Delaware and the Budweiser at the Glen in Watkins Glen, New York. Its champion Indy car drivers have included Mario Andretti (1984) and Bobby Rahal (1986 and 1987). Other company-sponsored sports events are the Budweiser Irish Derby in Dublin, Ireland; the Anheuser-Busch Golf Classic in Williamsburg; the Michelob Light Cup women's pro ski races; the Budweiser Hall of Fame Bowling Tournament; the ABC Bud Light Masters (bowling) Tournament; the Budweiser International horse race in Washington, DC; the Busch Pool League; and the Bud Light Ironman Triathlon World Championship at Kona, Hawaii.

No mention of Anheuser-Busch leisure time activities would be complete without the company's Busch Gardens theme parks. The Dark Continent, ranked among the top four zoos in the United States, opened in Tampa, Florida in 1959, followed by The Old Country in Williamsburg, Virginia in 1975. Two additional Busch Garden parks opened in 1980: a 13-acre outdoor water park called Adventure Island, constructed adjacent to the Dark Continent in Tampa; and Sesame Place, a family-oriented play park for children that combines physical play elements, live entertainment and challenging computer games, located in Langhorne, Pennsylvania near Philadelphia.

Aspen Beer Company was founded in 1988 in Aspen, Colorado. Its Aspen Silver City Ale is brewed under contract at Boulder Brewing. ■

Back Alley Brewery & Bistro opened in Davis, California in 1990, with brewing training conducted on the premises under the direction of Professor Michael Lewis, whose brewing school at the University of California at Davis has graduated many of the current generation of North American microbrewers. ■

Ballantine (see **Falstaff**)

Bayern Brewing operates the Northern Pacific Brewpub, an establishment with a predictably Bavarian theme. Brewing is under the direction of master brewer Jurgen Knoller. Opened in August 1987 in

the former Northern Pacific Railway station in Missoula, Montana, Bayern's 1500-barrel brewpub produces about 12 types of beer, including German Style Lager, Bayern Amber and Bayern Wheat. ■

Bayfront Brewery & Public House is a brewpub founded in 1989 in the coastside town of Newport, Oregon by Oregon Brewing, which also owns the Rogue Brewery in Ashland, Oregon. With brewing under the

direction of John Maier, 1988 American Homebrewer of the Year, Bayfront's principal brands are Pacific Lighter, Yaquina Golden, Oat Meal Lager Ale and Oregon Golden Coast. ■

Bell's (see **Kalamazoo**)

Belmont Brewing opened in Long Beach, California in 1990. ■

The **Berghoff** is an old Chicago restaurant famous for its 100-foot bar and for its private label Berghoff Beer, which is regarded by many as Chicago's 'hometown beer.' It traces its heritage to the brewery started in 1887 in Fort Wayne, Indiana by Herman Josef Berghoff of Dortmund, Germany. Berghoff introduced his beer to the Windy City at the 1893 Chicago World's Fair and opened the restaurant at its present site in 1898. In 1933, after Prohibition, Berghoff reopened with Chicago Liquor License No 1, and sold 24,000 glasses of beer the first

day. The Berghoff Brewery in Fort Wayne was sold to Falstaff in 1955, and since 1960 Berghoff and Berghoff Dark have been brewed in Monroe, Wisconsin by Joseph Huber. In 1989 Berghoff bought Huber, forming the **Berghoff-Huber Brewing Company**. Huber is listed separately in this book. ■

Big Time Brewery & Ale House was opened in December 1988 in Seattle, Washington. Total annual production is 1000 barrels, with brewing under the direction of brewmaster Reid Martin (who is also brewmaster for Triple Rock in Berkeley, California) and head brewer Ed Tringali. The three principal brands brewed here are Atlas Amber Ale, Coal Creek Porter and Prime Time Pale Ale. ■

Bison (see **Buffalo Bill's**)

Blatz (see **Heileman**)

Blitz-Weinhard (see **Heileman**)

Blue Ridge Brewing, Virginia's first microbrewery, is located in the town of Charlottesville. In 1988 the brewery's total capacity was 500 barrels, with brewing under the direction of master brewer A Burks Summers II. The principal brands brewed here are Hawksbill Golden Lager, Piney River Amber Lager, Afton Ale and Humpback Stout. ■

Bohannon Brewing of Nashville, Tennessee, founded by Lyndsay Bohannon as the mid-South's first microbrewery, began distributing its Market Street Beer to local tav-

erns and retail outlets in 1989. Other products, also brewed under the direction of brewmaster Thomas Kunzmann (formerly of Greenshield's in Raleigh, North Carolina), include Market Street Light and the award-winning Market Street Oktoberfest. ■

Bolt Brewery is a brewpub founded by Paul Holborn and Chris Lave in the town of Fallbrook, near San Diego, California. Its principal brands are named after the historic and long extinct breweries of San Diego County and include Aztec Red Ale, Aztec Extra Special Bitter, Balboa Porter and Mission Wheat Ale. ■

Boston Beer Company was founded in 1985 by Boston entrepreneur Jim Koch. Initially, Koch's flagship brand, Samuel Adams Boston Lager, was available only in Boston, Massachusetts and Munich, West Germany, but is now in nationwide distri-

bution in the United States. After having had his beer contract brewed by Pittsburgh Brewing for two years, Koch moved production to a renovated 40,000-barrel brewery in Boston in 1987. The brewery's other brands include Samuel Adams Double Bock and Boston Lightship. ■

Boulder Brewing Company of Boulder, Colorado, which began operations in 1980, is the second largest Colorado-based brewer, although, as its vice president George 'Skip' Miller points out, 'We're not

trying to be Coors...Coors brews about three times as much beer in an average day as we will in a year.'

Boulder Brewing developed from an interest in home brewing and, like many of the smaller breweries that started in the 1980s, the company is dedicated to heartier European-style beers and does not brew a lager. The product line at the 10,000-barrel brewery (Coors has an 18-million-barrel capacity) includes Boulder Bitter, Boulder Stout, Boulder Porter, Boulder Sport and Boulder Extra Pale Ale.

Brewmaster's Pub Ltd is located in the town of Kenosha, Wisconsin, with brewing under the direction of master brewer Jerry Rezny. ■

Brewpub on the Green, in Fremont, California, is so named because it is the first brewpub in North America to be located on a golf course. Opened by John Rennels in September 1988, the brewery's total capacity was 15.5 barrels, with brewing under the direction of brewmaster Sean Donnelly.

Known as 'California's rendition of a New England tavern,' it has a seating capacity of 220 and an outdoor beer garden. The principal emphasis is on draft beer and the principal brands brewed are California Amber, Gold Coast Lager, Mission Peak Porter and specialty beers such as Wheat beer and Pumpkin beer. ■

BridgePort Brewing is a brewpub located in the city of Portland, Orgeon. In 1989 the brewery's total capacity was 5000 barrels, to be expanded to 10,000, with brewing under the direction of master brewer Karl Ockert. The principal brands brewed here are Old Knucklehead, a specialty barley

wine ale; Blue Heron Bitter, Blue Heron Pale Ale, BridgePort Ale, Golden Ale, Stout XX, and such seasonal beers as Spring Draught, Summer Wheat and Winter Warmer.

British Brewing was founded in 1988 in Glen Burnie near Baltimore, Maryland by brewmaster Stephen Parkes and his partner Craig Stuart-Paul, both late of Britain

and anxious to recreate familiar ales from their homeland. Using malt and hops imported from England, they brew their Oxford Class ale for the local draft market. ∎

Brooklyn Brewery was founded in 1988 by Stephen Hindy and Tom Potter in the New York City borough of Brooklyn, a 'city' whose colorful history has included many great breweries. The flagship product,

Brooklyn Lager, is a dry-hopped 'pre-Prohibition' style lager inspired by the 'ball park' beers of that era. The Brooklyn Brewery does not actually have a *brewery*, but rather has their brew produced under contract at the FX Matt Brewing facility in Utica, New York. ∎

Brown Street Brewery is a microbrewery which opened in Napa, California in 1990. ∎

Buffalo Bill's of Hayward, California became one of the first three brewpubs to open in the United States since Prohibition when brewmaster Bill Owens opened for business in September 1983. In 1988 Owens opened a second brewpub, **Bison Brewing Company** ∎, in nearby Berkeley, California. The unique concept of the brewpub, feeding draft beer directly from the brewery to the taps at the bar, ensures the freshest possible product. Unlike the

beers of most microbreweries, Buffalo Bill's unique unpasteurized lager is available only at the brewpubs, whose combined annual capacity is less than 2000 barrels. The principal brands brewed are Billy Bock, Buffalo Brew, Pumpkin Ale, Tasmanian Devil and a Christmas beer called Scrooge's Best Bitter.

Buffalo Brewpub, not to be confused with Buffalo Bill's California pubs, is located in the town of Williamsville, New York, near Buffalo. In 1988 the brewery's total capacity

was 1400 barrels, with brewing under the direction of master brewer Keith Morgan. The principal brands brewed here are Amber Ale, Oatmeal Stout, Roo Brew (Australian Stout), Oktoberfest Lager and Red Ale. ∎

Butterfield Brewing is a restaurant and brewery, which opened in March 1989 in the town of Fresno, California. The brewery's total capacity is 1300 barrels, with a seven-barrel system, with brewing under the direction of master brewer Kevin Cox. It is the first of two breweries to be opened by Jeff Wolpert in the San Joaquin Valley. The principal brands brewed here are Bridalvale Ale, San Joaquin Golden Ale and Tower Dark Porter, which won a gold medal at the 1989 Great American Beer Festival. ∎

Calistoga (see **Napa Valley**)

Capital Brewery is a microbrewery opened in June 1986 in the town of Middleton, Wisconsin. In 1988 the brewery's total production was 6500 barrels, with brewing under the direction of brewmaster Kirby Nelson. The principal brands brewed here are Garten Brau Lager, Pilsner and Dark, which took a gold medal at the 1988 Great American Beer Festival, as well as seasonal

Bock, Weiss and Oktoberfest beers. Bottling takes place at the nearby Stevens Point Brewery. Like Stevens Point, Capital sells most of its product within one hour's radius of its headquarters. ∎

Catamount Brewing of White River Junction, Vermont, which produced its first beer in 1987, was the first commercial brewery to operate in Vermont since 1893. Initial distribution included only Vermont and New Hampshire, but has been expanded to other New England states since 1988. Brewing is under the direction of partner and brewmaster Steve Mason, whose experience includes having worked at Swannell's in Hertfordshire, England.

The product line includes Catamount Amber, Catamount Gold and Catamount Porter, which evolved out of their 1987 Holiday Porter, and which noted world beer authority Michael Jackson describes as a 'definitive' porter. ∎

Champale (see **Heileman**)

Chesapeake Bay (Chesbay) (see **Virginia Brewing**)

Chinook Alaskan (see **Alaskan Brewing and Bottling**)

City of Angels Brewing was founded in January 1988 in Santa Monica, California, but takes its name from nearby Los Angeles. A restaurant brewery with a 2000-barrel capacity, City of Angels produces its Angel Amber, City Light, Heavenly Gold and Imperial Stout under the direction of brewmaster Dennis Miller, a graduate of Dr Michael Lewis's brewing school at the University of California at Davis. ∎

Clark's USA was established in 1985 in Washington, DC by entrepreneur Lyman

Clark. Clark had contracted with Dr Joseph Owades of San Francisco's Center for Brewing Studies to develop an alcohol-free beer. Traditional 'non-alcoholic' or 'near' beer contains about one-half of a percent of alcohol, but the 'unbeer' developed by Owades and trademarked by Clark is the only beer produced in the United States that has *no* alcohol. ■

Cleveland Brewing was founded in May 1988 in the city of Cleveland, Ohio. With brewing under the direction of master brewing consultant Dr Joseph Owades, the

only brand is Erin Brew, a lager currently brewed under contract by Pittsburgh Brewing, and available regionally on draft or in bottles. ■

Coeur d'Alene Brewing operates 'TW Fisher's, A Brewpub,' which opened in Coeur d'Alene, Idaho in July 1987, three weeks after brewpubs officially became legal in Idaho. With brewing under the

direction of owner Tom Fisher and brewmaster Steve Pollard, production more than doubled within the first year, and today over 125 other taverns and pubs in Idaho and Washington serve Coeur d'Alene's draft ales, which include TW Fisher's Weitzen Light, TW Fisher's Festival Dark and TW Fisher's Centennial Pale Ale, a gold medal winner at the 1988 Great American Beer Festival in Denver. ■

Cold Spring Brewing of Cold Spring, Minnesota dates back to the brewery started by George Sargel in 1874 and evolved to its present name by 1898. Today brewing is under the direction of brewmaster James Schorn. With a 350,000-barrel annual capacity, it is the largest of the locally-owned Minnesota breweries. The brewery's products include Cold Spring, Cold Spring Export, Cold Spring Light, Fox Deluxe, Kegel Brau, North Star, White Label and North Star Sparkling Mineral Water.

Collin County (see **Reinheitsgebot**)

Commonwealth Brewing is located in Boston, Massachusetts, and brews Amber Ale, Bitter, Gold Ale, Stout and a seasonal Winter Warmer. ■

Adolph Coors Company of Golden, Colorado operated for 114 years at the same site high in the Rocky Mountains that was selected by Adolph Coors himself in 1873. From its founding, until the first edition of this book in 1986, Coors grew from one of scores of tiny, regional breweries that once dotted the nation's landscape, to the fifth

largest brewing company in the United States. At the same time, its brewing plant in Golden had become the single largest brewery in the world, with an annual output of 18 million barrels.

In 1987 Coors celebrated the grand opening of its second brewery in Virginia's Shenandoah Valley, near the town of Elkton, a plant with a 2.5 million-barrel capacity. This facility was part of a drive begun in the early 1980s to expand the company from a regional to a national brewer. By 1988 Coors was distributing in every state but Delaware, and had moved ahead of Heileman to become America's fourth largest brewing company. In September 1989 Coors announced its intention to purchase Stroh Brewing, ranked third in the United States, but the letter of intent expired in December 1989. Had such an acquisition taken place, Coors would have jumped from a nine percent to a 19 percent market share, putting it on the coattails of number two Miller Brewing, which, at that time, had a 22 percent market share. At press time, negotiations between Coors and Stroh were still said to be in progress, although on a reduced level.

Coors is operated by third and fourth generation Coors family members: William Coors is chairman; Joseph Coors is vice chairman; Jeffrey Coors is president; Peter Coors is president of the Brewing Company; and Joseph Coors Jr is president and CEO of Coors Porcelain Companies.

The Coors product line is headed by the flagship Coors Banquet brand, the complementary low-calorie Coors Light (which is known as the 'Silver Bullet' because of the natural aluminum finish of its can), and a seasonal beer called Winterfest. Other products include the distinctively colored George Killian's Irish Red, an ale brewed under license from the original Irish brewer, and three premium beers introduced in the 1980s called Herman Joseph's, HJ Light and Coors Extra Gold Draft. Because Coors products are not pasteurized, the brewery makes a special effort to see that its products are kept refrigerated during delivery and distributor warehousing to ensure freshness.

The Adolph Coors Company has its hand in a number of other activities, the largest of which is the Coors Porcelain Company (CPC), which is in turn one of the world's largest producers of technical ceramics. CPC has three factories in Colorado, one in California and offices in three other states and three foreign countries. Other activities include health care, food products, transportation and recycling. Coors' Container Operations division supplies most of the brewery's cans and bottles, and is the largest aluminum can manufacturing facility in the world.

Cornelius Pass (see McMenamin)

Crown City Brewery is a microbrewery that opened in Pasadena, California in July 1988. In 1989 the brewery's total capacity was 300 barrels, to be expanded to 400 barrels, with brewing under the direction of master brewer Mike Lanzarotta. The principal brands brewed here are Crown City Amber Ale, Mt Wilson Wheat, Yorkshire Porter and specialty beers. ■

Davis Brewing (see Back Alley)

Dead Cat Alley is a brewpub located on the street of the same name in the town of Woodland, California. In 1989 the brewery's total capacity was 1000 barrels, with brew-

ing under the direction of master brewer Jim Schlueter, who founded and later sold Hogshead Brewing in Sacramento. He began bottling his Dead Cat Lager, Cat Tail Ale and Fat Cat Stout in August 1989. ■

Devil Mountain Brewery is a brewpub located in the town of Walnut Creek, California. The principal brands brewed here are Gayle's Pale Ale, Iron Horse Alt, Devil's

Brew Stout and Railroad Ale, a gold medal winner at the 1988 Great American Beer Festival in Denver, as well as the seasonal Mighty Fine Barley Wine. ■

Dixie Brewing of New Orleans was established in 1907 and was, until recently, the only remaining brewery in the Louisiana city that once was the brewing capital of the entire South. The flagship brand of this 300,000-barrel brewery is Dixie Beer,

hich is complemented by a Dixie Light. Other brands, brewed under the direction of master brewer Guy Hagner, are Coy International Private Reserve, Coy International Marathon (Light), Britt Iced Tea Breeze, Schwegmann, Schwegmann Light, K&B, K&B Light, Fischer, Fischer Light, Coy Marathon, New Orleans Best and New Orleans Best Light.

Dock Street Brewing was founded in 1986 by Philadelphia chef Jeffrey Ware. Dock Street Amber Beer, created by Ware and brewed under the direction of brewmaster

Mortimer Brenner, is produced under contract by FX Matt Brewing in Utica, New York and is widely available in the Philadelphia area. In 1988 Ware began 'exporting' his beer to California. ■

Dubuque Star Brewing in Dubuque, Iowa was established as Star Brewing in 1898 and took the name of its hometown in 1904. With a 50,000-barrel annual capacity (down from 85,000 in 1985), it is the only remaining brewery in a state that has boasted 249 licensed breweries through the years. With brewing under the direction of master brewer Michael C Jaeger, the principal brands brewed here are Dubuque Star, Golden Star Light, Erlanger (a premium Märzen Bier) and Rhomberg. The company also does private label brewing for microbrewing companies with require-

ments of 100 cases or greater. Among these projects is Wild Boar Special Amber, which is brewed for the Atlanta, Georgia market.

Eastern Brewing of Hammonton, New Jersey was established as Eastern Beverage Corporation in 1933 at the end of Prohibition and has brewed under a wide variety of brand names over the ensuing years. These

have included Circle, Colonial, Colony House, Dawson, Fisher, Fox Head, Garden State, Hampden, Hedrick, Polar, Tube City, Waukee and San Juan Cerveceria. Brands being produced under the direction of brewmaster Carmine Penza at the 400,000-barrel brewery in 1989 included Canadian Ace, Milwaukee Premium, Old German, Old Bohemia and 704 Head Beer.

Emery Pub is a brewpub which opened in April 1989 in Emeryville, California. With brewing under the direction of brewmaster Roger Bergen, the principal brands brewed

here are amber, pale ale, porter and specialty brews, which have included a raspberry beer reminiscent of a Belgian framboise lambic, although wild yeast is not used as it is in lambics. ■

Eugene City Brewing, founded by John Karlick in Eugene, Oregon, began sales of Eugene Ale in January 1988. Since that time, the firm has added Eugener-Weizen wheat beer and has released such specialty products as Bach's Bock, a doppelbock to coincide with the Oregon Bach Festival; 1988 Eugene Celebration Lager; and 1989 Oregon State Fair Ale. The Eugene beers are brewed under contract by Montana Brewing in Helena, Montana, but Karlick intends to build a brewery in Eugene. ■

Falstaff Brewing of Fort Wayne, Indiana traces its roots to the Forest Park Brewing Company of St Louis, Missouri that was established in 1910 and taken over by 'Papa Joe' Griesdieck in 1917. Renamed Falstaff (after the Shakespeare character) during Prohibition, the company expanded to become one of the Midwest's strongest multisite regional brewers. After World War II, Falstaff became a leading national brewer, and by 1960 it was the nation's third largest brewer, behind Anheuser-Busch and Schlitz.

Through its complicated association with General Brewing of Vancouver, Washington, the Falstaff brand became prominent in the West. After the 1960s, however, Falstaff's market position gave way to other brands such as Miller and Coors, and many of the company's breweries were sold or closed. By the early 1980s, when the company came under the control of the late Paul Kalmanovitz, only the Fort Wayne and Omaha, Nebraska breweries, with respective capacities of 1.2 and 1.25 million barrels, remained. Under the direction of

brewmaster Otto Chawat, Falstaff's Omaha plant brews Falstaff Lager, Ballantine Ale and Narragansett Lager. Under the direction of brewmaster Thomas Giroux, Falstaff's Fort Wayne plant brews the same products as the Omaha brewery, as well as Haffenreffer Malt Liquor. Both sites have also been used for brewing Lucky Lager, General Brewing's flagship brand. (also see **S&P**)

Florida Brewery, located in Auburndale, Florida, was founded in 1973 as the Duncan Brewing Company, but no longer brews its own brands, concentrating instead on contract brewing. In 1988 the brewery's total capacity was 150,000 barrels, with brewing under the direction of master brewer Alex Duncan. The principal brands brewed formerly were Dunk's Beer, Dunk's

Ale, Fischer's Beer and Ale, Regal beer, Master's Choice and ABC. Regal and Hatney are brands currently in production.

Florida Brewing (aka **Miami Brewpub**), not to be confused with the larger Florida Brewery, was opened in April 1989 by Elizabeth Yamanoha in Miami. She formerly brewed Miami Weiss (pronounced punfully 'Miami Vice'), but now brews Miami Brau, Old Prussia Pils, Old Prussia Alt and four seasonal brews, which include a dry cream ale, a holiday beer, a bock and another weiss. At press time, plans included another brewpub in Miami and one in Key West. ■

Frankenmuth Brewery was founded in 1987 to renovate and operate the former Geyer Brothers Brewery in the town of Frankenmuth, near Detroit, Michigan. The Geyer Brothers Brewery grew out of the Heubisch & Knaust Cass River Brewery, established on Main Street in 1862. Taken over by John G Geyer in 1874, the brewery operated under his name until 1908, at which time it became the Geyer Brothers Brewery. The first beer produced by the Frankenmuth Brewery appeared in 1988, although the Frankenmuth name was used as a brand name by Geyer Brothers. The brewmaster today is Fred Scheer, and the brewery has a 10,000-barrel annual production. Its brand names include Frankenmuth Natural Weiss, Frankenmuth Old German Style Pilsner, Frankenmuth Old German Style Dark and Frankenmuth Old German Style Bock. ■

Friend's Brewing is a small microbrewery in Helen, Georgia, which began brewing in 1989. ■

Fulton (see **McMenamin**)

Garden State Brewing of Bordentown, New Jersey was founded in 1988 by Robert Gerson and Daniel Vanderbilt. Their Premium Jersey Lager is produced under contract by The Lion in Wilkes-Barre, Pennsylvania. ■

DL Geary Brewing was founded in 1988 in Portland, Maine. Brewing of Geary's Pale Ale is under the direction of brewmaster David Geary. ■

General Brewing Company (see **Falstaff**, **Pabst**, **Pearl**, **S&P**)

Genesee Brewing of Rochester, New York is the seventh largest brewer in the United States. Among the nation's regional brewers it is second only to Coors, although the latter produces four times as much beer and distributes to a larger part of the country. The company traces it heritage back to the brewery established on North St Paul

Street in 1855 by Jacob Rau. This business evolved into the Genesee Brewing Company in 1878, and in the latter years of the nineteenth century, Genesee's Liebotschaner Beer was famous throughout western New York State. After Prohibition, the company was reorganized under the same name but under the new management of a former Genesee assistant brewmaster, Louis Wehle. Genesee was one of the first breweries in operation after repeal in April 1933 and was the winner of the first post-repeal taste test.

After World War II, as regional breweries collapsed throughout the country, Genesee flourished. Between 1960 and 1965, for example, the company went from twenty-eighth to nineteenth place nationally.

By 1987 the Rochester brewery was producing 2.7 million barrels annually (down from 3.5 million in 1985) and storing its lager in 9000-barrel storage tanks, the largest such tanks in the world. The brewmaster is Ekkehard Luck. The company's brands include Genesee Lager, Genesee Light, Genesee Cream Ale, Genesee Cream Ale Light and Genesee Twelve Horse Ale.

In February 1985 Genesee bought the Fred Koch Brewery of Dunkirk, New York and moved production of the latter's Golden Anniversary Beer and Black Horse Ale to the Rochester plant. The Fred Koch Brewery, established in 1888, had been owned and operated by the Koch family for 97 years and had grown to a 70,000-barrel annual capacity. Young Jim Koch in turn founded Boston Brewing.

Georgia Brewing is a small microbrewery in Atlanta Georgia which was scheduled to open in 1990. ■

Geyer Brothers (see **Frankenmuth**)

Gibbons (see **The Lion**)

Golden Pacific Brewing is a microbrewery begun in 1985 in Emeryville, California.

With brewing under the direction of brewmaster Tad Stratford, Golden Pacific produces over 800 barrels annually. Products include Bittersweet Ale and Pacific Cascade. In 1989 Stratford signed an agreement with Charles Rixford of Thousand Oaks Brewing to begin producing Thousand Oaks products in Emeryville. ∎

The **Gordon-Biersch Brewery** of Palo Alto, California is a microbrewery and restaurant founded in 1988 by Dean Biersch and his brewmaster partner Dan Gordon, a graduate of the brewing engineering school at the Technical University of Munich.

In 1989 Gordon-Biersch acquired the former **Biers Brasserie**, a failed brewpub in nearby San Jose. As this book was going to press, Gordon-Biersch was eyeing a third site for possible expansion to San Francisco as well. Highly rated among San Francisco Bay Area microbreweries, Gordon-Biersch produces Export, Dunkles, Märzen, Weiss and a holiday Doppelbock. ∎

Goose Island Brewing, named for Chicago's only island, is a brewpub opened in May 1988 in Chicago. In 1989 the brewery's total capacity was 2000 barrels, with brewing under the direction of brewmaster Victor Ecimovich. The principal brands brewed here are Golden Goose Pilsner, Honkers Ale and Lincoln Park Lager. The brewery's list of 12 specialty beers often includes Old Clybourne Porter, Brown Ale, Doppelbock, Porter, Weizen, Oktoberfest and Christmas Ales. ∎

Gorky's Russian Brewery is a pair of brewpubs located in Hollywood and down-

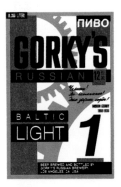

town Los Angeles, California, with brewing under the direction of brewmaster Fred Powers. Powers uses a Russian theme in his establishments and has gone so far as to propose to Soviet State Breweries that his beer be brewed in Leningrad. The principal brands brewed here are Gorky's Russian Imperial Stout, Red Star Ale and Baltic Light. ∎

Grant's (see **Yakima**)

Grapevine Brewery is a brewpub located in the town of Lebec, California. In 1989 the brewery's total capacity was 725 barrels, with brewing under the direction of

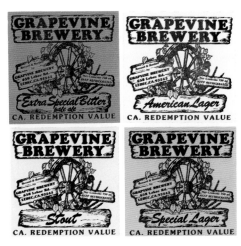

brewmaster John Benson. The principal brands brewed here are American Lager, ESB, Special and Stout. Seasonal beers on tap include Oktoberfest, Mild Ale and Winterfest. ∎

Greenshield's Brewery & Restaurant was founded by Gary Greenshield in Raleigh, North Carolina. Since its opening in July 1989 the brewery's total capacity has expanded from 400 to 2000 barrels. The principal types brewed here include Christmas bitter, porter, brown ale, Scotch ale, Munich amber pale ale and wheat beer. ∎

Hales Ales, Ltd is a microbrewery located in Colville, north of Spokane, Washington. Established in 1984, the company produces a variety of products under the direction of brewmaster Michael Hale, including

Hale's Pale American Ale, Hale's Special Bitter, Hale's Celebration Porter, Hale's Wee Heavy Christmas Ale, Hale's Irish Ale, Moss Bay Amber Ale, Moss Bay Stout, O'Brien's Harvest Ale, Sheimo's Special Bitter and such private label tavern brews as 64th Street Ale.

Hamm's (see **Falstaff, Pabst**)

Hart Brewing Company of Kalama, north of Vancouver, Washington, is another of the many microbreweries that sprang up in the Pacific Northwest during 1984 and 1985. Under the direction of Tom Baune, the 4000-barrel brewery produces Snow Cap Ale, Pacific Crest Ale, Sphinx Stout, Pyra-

mid Pale Ale and Wheaten Ale, the first draft wheat beer produced in he United States since Prohibition. Hart Brewing itself is the first brewery in Kalama since Prohibition. Kalama's previous brewer closed in 1880.

G Heileman Brewing Company of La Crosse, Wisconsin is a unique example of a small regional brewer that grew to national prominence, not through the vehicle of a single national brand like Anheuser-Busch or Miller, but through an amazing amalgam of important, formerly independent, regional brands. Established in La Crosse by Gottlieb Heileman and John Gund in 1858, the House of Heileman remained a small regional brewer until the early 1960s, when it began to acquire other smaller regional breweries, notably the acquisition of Associated Breweries in 1963 and Blatz in 1969. In 1960 Heileman was the thirty-first largest brewer in the United States, but by 1982 it was fourth. In 1987 Heileman was acquired by Alan Bond of Australia (owner of *Australia II*, the only non-American yacht ever to win the America's Cup), whose holdings constituted one of the world's largest multinational companies, and included brewers of Swan Lager. Pittsburgh Brewing Company, acquired by Bond in 1986, was then integrated into the Heileman regional network to further strengthen Bond's North American brewing operation. The Heileman acquisition made Bond Brewing the sixth largest in the world.

The House of Heileman is divided into three geographical divisions: the Central with five breweries, the Eastern with three breweries and the Western with two breweries. Of these 10 breweries (down from 11 in 1986), four are former Carling National breweries, which were acquired from the Canadian brewing giant in 1979. These plants still operate under the Carling national name and still produce, under license, Carling Black Label Beer, Carling Red Cap Ale and Tuborg, the beer that Carling has brewed in the United States under license from Tuborg of Denmark since 1973.

The Heileman Central Division includes the Carling National brewery under the direction of brewmaster Mark Ecker in Frankenmuth, Michigan, as well as the Heileman flagship brewery in La Crosse, under the direction of brewmaster Raymond Cyr, and Jacob Schmidt Brewing in St Paul Minnesota, under the direction of brewmaster Sig Plagens. The beers brewed in the Central Division include Heileman's original brand, their largest seller, Old Style, the complementary Old Style Light and the premium Heileman's Special Export. The Central Division produces other popular brands well known in the Minnesota/Pennsylvania/Kentucky triangle, such as Blatz, Falls City, Grain Belt, Red, White and Blue, and Wiedemann Bohemian Special. Meanwhile, in the same area, the Schmidt and Sterling breweries still produce beers under their own brand names. In 1986 work began on a unique sixth brewery in the Central Division. Built in Milwaukee, the brewery is named after Valentin Blatz, whose original brewery was one of the major historic Milwaukee breweries until it was closed in 1959. Heileman operated the new brewery as a specialty brewery, making beer from the original Blatz recipes and under the original brand names until 1989, when the project was terminated and the three-year-old Val Blatz brewery was closed.

The Heileman Eastern Division includes, and is headquartered at, the Pittsburgh Brewing Company in Pennsylvania, a former independent that was acquired by Bond in 1986, and was in turn integrated into the House of Heileman in 1987. Pittsburgh Brewing dates back to the brewery established by Edward Frauenheim and August Hoevler. By 1888 it had evolved into the Iron City Brewing Company. In 1899 Iron City Brewing was one of 21 brewing companies to merge into the Pittsburgh Brewing Company. As a result, each of the 21 became a 'brewery' of the Pittsburgh Brewing 'Company.' Iron City Brewing thus became the Iron City Brewery of the Pittsburgh Brewing Company. Today the former Iron City site is the only remaining brewery of the old Pittsburgh Brewing consortium, but because it uses the Pittsburgh Brewing name it is technically the descendant of *all* 21 of the formerly independent breweries in the consortium, even though the other 20 have since passed from the scene. For the sake of historical interest, some of the other breweries that joined Pittsburgh Brewing

in 1899 were Baeuerlein Brewing (originally established in 1845 and which survived as part of the consortium until 1934); Eberhardt & Ober Brewing (1852, 1952); Ernst Hauch's Sons (1849, 1904); Issac Hippley & Son's Enterprise Brewery (1859, 1899); Keystone Brewing (1887, 1920); Philip Lauer (1874, 1899); John Nusser's National Brewery (1852, 1900); Frank Ober & Brothers (1858, 1904); Phoenix Brewing (1845, 1920); John Seiferth & Brothers (1865, 1899); Herman Staub (1831, 1920);

Wainwright Brewing (1818, 1920); and Michael Winter & Brothers (1874, 1920).

Prior to being acquired by Heileman in 1987, Pittsburgh Brewing was the tenth largest brewer in the United States, up from twenty-seventh in 1960. Under the direction of brewmaster Michael Carota, the Pittsburgh plant, with its 1.25-million-barrel capacity, still uses Iron City as its flagship brand, producing an Iron City Beer, Iron City Light Beer and Iron City Dark Beer, as well as American Beer, Old Dutch

Beer, Old German Beer, Robin Hood Cream Ale, Mustang Malt Liquor, Hop'n Gator Tropical Flavor Malt Liquor, DuBois Premium, DuBois Export, Gambrinus, Augustiner, Mark V and Old Export. An Iron City Dry Beer was introduced in 1989.

Champale Incorporated of Trenton, New Jersey, acquired from Iroquois Brands in December 1986, evolved out of the brewery that Colonel AR Kuser established in 1891. The name evolved from Trenton Brewing to People's Brewing to Metropolis Brewery before becoming Champale in 1967. The brewmaster is currently John Ruhl. Over the years a wide variety of brands have emanated from the million-barrel plant, including Class A, Colony House, Gilt Edge, Hornell Old Bohemian and Tudor in the 1960s, and Banner and Rialto in the 1970s. Today's brands include Black Horse Ale (dating from 1973), nonalcoholic Metbrew and three varieties of Champale Malt Liquor: Golden, Pink and Extra Dry.

The Heileman Eastern Division also includes a Carling Brewery in Baltimore, Maryland, under the direction of brewmaster Peter Sowa, and the Lone Star Brewing Company in San Antonio, Texas, which was independent until 1976 and owned by Olympia until acquired by Heileman in 1983. Despite its absentee ownership from Washington and Wisconsin since 1976, the Lone Star brand developed a strong cult following within its home state during the 1970s. Immortalized in the songs of Willie Nelson, Waylon Jennings and Jerry Jeff Walker, Lone Star is reverently known as the 'National Beer of Texas,' and is brewed in San Antonio under the direction of brewmaster Guenter Sorge.

Heileman's Western Division includes two other breweries, which, like Lone Star in Texas, have strong cult followings. The Rainier Brewing Company of Seattle has been around since the nineteenth century, leading the Seattle brewery scene since Prohibition through a variety of owners, from Emil Sick to Molson of Canada to the House of Heileman. Rainier Beer is the largest selling beer brand in Washington, Montana and the Northwest as a whole, and the critically acclaimed Rainier Ale is the largest selling ale in the entire western United States.

Heileman acquired the West's oldest brewery (owned by Pabst for four years) in 1983. The Blitz-Weinhard Company brewery of Portland, Oregon was around for 10 years when Henry Weinhard became involved in 1862. In addition to the Blitz-Weinhard brand, the brewery, under the direction of brewmaster Robert Weisskuchen, produces a limited edition superpremium called Henry Weinhard's Private Reserve (also available in a dark beer), and an 'Ireland-style' ale. Henry's, as it is known to aficionados, ranks with San Francisco's Anchor Steam as one of the West Coast's most sought-after superpremium beers.

Falls City Brewing (established in 1905), which Heileman bought in 1978, is notable for having marketed Billy Beer, a product named for the younger brother of former President Jimmy Carter. The colorful Billy Carter was noted for his fondness for beer and his ability to distinguish between similar lagers. The idea that evolved at Falls City in 1977 seemed like a good one. They would formulate a product under Carter's specifications and license other regional

brewers to produce it. By using a network of regional brewers, Falls City hoped to be the power behind a national brand named for the brother of the president of the United States. It seemed like the most important blending of beer and government since Thomas Jefferson and James Madison were drawn into the National Brewery scheme. As it turned out, Billy Beer was a short-lived phenomenon. It received enormous media coverage but never managed to penetrate the market in the hoped-for quantities, and it was discontinued.

In addition to its own brands, the Carling brand and all the regional brands, the House of Heileman produces other related products. These include two national brands of higher-alcohol malt liquor (Colt 45 and Mickey's) and a blend of malt liquor and sparkling fruit wine marketed under the name Malt Duck. The company also produces a line of low-alcohol beers under the Old Style, Blatz and Black Label brands. At the opposite end of the spectrum, Heileman is the largest producer of nonalcoholic, or 'near' beer, in the United States. The company's near beers are sold under the Kingsbury, Schmidt Select and Zing brands. In 1989, responding to the 'dry beer' trend, Heileman introduced Old Style Special Dry, Colt 45 Dry, National Premium Dry and Lone Star Dry.

In other product areas the House of Heileman produces Country Cooler Wine Coolers, and La Croix and Cold Spring mineral waters. Heileman also produces several brands of snack foods from bakeries in Iowa, Minnesota, Illinois, Michigan and Wisconsin.

Hibernia Brewing of Eau Claire, Wisconsin began as Henry Sommermeyer's Dells Brewery in 1878 and became John Walter's City Brewery in 1890. Known simply as Walter Brewing from 1933 to 1985, the company was another rare example of a small family-owned brewery, but the 1970s and early 1980s were not good to Walter Brewing. In May 1985 Michael Healy purchased the brewery from the Walter family and renamed it Hibernia Brewing, after the

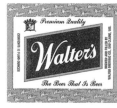 

Latin name for Ireland. He had wanted to build a brewery in Chicago, but found it easier to buy an existing facility elsewhere. The list of brand names from the former 100,000-barrel Walter Brewery included Walter's, Breunig's, Bub's, Master Brew and West Bend Old Timers Beer. Today Healy has his brewmaster Fred Scheer still brew Walters, Walters Special and Walters Light, as well as Eau Claire All Malt Lager, Hibernia Bock, Dunken Weizen, Oktoberfest and Winterbrau.

Highland (see **McMenamin**)

High Street (see **McMenamin**)

Hillsdale (see **McMenamin**)

Hogshead Brewing was founded in 1987 in Sacramento by Jim Schlueter, who sold it to brewmaster Phil Falmon before going on to found Dead Cat Alley in Woodland, California in 1989. Schlueter is remembered for

his short-lived River City Brewing, which he founded in Sacramento in 1980 and which was one of the original microbreweries. The principal styles brewed by Hogshead are lager, light lager, pale ale and dark ale. ∎

Honolulu Brewing of Honolulu, Hawaii was established as the **Koolau Brewery** in September 1988 and was sold to Wilson

Neill Ltd of New Zealand in May 1989. The brewery's total production was 5000 barrels in 1988, expanded to at least 10-15,000 barrels in 1989. 'Exports' to California began in 1989, with further distribution planned to Micronesia, New Zealand and Germany. With water naturally filtered through the lava of Oahu's Koolau Mountains, and brewing under the direction of German master brewer Hans Kestler, the principal brands brewed here are Koolau Light, Pali Hawaiian and Diamond Head Dry, which in 1989 was the first 'dry' beer to win a gold medal at the Great American Beer Festival. ∎

Honolulu Sake Brewery & Ice Company of Honolulu, Hawaii dates back to 1934 and survives today as the only commercial sake brewery in the United States. The 10,000-barrel brewery produces three brands of beer's closest relative, Takara Masamune, Takara Masamune Mirin and Takara Musume.

Hood River Brewing and its adjacent White Cap Pub opened in 1987 in the town of Hood River, Oregon, with brewing under the direction of partner and first brewer David Legsdon and brewmaster James Emerson. The principal brands brewed here are Full Sail Golden and Full Sail Amber, which are available in both bottle and draft forms, and Brown Ale, which, along with Full Sail, won a gold medal at the 1989 Great American Beer Festival. ∎

Hope Brewing, located in Providence, Rhode Island, began production in February 1988, and sold 5000 barrels of lager its first year in operation. Hope introduced seasonal, special brews to the New England market for the first time in decades. Not since Rhode Island's Narragansett Brewery closed in 1986, had New England seen beers like Hope's Bavarian Oktoberfest, Burton Christmas Ale and Springtime Bock. These limited production beers are available for a two to three month period in the fall, winter and spring.

Using the 300-barrel kettle at The Lion in Wilkes-Barre, Pennsylvania, Hope brewmaster Tim Morse (formerly with Anchor Brewing in San Francisco) formu-

lates the seasonals with imported hops, roasted malt and special yeast, as the type of beer requires. In 1989 Hope introduced a new ale, Red Rooster. Hope is the motto of the state of Rhode Island and the Rhode Island Red is the state bird. ∎

Hops Grill & Brewery was opened in Clearwater, Florida in November 1989, with brewing under the direction of brewmaster Ben Pierson. Principal brands produced here include Hammerhead Red, Hops Extra Pale Ale and Hops Golden Lager. ∎

Joseph Huber Brewing of Monroe, Wisconsin evolved from the Bissinger Brewery established in 1845. Between 1848 and 1906 it operated successively under the names John Knipschilt, Ed Ruegger, Jacob Hefty, Fred Hefty and Adam Blumer. It survived as Blumer Brewing until 1947, when it became Joseph Huber Brewing. In 1985, when Paul Kalmanovitz took over Pabst, the latter's president and vice president purchased Huber. In 1989 Huber was in turn purchased by the Berghoff in Chicago, a restaurant for whom it had long brewed a house brand beer. The resulting company is now known officially as **Berghoff-Huber Brewing**.

Today, under the direction of master brewer David Radzanowski, the 550,000-barrel brewery produces Alpine, Augsburger, Augsburger Bock, Augsburger Dark, Bavarian Club, Bohemian Club, Boxer Malt Liquor, Braumeister, Braumeister Light,

172

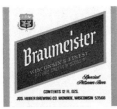

Pace Pilsner, Top Hat and Pace, a low-alcohol beer.

Humbolt Brewery is a brewpub located in the town of Arcata, California. It is owned by Mario Celotto, a former linebacker with the Oakland Raiders, with brewing under

the direction of master brewer John DeMarinis. The principal brands brewed here are Gold Rush Ale, Red Nectar Ale, Storm Cellar Porter and Oatmeal Stout, which was a gold medal winner at the Great America Beer Festival in June 1988. ∎

Jones Brewing of Smithton, Pennsylvania was established by Welsh immigrant William B 'Stoney' Jones in 1907 as the Eureka

Bengals of the National Football League.

Hudepohl originated with Gottfried Koehler in 1852 and was taken over as the Buckeye Brewery of Ludwig 'Louis' Hudepohl and George Kotte in 1885. The company became Hudepohl Brewing in 1899, and in 1934 a second Cincinnati brewery was added. In 1935 Hudepohl became one of the brewers that pioneered the use of cans for beer. During World War II, Hudepohl Beer was selected by the US War Department for use by American troops in the South Pacific. Special crates were developed for Hudepohl's cone-topped cans so that the beer could be dropped by parachute to soldiers in the field. In 1982 the company introduced Christian Moerlin, a superpremium brand named for one of Cincinnati's first great brewers, whose famous brewery was started on Elm Street in 1853 but did not survive Prohibition.

Schoenling Brewing of Cincinnati was established in 1934 on the heels of the repeal of Prohibition, under the name Schoenling Brewing and Malting, a name which was quickly changed to Schoenling Brewing and Ice, as the firm apparently decided that the ice-making was more lucrative an enterprise than the malting of barley. Schoenling dropped the reference to ice in 1937, the same year that it picked up the Top Hat brand name.

Today the principal brands are Big Jug, Burger, Burger Light, Christian Moerlein, Hudepohl Gold, Hudepohl Original Bock, Hudy Delight, Little Kings Cream Ale, Little Kings Premium, Ludwig Hudepohl Original Bock, Ludwig Hudepohl Special Oktoberfest, Midnight Dragon Malt Liquor,

Dempsey's Ale, Hi-Brau, Holiday, Huber Premium, Old Chicago, Regal Brau, Rhinelander, Van Merritt Light, Wisconsin Club and Wisconsin Gold Label, as well as Ambier products under contract. One of Huber's most unusual products is Harley Davidson Heavy Beer, brewed under contract for the motorcycle company of the same name. Huber also contract brews special house brand beers for such well-known Chicago eateries as Ed Debevik's and the venerable Berghoff. (see also **Berghoff**)

Hudepohl-Schoenling of Cincinnati, Ohio, known locally as 'Cincinnati's Brewery,' was created in December 1986 by the merger of Hudepohl Brewing and Schoenling Brewing. The combined capacity of the company is now 600,000 barrels. Among the company's recent activities have been to brew special beers for the Kentucky Derby and in commemoration of the Cincinnati

Brewing Company. The brewery's original brand was Eureka Gold Crown, but because Stoney Jones habitually made personal sales calls to taverns in the area, it came to be known unofficially as 'Stoney's Beer.' The brewery lost little time changing the official name. Until recently, the brewery was operated under the presidency of William B 'Bill' Jones III. The company subscribes to the notion that 'The beer most in demand is a product brewed in the traditional fashion [and] that this is why foreign or imported beers are gaining an increasing share of the market... as Americans become more and more disenchanted with American "fad" beers. The Jones Brewing Company, therefore, has chosen not to get involved in fads and gadgets, but instead will brew the finest natural (or traditional) beer possible!'

Because direct contact is still part of company policy, the products of the 175,000-barrel brewery are still distributed in a very small area. Those products include Stoney's and Stoney's Light, as well as Esquire, Esquire Light, Fort Pitt and Old Shay Golden Cream Ale. Jones Brewing also produces a variety of private label beers, such as Bubba's (Alabama Brewing of Chicago); Hinky Dink Kenna's (Alabama Brewing of Chicago); Olde Town Ocean City (Ocean City Brewing); and Penn Pilsner (Pennsylvania Brewing).

JV's Cafe is a brewery restaurant in Palm Beach Gardens, Florida, opened by John Vislocky in June 1989. With brewing under the direction of Flip Garry, JV's produces amber ale, pale ale, Summerfest Wheat beer and seasonal specialty beers. ■

Kalamazoo Brewing (aka **Bell's**) is a microbrewery in Kalamazoo, Michigan. In 1989 the brewery's total capacity was 600 barrels, up from 400 barrels in 1988. With brewing under the direction of head brewer

Larry Bell, the principal brands brewed here are Bell's Beer, Bell's Best Brown Ale, Bell's Special Double Cream Stout, Cherry Stout, Deb's Red Ale, Expedition Stout, Great Lakes Amber Ale, Hearted Ale, Kalamazoo Stout, Third Coast Beer and Third Coast Old Ale. ■

Kelmer's Brewhouse is a brewpub founded in 1987 by Bruce Kelm in Santa Rosa, California. In 1989 brewery's total capacity was 1700 barrels, with brewing under the direction of Timothy James O'Day. The principal brands brewed here are Klout

Dark, Krystal Light and Klassic Medium. Specialty beers have included Classic Continental Wheat Beers, English Bitter (hand pump), Five Boys, Independence Ale, Klydeside Strong Ale, October Pilsner, October Alt, Paddy's Pulverizer, Scottish Ale, Kris Kringle Christmas Ale and Klassic Amber Ale. Kelmer's also brewed a pilsen called California Gold, commissioned by Random House Publishers to commemorate the 1989 book of the same name by John Jakes. ■

Kemper Brewing on Bainbridge Island in Washington's Puget Sound is another of the microbreweries founded in the Pacific Northwest in 1984. Unlike many microbreweries, which tend toward top-ferment-

ing beers, Kemper brews a lager appropriately named Thomas Kemper Beer.

Kessler (see **Montana Beverages**)

Koch (see **Boston, Genessee**)

Lakefront Brewery is a tiny microbrewery with a 100-barrel capacity located in Milwaukee, Wisconsin, one of a growing trend of such establishments in the city that was once the center of American brewing. With brewing under the direction of Jim Klisch, Lakefront is noted for its distinctive Klisch Cherry Beer, a cherry lager which differs from the familiar kreiks of Belgium by being a lager rather than a top-fermented beer. Other products include Klisch Lager

and Riverwest Stein Beer. In October 1989 Lakefront debuted its 'October Classic,' Lakefront Pumpkin Beer, which is made from a recipe reportedly originating from Thomas Jefferson, and brewed by just a handful of brewers worldwide. This seasonal beer contains pumpkin, two-row barley, caramel malt, hallertauer and cascade hops. Cinnamon and nutmeg are used for flavoring. ■

Latrobe Brewing of Latrobe, Pennsylvania was established in 1893 at a time when the town's only other brewery was located at St Vincent's Abbey and operated by Benedictine monks. The brewery at St Vincent's closed in 1898 after 42 years of operation, but the brewery that took the name of the town survives to this day. In 1985 the company was sold to the Sundor Group of Darien, Connecticut, which initiated a vigorous advertising campaign for the flagship Rolling Rock brand, named for the nearby Rolling Rock Estate, a horse ranch. With its present 750,000-barrel capacity, Latrobe brewed 545,000 barrels in 1988, up from 466,000 in 1986. Under the direction of brewmaster Roland Mueller, the company produces Rolling Rock, Rolling Rock Light and Rolling Rock Light & Lo.

An intriguing detail about Rolling Rock is the presence of the mysterious '33' Symbol that appears on the back of the bottle. The company itself cannot remember why it was put there in the first place because the product was introduced in 1939. However, among the most popular answers to the riddle are that Prohibition was repealed in 1933; there are 33 words on the back of the 12 ounce Rolling Rock bottle; or that there are 33 letters in the ingredients of Rolling Rock—water, malt, rice, corn, hops, brewer's yeast.

Jacob **Leinenkugel Brewing** of Chippewa Falls, Wisconsin was built in 1867 by its namesake and John Miller, who was Leinenkugel's partner for the next 16 years. Located on top of Big Eddy Springs, the brewery was known as the Spring Brewery until 1898. In 1987 the company was purchased by Miller Brewing (no relation) of Milwaukee, but it remains autonomous as a separate operating unit. The 100,000-barrel brewery produces Chippewa's Pride,

Gawire, Gilt Edge, Leinenkugel's Beer, Leinenkugel's Light Beer, (Leinie's Light) and Leinenkugel's Bock. Every bottle and can of Leinenkugel's carries the distinctive Indian maiden head ('Leinie') motif. This reflects the brewery's location in 'Indian Head Country,' so named because of the Indian profile created on maps by the meanderings of the Mississippi River along the Wisconsin-Minnesota border near Chippewa Falls.

Lighthouse (see **McMenamin, Santa Cruz**)

Lind Brewing Company is a draft only microbrewery founded in August 1989 in the town of San Leandro, California. In 1989 the brewery's total capacity was 700 barrels per year, with brewing under the

direction of brewmaster Roger Lind, a homebrewer for 10 years, who had previously also brewed at Devil Mountain and Triple Rock. The principal brands brewed here are Drake's Ale and Sir Francis Stout. ■

The Lion, Incorporated, also known as **Gibbons Brewery**, of Wilkes-Barre, Pennsylvania, was founded in 1905 as the Luzerne County Brewing Company and became Lion Brewing in 1910. It was reconstituted as The Lion, Incorporated after

Prohibition, and has used the Gibbons, Stegmaier and Pocono brand names ever since. The 300,000-barrel capacity brewery today produces beer, ale and porter under both the Gibbons and Stegmaier names, as well as Bartel's Beer, Esslinger, Liebotschaner Cream Ale, Lionshead and Steg Light.

Lone Star (see **Heileman**)

Long Island Brewing is located in the town of Montauk, New York at the eastern tip of Long Island. Opened 22 May 1988, Long Island contracts for its production with FX Matt in Utica, New York and distributes its

only brand, the 105-calorie Montauk Light, to Long Island's two counties, but plans to supply its product to the five boroughs of New York City, as well as Connecticut, New Jersey, Maine and Washington, DC. ■

Maine Coast Brewing is a small company located in Portland, Maine, whose Portland Lager, a Vienna-style lager, is brewed under contract by the FX Matt Brewing Company of Utica, New York. ■

Manhattan Brewing of New York City opened its doors in November 1984, marking a return of brewing to the borough of Manhattan, which hadn't had a brewery operating within its borders since 1965. Located in a former Consolidated Edison substation on Thompson Street, the brewery has an annual brewing capacity of 40,000 barrels, but initial fermenting capacity was much less. Additional contract brewing is done at The Lion in Wilkes-Barre, Pennsylvania. Founded by Robert D'Addona, Manhattan Brewing was also the first brewpub located east of the Rockies and one of the largest in the United States, with two restaurants operating within a few feet of the huge German-made

copper brew kettles. Though Manhattan Brewing will be remembered in the history books as the first brewery in Manhattan in 19 years and as the first brewery in New York City in eight years (Schaefer's Brooklyn plant closed in 1976), it was most well known locally in the mid-1980s for its horse-drawn beer wagons, the first of their kind to make regular deliveries to Manhattan taverns since the turn of the century. Brewing is under the direction of brewmaster Mark Witty (formerly of Whitbred and Samuel Smith in England), who created the recipes and oversaw the production of the Manhattan Brewing Company's seven original ales—Manhattan Amber, Manhattan Royal Amber, Manhattan Special Porter, Manhattan Sports Ale, Manhattan Brown Ale, Manhattan Stout, D'Agostino Fresh and, seasonally, Manhattan Winter Warmer, as well as the company's first bottled beer, Manhattan Gold Lager, which won a gold medal at the 1989 Great American Beer Festival.

Marin Brewing Company of Larkspur (Marin County), California was founded in April 1989 by brewmaster Brendan Noylan, with a brewhouse designed by Dr Michael Lewis of the University of California at Davis. The brewery's total production was 1200 barrels, with the principal brands

brewed being Albion Amber, Marin Hefeweiss, Marin Weiss, Mount Tamalpais Ale, Miwok Weizen Bock, Old Dipsea Barley Wine, Point Reyes Porter, Raspberry Trail Ale, St Brendan's Ale, San Quentin Breakout Stout, which won a gold medal at the 1989 Great American Beer Festival, and various seasonal wines. ■

Massachusetts Bay Brewing, a microbrewery which calls itself simply **Mass Bay Brewing**, is located in Boston, Massachusetts, with distributions throughout New England. In 1988 the brewery's total capacity was 9000 barrels, with brewing under the direction of brewmaster Russ Heissner. The principal brands brewed here

are Harpoon Ale and Harpoon Winter Warmer. When Mass Bay introduced its first brew in June 1987, it became the first brewer to operate in Boston since 1964. Boston Beer Company produced its Samuel Adams Lager in Pittsburgh, Pennsylvania until late in 1987. ■

FX Matt Brewing of Utica, New York (also known as **West End Brewing**) evolved from the Columbia Brewery established by Charles Bierbauer in 1853. The company was taken over in 1888 by Francis Xavier Matt I (grandfather of the current president, FX Matt II) and organized as West End Brewing. The brewery was renamed for FX Matt in 1980, 22 years after his death, by which time it reached an 800,000-barrel capacity and ranked among the top 15 brewers in the United States. The brand name Utica Club, which was introduced for the soft drinks produced by the company

during Prohibition, became so popular that it was retained afterward for West End's beer products.

The brewery's brand names today include Utica Club, Utica Club Light and Utica Club Cream Ale, as well as Saranaca 1888, Matt's Premium and Matt's Premium Light. Other products include Maximus Super, a high alcohol malt liquor. FX Matt also brews small batches of dark beer and ale for local draft consumption, a Season's Best Amber Beer for sale in December, and contract brews for several small brewing companies in the Northeast. One other unique product is Fort Schuyler Beer, a product that was brewed by the Old Fort Schuyler Brewery (later named Utica Brewing) between 1886 and 1937. FX Matt is also one of the leading producers of beer under contract from East Coast boutique brewing companies, producing beer for Dock Street in Philadelphia, Brooklyn Brewery, Maine Coast Brewing and Old New York, among others.

McGuire's Irish Pub & Brewery is a restaurant established in 1974 that began brewing in March 1989. Located in the city of Pensacola, Florida, the brewery's total capacity was 24 to 26 kegs a week at the start. With brewing under the direction of

brewmaster Steve Fried and owner W McGuire Martin, the principal brands brewed here are McGuire's Ale, McGuire's Golden Ale, McGuire's Irish Red, McGuire's

Irish Stout and seasonal beers that include Oktoberfest Amber and Winterfest. ■

McKenzie River Corporation was founded in San Francisco, California in January 1987 to develop premium brands in specialty niches by Fred Wessinger, who owned and operated his family's brewery, the Blitz Weinhard Company in Portland, Oregon, before its sale to the Pabst Brewing Company in 1979. Through his career

Wessinger has developed and successfully introduced several premium brands, including Henry Weinhard's Private Reserve Beer and Olde English 800 Malt Liquor. The McKenzie River Corporation's first brand is St Ides Premium Malt Liquor. ■

Mike McMenamin of Portland, Oregon and his brother Brian operate more than a dozen restaurants and pubs in western Oregon. Among them are six brewpubs, making the McMenamin group the largest *chain* of seven brewpubs in the United States. Each of the locations brews beer that is common to all or several of the sites, as well as other beer that is indigenous only to that particular site. For example, the **Fulton** and **High Street** breweries each produce a beer that bears its name. The first of the McMenamin brewpubs was the **Hillsdale Brewery,** opened in Portland in October 1985, which was the first brewpub to be established in Oregon since

Prohibition. The other McMenamin sites are the **Cornelius Pass Roadhouse & Brewery** at Hillsboro; the **Fulton Pub & Brewery** in Portland; the **Highland Pub & Brewery** at Gresham; the **High Street Brewery & Cafe** in Eugene; and the **Lighthouse Brewpub** overlooking the Pacific at Lincoln City. At press time, the **Thompson House Brewpub** was about to open in Salem, and another brewpub was being considered for a site in the Columbia River Gorge. Among the beers brewed at these sites are Cascade Head Ale, Crystal Ale, Hammerhead, King Crimson, Maid Marion, Ruby (originally Ruby Tuesday), and the remarkable Terminator Stout. Seasonal beers, such as bocks, are also often available. ∎

Mendocino Brewing in Hopland, California was founded by Michael Laybourn, Norman Franks and John Scahill in 1982, and is today under the direction of master brewer Don Barkley. It was California's first brewpub since Prohibition and produces about 8000 barrels a year. Its brands are typically named for birds of the region and

include Black Hawk Stout, Blue Heron Pale Ale, Eye of the Hawk, Peregrine Pale Ale, Red Tail Ale, Yuletide Porter and Springtime Celebration. All are available on draft at the brewpub and occasionally in quart bottles. Red Tail, the flagship brand, has been widely available in bottled form, and has been marketed in six-packs of 12-ounce bottles since July 1989.

Miami Brewpub (see **Florida Brewing**)

Mill Bakery, Eatery & Brewery of Huntsville, Alabama operates five Mill stores, two of which have breweries. All brewing is under the direction of brewmaster John Stuart who commutes between the breweries in Tallahassee and Gainesville, Florida. The brewery is now an integral part of the Mill concept. The first to open was the Gainesville Mill on Valentine's Day 1989. The second, at Tallahassee, opened on 4 July 1989. It was added to the existing Mill Bakery & Eatery, which had been in operation for three years. Each brewery's capacity is 400 barrels a year. At the time of this writing, they were operating at 60 to 65 percent capacity. Three brands are brewed on premises: Seminole Gold, Gator Tail Ale and a brewmaster's Special. The Mill Bakery, Eatery & Brewery also has an Amber Lager and Harvest Gold Light, which is a low calorie Pilsner, that are contract brewed by Jones Brewing of Smithton, Pennsylvania. Three additional sites are planned in Baton Rouge, Louisiana, and Charlotte and Greensboro, North Carolina. ∎

Miller Brewing of Milwaukee has been the second largest brewing company in the

United States since the late 1970s after a long climb from eleventh place in 1965. The brewery originated in suburban Milwaukee, Wisconsin in 1855 as Charles Best's Plank Road Brewery. It was purchased in 1855 by Frederic Miller, who turned it into one of the region's leading breweries. In 1969 the Philip Morris Tobacco Company acquired 53 percent of Miller Brewing, and the following year they bought the remaining 47 percent.

In 1988 Miller produced 40.7 million barrels, up from 38 million in 1985. The company operates six plants located at Albany, Georgia; Eden, North Carolina; Irwindale, California; Fort Worth, Texas; Fulton, New York; and Milwaukee, Wisconsin. The Milwaukee brewery is the largest, producing 8.5 million barrels annually, but the Eden and Albany plants are close behind with an annual production rate of eight million barrels each. The company's flagship brand is Miller High Life, a premium national lager brand that has existed since before Prohibition. In 1975 Miller introduced Lite, the first nationally marketed reduced-calorie beer. It went on to become the leading reduced-calorie beer, as well as the second best selling beer of any kind, in the United States. (Budweiser is first.) Miller also markets two budget lager brands (Milwaukee's Best and Meister Brau), a regional malt liquor (Magnum) and a reduced-alcohol beer (Sharp's LA). Milwaukee's Best is a reformulation of a beer originally brewed by A Gettelman in the 1890s. The brewery was acquired by Miller in 1961, but Miller still uses the Gettelman name. In 1985 Miller introduced another 'historical' product. A nonpasteurized draft-style beer, it was called Plank Road after the original brewery acquired by Frederic Miller in 1855. This was phased out in favor of Miller Genuine Draft, a nonpasteurized beer with the Miller name that has become an extremely successful product. Miller also produces Matilda Bay Cooler.

An important Miller product since 1975 is Lowenbrau, produced under license from the brewer of the same name in Munich, Germany, where it has been produced since 1383. (In Canada, Molson brews Lowenbrau.) While Miller brews a German beer in the United States, Miller High Life is brewed in Canada by Carling-O'Keefe and in Japan by Sapporo. In 1987 Miller acquired Jacob Leinenkugel Brewing of Chippewa Falls, Wisconsin, a long-standing family brewer. It remains autonomous as a separate operating unit and is listed separately in this book.

Like industry leader Anheuser-Busch, Miller Brewing actively sponsors sports. It alone sponsors US Olympic Training Centers in Colorado Springs and Lake Placid, New York. Miller also sponsors the US Hockey Team, the US Rifle Team, the US Track and Field Team and the US Ski Team, as well as a number of auto and power boat racing teams. Among Miller-sponsored sporting events are the Miller High Life 200 and 500 auto races, the Miller High Life National Doubles Bowling Tournament, the Lite Bartender's Cup ski races, the Lite Major League Fun Runs and the Lite Beer World Series of Tavern Pool.

Millstream Brewing of Amana, Iowa was founded by Joe Pickett, Sr, with the first bottling in December 1985. With brewing under the direction of Larry Schantz, Millstream has a capacity of 2200 barrels for its Millstream Lager, Millstream Wheat Beer and Schild Brau. ∎

Montana Beverages of Helena, Montana was established in 1982 by Dick Burke and Bruce DeRosier. In 1983 they hired brewmaster Dan Carey, a graduate of Dr Michael Lewis's brewing school at the University of California at Davis, to develop their first beer, which was marketed under the brand name Kessler. It was first produced in 1984 and is a reference to the original Kessler brewery, which was started in 1865 by Luxembourg native Nick Kessler and later grew into one of Montana's most important breweries. By 1957 the market for small breweries in Montana, as in most of the rest of the United States, had been reduced to the point where it was no longer economically viable. Kessler Brewing closed, and its copper kettles were shipped to South America. When Montana Beverages revived the Kessler brand 27 years

later, it was an entirely new beer and an entirely new market.

A new generation of Americans was ready for local brews produced on a smaller scale and Montanans were particularly ready for a 'Made in Montana' beer. Starting with a 300-barrel capacity in 1983, Montana Beverages had grown to 15,000 barrels in 1989. Today, under the direction of master brewer Julius Hummer, the brewery produces Winter Kessler, Kessler Bock, Wheat, Holiday, Lorelei Extra Pale and Oktoberfest beer. In 1989 Kessler Grand Teton Doppelbock won a gold medal at the Great American Beer Festival. The company also brews Santa Barbara Lager, which is distributed by Terry Allen's RAM Distributing of Santa Barbara, California, as well as brewing under contract for companies in Eugene, Oregon and Jackson Hole, Wyoming.

178

Monterey Brewing is a microbrewery and brewpub located on the legendary Cannery Row in Monterey, California. The principal brands brewed here are Great White Light, Killer Whale Amber Ale, Pacific Porpoise Porter, Sea Lion Stout and Whale's Tail Pale Ale. ■

Napa Valley Brewing of Calistoga, California also operates the historic 1882 Calistoga Inn, a brewpub, restaurant and hotel. A brewery located in the heart of North America's premier wine-producing region may seem to be an anachronism, but Napa Valley Brewing's beers are just as world

class as the wines being produced from the adjacent fields. Under the direction of brewmaster Phil Rogers, until he sold his interest in 1989, the brewery's products include Calistoga Lager and Calistoga Red Ale. ■

Nevada City Brewing, a tiny sister brewery to Truckee Brewing, is located in Nevada City, California. Opened in 1989 under the direction of Gene Downing, it has a 200-barrel capacity and brews the same products as Truckee Brewing. ■

New Haven Brewing of New Haven, Connecticut began brewing in September 1989 with a total capacity of 3000 barrels, but was designed to be expanded to 10,000 barrels. With brewing under the direction of

brewmaster Drew Lisher, the principal brands brewed are Elm City Connecticut Ale, Blackwill Stout and a Golden Ale. These were on draft until 1990, when bottling began. ■

William S Newman Brewing, established in Albany, New York in 1981, was the first microbrewery in the East and, incredibly, the first new company to establish a brewery in New York State since Prohibition. Older breweries had changed hands or built new plants during that period, but all of the more than 700 previous breweries in

New York had roots before 1934, and the majority of those had both opened and closed prior to Prohibition. Serving as head brewer, William S Newman himself brewed the company's products in a brewhouse whose 6500-barrel capacity certainly made it one of the nation's smallest. However, demand for Newman's products eventually increased to the point where Newman

closed the brewery in 1988 and moved to contract production at FX Matt in Utica, New York. Brand names include Albany Amber Ale, Newman's Albany Amber Beer, Newman's Tricentennial Pale Ale and Newman's Winter Ale.

Noggins Breweries are a pair of brewery restaurants in Seattle, Washington owned by the Spinnakers Brewing Corporation of Victoria, British Columbia. Brewing at both of the 3200-barrel facilities is under the direction of Spinnakers' master brewer Brad McQuhae. The Westlake District Noggins Brewery was opened in October 1988, where production consists of Autumn Amber Ale, Fitzpatrick Stout, McQuhae's Scottish Ale, Medieval Ale, Noggins Ale, Noggins India Pale Ale, Olde Preston Strong Ale, Pine Street Porter, Steiner Dark Lager, Summer Light Ale, Taylor's SOB, Weizenbrau and Westlake Dark. The University District Noggins, which opened in March 1989, produces Brooklyn Dark Ale, Burke Bitter Ale, Felton's Pale Ale, McQuhae's Scottish Ale, Noggins Ale, Noggins India Pale Ale, Union Stout, Weizenbrau and Husky Lager. The latter is a reference to the University of Washington mascot. ■

North Coast Brewing was founded in Fort Bragg on California's Mendocino County coast in 1988 under the leadership of brewmaster Mark Ruedrich and his associ-

ates Joe Rosenthal and Tom Allen. Situated in an old nineteenth century mortuary, the brewery has an annual capacity of 700 barrels, and is the proud home of Ruedrich's Red Seal Ale, Scrimshaw Pilsner Style Beer and Old No 45 Stout. Seasonal brews are offered as well, including an India Pale Ale, Weiss Beer, Bock, a Vienna Style Ale and an annual Christmas Ale, among others. Using the British single stage infusion system, all the beers are available on tap. Red Seal and Scrimshaw are also sold in 750 ml bottles. ■

Northampton Brewery on Brewster Court in Northampton, Massachusetts is associated with, and brews its all-malt lagers for, the appropriately named Brewster Court Bar & Grill. These beers include Amber Lager, Bock, Gold Lager and Steamer. ■

Ocean City Brewing (see **Jones**)

Old Columbia Brewery & Grill is a brewpub located in downtown San Diego, California. In 1988 the brewery's total capacity was 1500 barrels, with brewing under the direction of master brewer Karl

Strauss and brewmaster Martin Johnson. The principal brands brewed here are Black's Beach Extra Dark, Downtown After Dark, First National Bock, Gaslamp Gold, Lighthouse Light and Old Columbia Amber Lager. ■

Old Marlborough Brewing of Marlborough, Massachusetts was founded in 1989 by Larry Bastien and three partners: Joseph Cunningham, AJ Morgan and Barry

McCarthy. Their Post Road Real Ale—named for the old New York to Boston thoroughfare—is produced under contract by Catamount Brewing in White River Junction, Vermont. ■

Old New York Beer Company is headquartered on Washington Street in New York City, but its New Amsterdam Amber Beer is actually brewed under contract by the FX Matt Brewing Company in Utica, New York. Introduced in 1982, New Amsterdam

Amber is available only in New York City at specialty food stores, restaurants and what the company describes as 'society' saloons. Additional brands, all introduced in 1988, include Baja (a Mexican-style premium), Whyte's Pale Ale and El Paso (a Mexican-style premium).

Olde Heurich Brewing was founded in 1986 in Washington, DC by Gary Heurich, the grandson of Christian Heurich, who started a brewery in 1873 that overlooked the Potomac on the site now occupied by the Kennedy Center. Christian Heurich supervised the brewery until his death in 1945 at the age of 102. His son kept the brewery in business until 1965. With brewing under the direction of master brewing consultant Dr Joseph Owades, the revived company now markets Olde Heurich Amber Lager, which is produced under contract at Pittsburgh Brewing. ■

Oldenberg Brewery is a 'brewery and entertainment complex' of restaurants, a beer hall and beer garden, located on Buttermilk Pike in the town of Fort Mitchell, Kentucky. In 1987 the brewery's total capacity was 30 barrels daily and 12,500 barrels yearly. With brewing under the direction of master brewer Hans Bilger, the principal brands

brewed here are Master Brewer's Special, Oldenberg Premium Verum and Schenk. Oldenberg's Cherry Lager was the first beer to win a gold medal in the Great American Beer Festival's fruit beer category when it was debuted in 1989. ■

Olympia (see **Falstaff**, **Pabst**)

Oregon Brewing (see **Bayfront**, **Rogue**)

Oregon Trail Brewing is a microbrewery founded in July 1987 in the university town of Corvallis, Oregon. In 1988 the brewery's total capacity was 900 barrels, with brewing under the direction of brewmaster Jerry Shadomy. The principal brands brewed here are a seasonal Summer Ale, as well as four principal beers: Oregon Trail Ale, Oregon Trail Nut Brown Ale, Oregon Trail Porter and Oregon Trail Stout. ■

Pabst Brewing Company of Milwaukee, Wisconsin was the largest brewery in the United States at the turn of the century and has remained in the top six ever since. In 1988 Pabst brewed just over six million bar-

rels of beer at four plants with an aggregate capacity of 14.7 million barrels. The original brewery was started in 1844 by Jacob Best and later run by Philip Best in partnership with Captain Frederick Pabst. The Captain essentially ran the brewery himself after Philip retired in 1866. Pabst acquired Olympia Brewing in 1983 (which had recently acquired the Theodore Hamm brewery in St Paul, Minnesota) and was itself taken over in February 1985 by the reclusive California millionaire Paul Kalmanovitz, who already owned the Falstaff, General and Pearl breweries. After Kalmanovitz died in 1987 all four companies passed to the S&P holding company. (see **S&P**)

The Pabst breweries include the six-million-barrel flagship brewery in Milwaukee; satellite Pabst breweries in Tampa, Florida

(1.5 million barrels) and Newark, New Jersey (2.5 million barrels); as well as the Olympia Brewery at Tumwater, Washington (4.5 million barrels), which continues to produce under its own brand name. The major Pabst brand is Pabst Blue Ribbon, one of the oldest name brands in American history. Other Pabst-owned brands include

Pabst Light, Pabst Extra Light, Pabst Special Dark, Buckhorn, Buckhorn Light, Hamm's, Hamm's Special Light, Hamm's Draft, Ice Man Malt Liquor, Jacob Best Premium Light, MAXX Special Lager and Old English 800 Malt Liquor. The former Olympia Brewery at Tumwater (now known as a Pabst Brewery) brews Olympia (aka 'Oly'), Olympia Light and Gold Light. In October 1985 Paul Kalmanovitz closed the General Brewery at Vancouver, Washington and transferred production to the Tumwater Pabst plant.

In 1989 Pabst worked with Kalsec Foods, a large seasoning company, to develop a product called Original Cajun Beer. Developed by Ken Needham initially for the Louisiana market, Original Cajun is intended to eventually be available in as many as 20 states. It is a unique spice and pepper-seasoned beer with a predictably distinctive flavor—and aftertaste.

Pacific Brewing of Wailuka, Hawaii first began brewing in July 1986 on the island of Maui by German immigrant Aloysius Klink. It was the first *beer* brewery (Honolulu still has a sake brewery) in Hawaii since Schlitz closed the Primo Brewery in

1980. The 6500-barrel brewery is under the direction of brewmaster Dan Lacanienta. Klink produces his Maui Lager with Hallertau hops flown in (it costs as much to to ship by boat) from Germany, with malt from Canada and Belgium and water from Maui's famed Iao Valley. ■

Pacific Coast Brewing is a brewpub located in Oakland, California, with brewing under the direction of brewmaster Barry Lazarus. The principal brands

brewed here are Blue Whale Ale, Grey Whale Ale, Orca Porter and Rejuvenator Doppelbock. Also produced are Amethyst (blackberry) Ale and Heartthrob Ale, produced for Valentine's Day. A Holiday Ale, released in 1988, was Pacific Coast's first, limited, venture into bottled beer. ■

James Page Brewery is a microbrewery founded in October 1987 in Minneapolis, Minnesota. In 1989 the brewery's total production was 1500 barrels, with brewing

under the direction of brewmaster John Page. The principal brands brewed here are Boundary Waters Beer, Boundary Waters Bock and James Page Private Stock. ■

Pasadena Brewing, founded by Edward Ojdana in Pasadena, California, is a small brewing company whose Pasadena Lager is brewed under a unique international contract agreement by Granville Island Brewing in Vancouver, British Columbia. ■

Pearl Brewing of San Antonio, Texas developed out of the brewery started by JB Behloradsky in 1881 and evolved into San Antonio Brewing in 1883. The company became Pearl Brewing in 1952, although the Pearl brand name had been used since 1886 by San Antonio Brewing. In 1961 Pearl acquired Goetz Brewing of St Joseph, Missouri, which was operated until 1976. Having become associated with General Brewing in 1978, Pearl became part of the group of breweries assembled by Paul Kalmanovitz prior to his death in 1987.

Today, Pearl, as well as Falstaff, General and Pabst, are sister companies under the

S&P holding company (see **S&P**). Under the direction of master brewer John Riley, the 1.6-million-barrel capacity San Antonio brewery produces Pearl Premium and Pearl Light, as well as Country Club Malt Liquor, Goetz, 900 Super Premium Malt Liquor, Pilsner Club, Texas Pride and Jax Beer, a brand produced by the now-defunct Jackson Brewing of New Orleans. Keys Lite, a contract-brewed product for Keys Beverage in Key West, Florida, was also brewed here in 1984. The Pearl brewery also has produced Pale Nonalcoholic Beer and General's Lucky Lager.

Pennsylvania Brewing was established by Thomas V Pastorius in Philadelphia in 1986 to oversee the production of Pennsylvania Pilsner, which was brewed under contract by Jones Brewing in Smithton,

Pennsylvania until Pastorius opened his own plant in Pittsburgh in 1989. Pennsylvania Pilsner is based on German Erbacher beer and was developed jointly by Pastorius and Dr Joseph Owades of the Center for Brewing Studies in San Francisco. The brewmaster is Alexander Deurl. ■

Pete's (see **August Schell**)

Pike Place Brewery is a microbrewery which opened in the historic Pike Place Market in Seattle, Washington in October 1989. It is owned jointly by internationally-known beer importer Charles Finkel and brewmaster John Farias, who oversees the brewing of Pike Place Pale Ale and other specialty beers. ■

Pittsburgh Brewing (see **Heileman**)

Portland Brewery is a brewery and brewpub founded in January 1986 in Portland, Oregon. In 1989 the brewery's total capacity was 3100 barrels, to be expanded to 4500 barrels, with brewing under the direction of brewmaster Fred Bowan. The principal brands brewed here are Oregon Dry Beer, Portland Ale and Timberline Ale. ■

Post Road (see **Old Marlborough**)

Rainier (see **Heileman**)

Red Hook Ale Brewery of Seattle, Washington was established by Paul Shipman in 1982 in the city's Ballard district. This microbrewery's 7500-barrel annual capacity is divided among its original Red Hook Ale, Black Hook Porter and Ballard Bitter.

 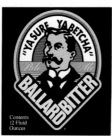

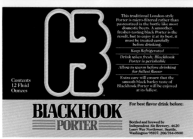

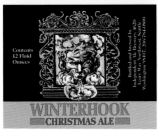

For the first three years of its operation, the brewery's products were available only in draft form, but a bottle line was installed in 1985, in time for the introduction of Winterhook Christmas Ale.

Redwood Coast Brewing operated the Tied House Cafe, a brewpub located in Mountain View, California. In 1988 the brewery's total capacity was 3120 barrels, with brewing under the direction of senior brewmaster Tom Cheuch, who had 28 years of experience with San Miguel and six years with Anheuser-Busch. The principal brands brewed are Tied Amber, Tied Dark and Tied Pale, as well as special brews. The company has plans for another brewery in San Jose, California, with eight to 10 brands to be swapped between the two. ■

Reinheitsgebot Brewing produces its Collin County beers in the town of Plano, Texas. Named for the German Purity Law of 1516, the brewery had a total capacity in 1986 of 1600 barrels, which was expanded to 2500 in 1989. With brewing under the

direction of brewmaster Donald Thompson (the first place winner in the 1982 American Home Brewers Association contest) and his wife Mary, the principal brands brewed here are Collin County Black Gold, Collin County Emerald Beer, Collin County Pure Gold, Special Bock Beer for Spring, Fourth of July Beer and Christmas Beer. The Thompsons have also discussed a light beer to be called Collin County Fool's Gold. ■

Rhomberg (see **Dubuque Star**)

River North (see **Sieben's**)

Rogue Brewery is located near Oregon's Rogue River in the town of Ashland, Oregon, and is owned by Oregon Brewing, which started a second brewpub, the Bayfront, in Newport in 1989. With brewing under the direction of master brewer

ing under the direction of master brewer Greg Kebkey, the principal brands brewed here are Ashland Amber, Doppelbock, Jackson Pale, Rogue Golden, Shakespeare Stout and Weitzen as well as such specialty beers as Roguenberry and Rogue Mogul Madness. ■

Roslyn Brewing of Roslyn, Washington was originally founded in 1889 (some sources say 1891) by William Dewitt and Frank Groger. Closed in 1915 prior to Prohibition, Roslyn Brewing was re-established

in its centennial year by Roger Beardsley and Dino Enrico. The brewery is located in a rugged nineteenth-century-style building built by Enrico, where the company's appropriately named Roslyn Beer is produced. ■

Rubicon Brewing is a microbrewery located in the city of Sacramento, Califor-

nia, with brewing under the direction of master brewer Phil Moeller. Styles include a Wheat Ale, an Amber ale, a Stout and an India Pale Ale, for which Rubicon won a gold medal at the 1989 Great American Beer Festival. ■

Saint Michael's of Philadelphia is a small brewing company devoted to the production of Saint Michael's Non-Alcoholic Malt Beverage. ■

S&P Company of Corte Madera, California and Vancouver, Washington is the holding company established by the late Paul Kalmanovitz as an umbrella for his extensive acquisitions in the American brewing industry. These include the Falstaff/General/Pearl group of companies and Pabst, which incorporates Olympia and Hamm's. No actual brewing takes place at either site. Corte Madera, California, near San Francisco, was Kalmanovitz's home and when he died in 1987, the corporate offices remained there. Vancouver was the site of the General Brewing Company, which was acquired by Kalmanovitz in 1985. He closed General Brewing the same year and moved all of its operations to his Pabst/Olympia brewery at nearby Tumwater, Washington.

By the time he made headlines with his 1985 acquisition of Pabst, Kalmanovitz

had already assembled an impressive collection of breweries that included Pearl Brewing of San Antonio, General Brewing of Vancouver, Washington and Falstaff of Fort Wayne, Indiana (which in turn owned the formerly independent East Coast brand names Ballantine and Narragansett). The cost-cutting and brewery closings that came in the wake of his takeover of these three breweries saddened many in the industry, but such measures did enhance the profitability of the breweries. The reclusive multimillionaire also ruffled some feathers when he bought the ailing Pabst Brewing and eliminated white collar jobs and public tours at Pabst's big Milwaukee brewery.

The Falstaff/General/Pearl group constitutes the eighth largest brewery in the United States, with an output of two million barrels, despite a reduced number of brewing sites. Sixth-ranked Pabst (which includes formerly independent Olympia and Hamm's), meanwhile, has an annual output of more than eight million barrels of beer. (see also **Falstaff**, **General**, **Pabst**, **Pearl**)

San Andreas Brewing operates the Earthquake Country brewpub that opened in the central valley town of Hollister, California in September 1988. During its first year, the brewery's total capacity was 1500 barrels, to be expanded to 4000 barrels, with brewing under the direction of brewmaster

Mitch Steele. Named for California's famed San Andreas earthquake fault, which is not actually near Hollister, the brewery's principal draft brands were named with an 'earthquake' theme. They include Earthquake Pale, Earthquake Porter, Kit Fox Amber and Seismic Ale. Special brews include Apricot Ale, Cherry Ale and Courtley Stout. In September 1989 San Andreas released an Oktoberfest beer called October Quake. On 17 October 1989 Northern California was struck by the worst earthquake since 1906, an event for which San Andreas was blamed (tongue-in-cheek, of course). ■

San Francisco Brewing Company is located on the site of the historic Albatross Saloon on Columbus Avenue in San Francisco. America's fourth brewpub, brewing

began here in November 1986 under the direction of owner and master brewer Allen Paul. The brewery has a 900-barrel capacity that is used almost exclusively to service

the brewpub, although there is a limited distribution of bottled beer. San Francisco Brewing produces Albatross Lager, Emperor Norton Lager, Gripman Porter, and a variety of outstanding specialty beers, which have included Andromeda Wheat Beer, Serpent Stout and Gold Rush Ale. ■

Santa Barbara (see **Montana Beverages**)

Santa Cruz Brewing brews bottled beer for the local, northern California market and operates the Front Street Pub in Santa Cruz, California. In 1989 the brewery's total

capacity was 2000 barrels, with brewing under the direction of brewmaster Scotty Morgan. The principal brands brewed here are Lighthouse Amber, Lighthouse Lager and Pacific Porter. ■

Santa Fe Brewing was founded in June 1987 by Mike Levis at Gallisteo, New Mexico. Levis brews 150 cases a month for principal distribution to 113 restaurant

accounts in the Santa Fe/Albuquerque area, although he has accounts as far away as northern Virginia. The only brand brewed here is Santa Fe Pale Ale. ■

Sarasota Brewing is a brewery restaurant opened in Sarasota, Florida in September 1989. With a total capacity of 1400 barrels, brewing is under the direction of Gisele

Budel. The principal brands are Cobra Light, Presidential Pale Ale, Sequoia Amber

Lager and such specialty beers as Christmas Cream Ale, Autumn Harvest Dark and a weizenbier. ■

Saxton Brewery is located in the town of Chico, California. In 1988 the brewery's total capacity was 300 barrels, with brewing under the direction of DeWayne and Stacy L Saxton. DeWayne was Homebrewer of the Year (Best of Show) in 1984. The principal brands brewed here are

Excalibur, DüBrü, Grail Pale Ale and Lion Hearted Ale. Special brews include Ivanhoe Ale, Fasching, Summer Solstice, Oktoberfest and Lion Hearted Yule-Fest. The Saxtons also operate Sherwood Brewing in Chico, California. ■

August Schell Brewing of New Ulm, Minnesota was established in 1860. The brewery survived the 1862 Sioux uprising because of August Schell's good relations with the Indians, and has existed as a small regional brewery ever since. The 50,000-barrel annual output is divided among the

highly-regarded, prize-winning August Schell Pilsner, Schell's Light, Schell's Export, Ulmer Lager and Ulmer Braun, as well as August Schell Bock, August Schell Weiss, August Schell Light, Deer Brand Export, Steinhaus and Twins Lager. Prior to 1985 August Schell's products were available only in Minnesota, North Dakota

183

and Illinois, when Charles Finkel of Merchant du Vin Corporation convinced the brewery that a national market existed for their products and began a national distribution campaign. August Schell also produces Pete's Wicked Ale for Pete's Brewing in Los Gatos, California.

Schirf Brewing, located in Park City, Utah, is the only brewery to operate in Utah since 1967. Founded as a microbrewery in October 1986, Schirf expanded into its Wasatch brewpub in July 1989. In 1988 the brewery's total capacity was 2750 barrels, but this is expected to be expanded to 6000 barrels, under the direction of brewmaster

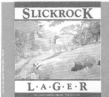

Mellie Pullman. The principal brands brewed here are Park City Silver Reserve, Slickrock Lager, Wasatch Gold, Wasatch Premium Ale and Wasatch Irish Stout. ■

C Schmidt & Sons of Philadelphia (not to be confused with Jacob Schmidt of St Paul, Minnesota) originated with Robert Courtenny in 1859, was acquired by Christian Schmidt in 1863 and has used its present name since 1892. In 1954 the company bought Scheidt Brewing (later Valley Forge Brewing) of Norristown, but closed the facility in 1975. A former Schaefer of Ohio brewery in Cleveland was purchased in 1974 and was operated until 1984.

The brewery has today grown to a million-barrel capacity. The company brews Schmidt's Beer, Schmidt's of Philadelphia Light, Schmidt's Bavarian, Schmidt's Bock, Schmidt's Oktoberfest, Christian Schmidt Golden Classic, Christian Schmidt Select and Tiger Head Ale. The Valley Forge brands of the old Norristown brewery still being brewed are Rheingold Extra Dry and Rheingold Extra Light (a brand name once used by the old Ruppert empire in New York City), that Schmidt has been brewing in Philadelphia since the 1970s.

The Schmidt, Valley Forge and Rheingold brands may be the highest flags flying from the flagship, but other brands are on hand to give the brewery the largest roster of names in the United States. These others include Bavarian Beer, Bergheim, Brew 96, Casey's Lager, Classic Golden Hawk Malt

Liquor, Coqui 900 Malt Liquor, Duke Ale, Duke Beer, Erie Light Lager, Gablinger's Extra Light, Kaier, Knickerbocker Beer, Koehler's, Kool Premium, USA and Yacht Club, as well as two nonalcoholic brews, Birell and Break Special. In 1986 Schmidt brought back Twentieth Century Ale, a beer brewed at the turn of the century by Adam Scheidt Brewing, a firm that Schmidt bought in 1954.

Schoenling (see **Hudepohl-Schoenling**)

Seabright Brewery is a seven-barrel brewery, as well as a brewpub and restaurant, which is located in Santa Cruz, California. Brewing is under the direction of brewmaster Michael Clifford, whose Pelican Pale Ale is presented along with various specialty beers. ■

Seacliff Cafe and Brewery was founded in 1987 by noted San Francisco chef Klaus Lange, who describes his establishment as a 'vest pocket brewery' with a cafe whose menu is devoted to 'beer cuisine.' Unlike most other brew publicans, Lange initially

brewed his Seacliff Dutch Brown Ale to be bottled, but began serving it on draft in 1989. Says Lange: 'Beer cuisine is my contribution to the California beer renaissance. It is meant to invite the exploration of the complex range of beers without getting philosophical about it. Beer is elevated to wine status, meat and potatoes are king, and the brew kettle is back in the kitchen.' ■

Sherwood Brewing Company is a brewpub with a Robin Hood theme located in Chico, California. Opened in 1989, the brewery's total capacity is 14 barrels. The Sherwood Brewing Company is one of two breweries operated in Chico by DeWayne and Stacy L Saxton. ■

Sieben's River North Brewery is a 3200-barrel microbrewery and restaurant which

opened in Chicago in September 1987, the first brewpub in Chicago since Prohibition. With brewing under the direction of brewmaster Al Busch, the principal brands brewed here are Amber Ale, Golden Ale, Lager, Pilsner Light and Stout. Ten to 12 Seasonal beers are also brewed, including Alt, Bock, Cherry Beer, Irish Ale, Maibock, Orange Beer and Weissbier. ■

Sierra Nevada Brewing of Chico, California was founded in 1980 by Paul Camus and Ken Grossman as one of the nation's first microbreweries. As with most microbreweries, Sierra Nevada uses only pure malted barley, Yakima Valley hops and topfermenting yeast. As of 1989 Sierra Nevada's brewing capacity was 50,000 barrels, up from 10,000 in 1987. The firm's major products are Sierra Nevada Pale Ale, Sierra

Nevada Porter and Sierra Nevada Stout, but it also brews Sierra Nevada Draught Ale (a keg-conditioned version of the Pale Ale), an annual Sierra Nevada Celebration Ale, and an award-winning barley-wine-style ale called Bigfoot Ale, that was introduced in 1985.

SLO Brewing is a a brewpub opened in September 1988 in the city of San Luis Obispo, California. In 1988 the brewery's total capacity was 1000 barrels, with brewing under the direction of brewmaster Mike Hoffman. The principal brands brewed

here are SLO Amber, SLO Pale Ale and SLO Porter, as well as seasonal brews that include Cherry Bomb Ale, Extra Special Bitter, Nagal's Nutty Brown Ale, Holiday Ale, Wheat Beer and Lighter Shades of Pale Ale. ■

Smith & Reilly of Vancouver, Washington markets Smith & Reilly Honest Beer, an all-malt beer that has been produced under contract by the Pabst brewery in nearby Tumwater since 1984. ■

Snake River Brewing, a 1000-barrel microbrewery, is located in the town of Calwell, Idaho, with brewing under the direction of Tim Batt. The principal brands brewed here, Amber Lager and Premium Lager, were first marketed in 1985. ■

Spoetzl Brewery of Shiner, Texas evolved from the Shiner Brewing Association started in 1909. Taken over by the Petzold and Spoetzl partnership in 1915, it emerged from Prohibition as the Spoetzl Brewery

and Ice Factory. The Ice Factory tag was dropped from the name in 1934. By 1980 Spoetzl had a 60,000-barrel annual capacity for its Shiner Premium and Shiner Bock beers. In 1989 the company was purchased by Gambinos Imports, the San Antonio-based importer of Modelo's Corona brand.

Sprecher Brewing is a microbrewery located in Milwaukee, Wisconsin, with brewing under the direction of master brewer Randy Sprecher. The principal

brands brewed here are Black Bavarian Style, Donkleweizen, Milwaukee Weiss, Special Amber, Maibock (winter/spring), Oktoberfest (summer/fall) and Winterbrew (fall/winter), and a nonalcoholic root beer soda. ■

St Brendan Brew of Berkeley, California is a tiny microbrewery named for the Irish

monk St Brendan, who is alleged to have 'discovered' America before either Columbus or Leif Erikson. The company was founded by former homebrewer George Draper, who began bottling his Navigator Pale Ale in 1989. ■

Stanislaus Brewing of Modesto, California was established by Garith Helm, who began commercial production in 1984. The 'patron saint' of Stanislaus Brewing is 'St Stan,' a bearded public relations man whose character—a brewer named Brother Stanislaus—is said to have brewed for Frederick the Great a beer inspired by divine intervention.

Stanislaus Brewing produces only altbier, a German-style, top-fermented brew similar to ale. Under the direction of Garith and Romy Helm, capacity increased from 1000 barrels in 1985 to 3000 in 1988, with plans afoot for an expansion to in excess of 10,000 barrels, which will include a brewpub. Production is divided between the St Stan's Amber and St Stan's Dark brands, as well as St Stan's Fest.

Stevens Point Brewery of Stevens Point, Wisconsin dates from the brewery established prior to 1857 by Frank Wahle and George Ruder. By 1902 the brewery had taken its present name. Soon afterward,

the Stevens Point Brewery began producing beer under the brand name Pink's Pale Export, a reference to general manager Nick 'Pinky' Gross and his decision to 'export' the beer to faraway Amhearst Junction, Wisconsin. Felix 'Phil' Shibilski joined the company at the end of Prohibition and worked his way to the presidency. Today his son Ken is president and general manager.

During his tenure with the company, Felix Shibilski watched the number of small breweries in Wisconsin dwindle from 44 in 1948 to four in 1980. However, the success of the Stevens Point Brewery and its Point Special Beer is due, at least in part, to its decision to limit distribution to a very narrow geographical area, permitting demand to exceed supply. The brewery in the little white hop-covered building at the corner of Beer and Water streets has a 55,000-barrel annual capacity for its Point Special, Eagle Premium Pilsner and its seasonal Point Bock.

Stoudt Brewing Company serves a brewpub called Stoudt's Black Angus, which is located in Adamstown, Pennsylvania. In 1988 the brewery's total capacity was 1500 barrels, with brewing under the

direction of master brewer Carol Stoudt. An outdoor beer garden features live German bands on summer weekend evenings. The principal brands brewed here are Golden Lager, Pilsner, Vienna Amber and the award-winning Weizen, as well as specialty beers. ■

Straub Brewery in St Mary's, Pennsylvania was started by Captain Charles Volk in 1872 as an extension of his City Hotel, and was taken over by Peter Straub, Volk's former brewmaster, in 1876. Thereafter, except for two years (1911-1913) as the Benzinger Spring Brewery, the brewery has carried the Straub name. The brewery is still a

family affair, with Herbert Straub currently serving as president, general manager and master brewer. Straub and Straub Light, known locally as 'high test' or 'greenie,' are the only brand names used by the 40,000-barrel brewery.

Stroh Brewery of Detroit became the third largest brewing company in the United States in May 1982 when it purchased the much larger, but financially ailing, Joseph Schlitz Brewing Company. Schlitz, whose brand name Stroh retained, had been one of the two largest brewers in the United States since the nineteenth century. Despite its being in third place after the Schlitz acquisition, Stroh's market share declined through most of the mid-1980s.

By 1987 only about two-thirds of its 31.5-million-barrel national capacity was being utilized. Thus, in 1989 Stroh began look-ing for a buyer for some, or all, of its assets. Several foreign groups expressed interest, but in September it was announced that America's fourth largest brewer, Adolph Coors of Golden, Colorado, was interested. However, Coors' letter of intent to acquire Stroh expired in December 1989. At press time, negotiations between the two brewers were said to be continuing.

Started in 1850 by Bernhard Stroh, the company survived Prohibition but remained a regional brewery until well after World War II. The acquisition of Schaefer in 1981 and of Schlitz the following year catapulted Stroh from seventh to third place among United States brewers.

The Stroh Brewery Company's own brand name products (Stroh's Premium and Stroh Light) have long been noted for the use of direct flame rather than steam in the heating of the brew kettles. This process is used by European brewers but has been less common in North America, so the company uses it in its advertising, referring to these two products as 'fire brewed beers.'

Stroh's interesting variety of other products include the upscale Erlanger Premium Beer and the Signature Super Premium Beer, which was first introduced in 1983. From the Schaefer acquisition, the company gained not only Schaefer and Schaefer Light, but Piel's Draft Style, Piel's Light and Goebel Golden Lager. In the Schlitz takeover, the Schlitz flagship brand was retained, as well as Schlitz Light, Schlitz Malt Liquor and the famous former Hawaiian brand, Primo, which Schlitz had been brewing in California. Despite its large repertoire of famous brands, the best-selling Stroh-owned brand is the budget brand Old Milwaukee, which is complemented, of course, by an Old Milwaukee Light.

The original Stroh brewery in Detroit was finally closed in 1985, doomed to the wrecker's ball by age and inefficiency. This left Detroit's one-time premier brewer with a new corporate headquarters but no actual brewery in the Motor City. With the demise of the old Detroit flagship, America's third largest brewer was left with six breweries: the Allentown, Pennsylvania plant that Schaefer had built in 1972 and which Stroh acquired in 1980; the old Theodore Hamm Brewery in St Paul, Minnesota that Stroh acquired from Olympia by way of Pabst in 1983; and the former Joseph Schlitz breweries in Longview, Texas; Memphis, Tennessee; Van Nuys, California; and Winston-Salem, North Carolina.

With the Schlitz acquisition behind it, the Stroh company began a spirited marketing campaign that saw a blizzard of new media advertising and the sudden appearance of Stroh's neon signs in the windows of taverns and corner groceries in select markets in California and New York, places far removed from the brewery's midwestern stronghold. By 1984 fire brewing was introduced to the old Schlitz plant at Van Nuys. Schlitz, Schlitz Light and Schlitz Malt Liquor are still brewed at the former Schlitz plants, while the Stroh and Schaefer brands are divided among these and the other breweries. The other brands include Stroh Light, Schaefer, Schaefer Light,

186

Schaefer Low Alcohol, Goebel, Piel's, Red Bull Malt Liquor and Old Milwaukee, Stroh's nationally marketed budget brand which is not brewed in Milwaukee.

Summit Brewing is a 26-barrel microbrewery located in St Paul, Minnesota. The principal brands brewed here are Extra Pale Ale, the award-winning Great Northern Porter, Summit Sparkling Ale and Christmas Ale. ∎

Sun Valley Brewing is a 35-barrel microbrewery located in the town of Wood River, Idaho, near the Sun Valley ski resort. The brewery has been in operation since November 1986, and the principal brands brewed here are Our Holiday Ale, Sawtooth Gold Lager, White Cloud Ale and Yule Ale. ∎

Tampa Bay Brewing is a 150-seat restaurant brewery that was opened by award-winning homebrewer Ben Meisler in Carrollwood, Florida on Christmas day in

1989. Brewing is under the direction of Gary Vaughn, who produces Pilsner, British Red Ale, Wheat Beer, Porter, Bock and Christmas Ale. ∎

Telluride Beer Company of Telluride, Colorado markets a beer of the same name that has been produced under contract by

Huber (later Berghoff-Huber) since 1986. Limited quantities of Telluride Winter Ale are also produced. ∎

Thousand Oaks Brewing of Berkeley, California is a 400-barrel microbrewery that was started in 1981 and was, for many years, considered to be the smallest microbrewery in the United States, although it now has several serious rivals. Located in the home of Charles and Diana Rixford, the brewery probably still qualifies for distinction as North America's only commercial home brewery. Despite its size, the brewery's products, which include Golden Gate Malt Liquor, Golden Bear Dark Malt Liquor and Thousand Oaks Lager, are widely available throughout the San Francisco Bay Area.

Tied House (see **Redwood Coast**)

Triple Rock Brewery is a brewpub that opened under the name **Roaring Rock** in

March 1986 in the town of Berkeley, California adjacent to the campus of the University of California. The name was changed in April 1987 to avoid possible confusion with Latrobe Brewing's Rolling Rock brand name. In 1988 the brewery's total production was 1550 barrels, with brewing under the direction of brewmaster Reid Martin and head brewer Teri Fahrendorf. The principal brands brewed here are Agate Ale, Black Rock Porter, Pinnacle Pale Ale and Red Rock Ale, as well as specialty beers which include Reindeer Ale for Christmas and Resolution Ale for New Year's. Every 100th brew is a Century Ale. In September 1989, Triple Rock reached its 800th brew. ∎

Truckee Brewing is a microbrewery founded in 1985 in the town of Truckee, California. In 1989 the brewery's total capacity was 500 barrels, with brewing under the

direction of Gary Rausch. Using a boxcar for a brewhouse, Rausch brews Truckee Lager, Truckee Dark Lager and Boxcar Bock for Christmas. ∎

Vernon Valley Brewing is a microbrewery located in the resort town of Vernon, New

Jersey. In 1988 the brewery's total capacity was 14,000 barrels, with brewing under

the direction of brewmaster Reinhard Schrimpf. The principal brands brewed here are Blonde Bock, Doppelbock, Dark, Kristall Classic Lite and Pilsner. ∎

Virginia Brewing Company, formerly the Chesapeake Bay (Chesbay) Brewing Company, was opened in September 1988 in the town of Chesapeake, Virginia. In 1988 the brewery's total capacity was 5000 barrels, with brewing under the direction of brewmaster Wolfgang Roth. The principal brands brewed here are Chesbay Oktoberfest, Chesbay Gold Pilsner and Skipjack Doppelbock. Current brands include Gold Cup Premium Pilsner and Dark Horse Doublebock. Virginia also produces People's Choice, a private label contract brew for the Clyde's Restaurant Group in Washington, DC. ∎

Walter (see **Hibernia**)

Weeping Radish Restaurants and Brewpubs are a chain of such establishments located in Manteo, North Carolina (established 1985); Durham, North Carolina (established 1988); Virginia Beach Virginia (established 1989); and Fayetteville, North Carolina (established 1989). The Durham facility is the largest, with a 4000-barrel capacity, four times that of the original Manteo site. Weeping Radish brews

Light lager, Bock Beer and a mild Black Beer, as well as specialty and Christmas beers. Weeping Radish has purchased the Hopfen brewery and has transported it—lock, stock and lauter tun—from Germany. ∎

Henry Weinhard (see **Heileman**)

West End (see **FX Matt**)

Widmer Brewing of Portland, Oregon was established by Kurt Widmer in 1984. It was the second microbrewery to be established in Portland and the second brewery (after Stanislaus in California) to brew altbier, or German-style ale, outside of Germany since Prohibition. With a 4000-barrel annual

 Hefeweizen Bier   Festbier

 Oktoberfest   Maerzen Bier

 BOCK   Weizen Bier

output, Widmer is the largest microbrewery in Oregon, a state noted for its vast proliferation of small breweries. In 1990 production doubled, and Widmer expanded to include a large brewpub and outdoor beer garden. In addition to Widmer Altbier, the brewery also produces Widmer Weizen, Hefeweizen and seasonal brew such as Bock, Oktoberfest, Festbier and Märzen.

Wild Boar (see **Dubuque Star**)

Winchester Brewing is a brewpub which opened in July 1988 in San Jose, California and began selling packaged beer in December 1989. Winchester was the first brewpub to sell its beer in a refillable, mug-like container. In 1989 the brewery's capacity was 3000 barrels, with brewing under the direction of master brewer Roger Gribble.

The principal brands brewed here are Winchester Pale Ale, Winchester Red Ale, Winchester Midnight Stout and Winchester Special Porter. ∎

Xcelsior Brewing of Santa Rosa, California was a 36,000-barrel brewery established by Pete Ireman in 1987 to revive the great old San Francisco Acme Lager brand. The brewery and the resurrected Acme Lager survived for about two years, but succumbed at the time this book was in preparation. ∎

Yakima Brewing & Malting, a 5000-barrel microbrewery, was established in 1982 in Yakima, Washington in the heart of North America's greatest hop-growing region. Under the direction of founder Herbert Grant, the brewery produces beer for both the retail market and for Grant's own brewpub. The brands include Celtic Ale, Christmas Ale, Grant's Scottish Ale, India Pale Ale, Light American Ale, Nut Brown

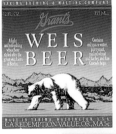 

Ale, Russian Imperial Stout and Weiss Beer, as well as Yakima Hard Cider.

Yuengling & Son was established in 1829 by David G Yuengling. It stands as the oldest brewery in the United States and, after Molson in Canada (1786), as the second oldest in North America. Today the 200,000-barrel brewery is still family owned and operated under president Richard Yuengling. With brewing under the direction of N Ray Norbert, Yuengling's product line includes such brand names as

Yuengling Premium, Yuengling Premium Light, Yuengling Porter ('brewed expressly for tavern and family trade'), Bavarian Premium Beer, Old German Beer, Lord Chesterfield Ale and the newer Traditional American Amber Lager.

CANADA

Long the second biggest brewing nation in North America, Canada yielded that distinction to Mexico in the mid-1970s. In 1986, for example, Canada brewed 18 million barrels of beer, compared to 23 million in Mexico and 182 million in the United States. Canada is, however, a larger net exporter of beer to the United States, with two million barrels, versus 1.5 million for Mexico.

Canada can also boast the oldest brewer in North America in Molson, which was established in 1786. For most of the twentieth century, Canadian brewing was overwhelmingly dominated by its big three, Carling O'Keefe, Labatt's and Molson. Labatt's

was Canada's number one brewer and Molson traditionally had the largest Canadian share of the lucrative export market to the United States. In 1989, however, Molson and Carling O'Keefe announced their intention to merge into a single entity to be called Molson Breweries. This new entity would then become Canada's premier brewer, with better than half the market. (For the sake of clarity, Carling O'Keefe and Molson are considered here in their pre-merger configurations.)

Despite the dominance of the big three, several smaller breweries still exist and new microbreweries have been started in British Columbia and

Nova Scotia since the mid-1980s. The big three were, however, the only brewing companies with breweries in more than one province, and as a result, they are the only brewers with national distribution. An interesting aside to the big three is that each had a flagship or most popular brand which was identified by a color. These were Carling O'Keefe's *Black* Label, Labatt's Pilsen *Blue* and Molson *Golden*.

The breweries are listed in alphabetical order with minimum cross-referencing. Specific brands and non-extant brewery names are noted and are included in this edition's general index.

Amstel Brewery Canada, formerly Hamilton Breweries, began operations in 1981 and is now owned entirely by Heineken NV of the Netherlands. Headquartered in Hamilton, Ontario, the brewery has an annual capacity of 300,000 barrels and is one of Canada's fastest growing brewing companies. The products brewed here include Steeler Lager, which is considered Hamilton's 'hometown' beer, and Grizzly, a lager originally brewed only for the United States export market but now available in Ontario

as well. A major part of Amstel's operation, of course, is devoted to brewing the parent company's Amstel and Amstel Light brands, but it also brews Henninger and Peroni beers under license from the respective German and Italian breweries who originated these brands.

Big Rock Brewery was founded in 1985 by Ed McNally and is located in Calgary, Alberta. In 1989 the brewery's total capacity was 30,000 barrels, having sold 6000 bar-

rels in its first year. Big Rock takes advantage of the fact that Calgary is in the heart of a fertile grain-growing region. Brewing is under the direction of Bernd Pieper, who was formerly associated with Lowenbrau Zurich. The principal brands brewed here, and packaged with Dirk van Wyk labels, are Big Rock Pale Ale, Big Rock Bitter Pale Ale, Big Rock XO Lager, Cock o' the Rock Porter, Cold Cock Winter Porter, McNally's Extra, Royal Coachman Dry Ale and Traditional

Ale. In 1988 Big Rock brewed the Banff Springs Hotel Centennial Ale. ∎

Brick Brewing is a small brewery located in Waterloo, Ontario. Brewing began in 1984, and in 1989 the brewery's total capacity was 30,000 barrels, to be expanded to about

60,000 barrels. The principal brands brewed here are Brick Anniversary Bock, Brick Premium Lager, Brick Red Baron and Brick Spring Bock. ∎

Carling O'Keefe Ltd (**Brasserie O'Keefe L'tee** in Quebec) is the result of the nineteenth century merger of the breweries of Sir John Carling (established by his father, Thomas Carling, in 1840) and Eugene O'Keefe (established in 1862). In the 1950s and 1960s Carling O'Keefe expanded its operations into the United States through its subsidiary company, **Carling National Brewing**, which once operated 14 breweries in 11 states. In fact, in 1960 Carling National was the fourth largest brewer in the United States. After this high point, the market share of the American subsidiary declined, and Carling, like many other brewers, was forced into closing plants. In 1979 the Carling National Brewing subsidiary, four remaining breweries and a license to brew Carling Black Label Beer and Carling Red Cap Ale were sold to the Heileman Brewing Company of La Crosse, Wisconsin.

Carling O'Keefe Ltd is headquartered in Toronto, with breweries located in Toronto, Ontario (2.5-million-barrel capacity); Montreal, Quebec (2-million-barrel capacity); Vancouver, British Columbia (815,000-barrel capacity); Winnipeg, Manitoba (385,000-barrel capacity); Calgary, Alberta (290,000- barrel capacity); Saskatoon, Saskatchewan (200,000-barrel capacity); and St John's, Newfoundland (175,000-barrel capacity).

The company's flagship brand is Black Label Beer, which is brewed at all seven Carling O'Keefe breweries across Canada. Other brands in regional distribution include Red Cap Ale, Alta 3.9, Black Horse,

Calgary Lager, Carling Pilsner, Champlain, Dominion Ale, Dow Ale, Heidelberg, Kroenbrau 1308, O'Keefe Ale, O'Keefe Extra Old Stock Malt Liquor, O'Keefe Light, Old Vienna, Standard Lager, Trilight and Toby.

In addition to its own brands, Carling O'Keefe brews Colt 45 under license from Heileman in the United States, Miller High Life under license from Miller Brewing in the United States.

In 1989 Carling's distribution company, Century Importers, significantly expanded its business with the launching of two new brands, Calgary and Glacier Bay. In the Canadian market, the introduction of Foster's Lager on tap to British Columbia, Ontario and Alberta was an immediate success, as Foster's Light had been when introduced in late 1988.

In the province of Quebec, O'Keefe Ale continues as the long-time sales leader. O'Keefe is the also the major sponsor for the Quebec Nordiques, the National Hockey League team based in Quebec City.

Conners Brewing began brewing in 1985 in Don Mills, near Toronto, Ontario. With brewing under the direction of brewmaster Doug Morrow, the principal brands brewed here are Best Bitter, Conners Ale, Conners

Pale Ale and Imperial Stout, as well as a seasonal Conner's Light, all of which are available in returnable plastic bottles. ∎

Drummond Brewing is located in Red Deer, Alberta. In 1989 the brewery's total capacity was 200,000 barrels, with brewing under the direction of master brewer

J Spiers. The principal brands brewed here are Drummond Premium, Drummond Light, Draught, No Name, No Name Light and Special Gold. ∎

Granite Brewery of Halifax, Nova Scotia was established in 1985 and was the first Canadian microbrewery and brewpub outside British Columbia. Head brewer Kevin Keefe

is also the proprietor of neighboring Ginger's Tavern. Keefe opened the brewpub after noting the resurgence of interest in ale brewing in North America and Britain.

Granville Island (see **Pacific Western**)

Hamilton (see **Amstel**)

Horseshoe Bay Brewery in Horseshoe Bay, British Columbia became Canada's first brewpub when the trend first crept north from the American Northwest in 1982. The products of this 850-barrel brewery, presided over by brewmaster John Mitchell, were originally available only in the adjacent Troller Pub but are now exclusive to Yaya's Oyster Bar. They include the original Bay Ale, Royal Dark Ale and Royal Light Ale.

Island Pacific Brewing of Victoria, British Columbia is one of the province's better known microbreweries. Well situated in the provincial capital, Island Pacific has a 9600-barrel capacity, which serves primar-

ily a draft market, although bottled beer from Island Pacific debuted in 1990. The principal brands brewed here are Hermann's #1, Key Lager, Viking Premium Lager and Piper Richardson Draught Ale.

John Labatt Ltd (**Brasserie Labatt L'tee** in Quebec) was founded by John Labatt in London, Ontario in 1853 and still maintains the corporate headquarters there. Although the brewing headquarters for the company are in Toronto, Labatt's breweries are located in Lasalle, Quebec (2.7-million-barrel capacity); London, Ontario (1.4-million-barrel capacity); Weston, Ontario (1.4-million-barrel capacity); New Westminster, British Columbia (940,00-barrel capacity); Waterloo, Ontario (750,000-barrel capacity); Edmonton, Alberta (500,000-

barrel capacity); Creston, British Columbia (365,000-barrel capacity); St John's, Newfoundland (300,000-barrel capacity); and Saskatoon, Saskatchewan (200,000-barrel capacity). The Oland Brewery in Halifax, Nova Scotia is a subsidiary of Labatt

and functions as a brewing site for major Labatt products. The Oland subsidiary also operates the Labatt brewing in St John, New Brunswick.

Labatt's flagship brand, and the leading single brand of beer, is Labatt's Pilsen, which is better known (because of its label) as 'Labatt's Blue.' As with many United States brews, Labatt's leading brand is complemented by a low-calorie beer appropriately named Blue Light. The company's other brands fall into three categories: other company-owned national brands (like 'Blue' and Blue Light); foreign brands brewed under license by Labatt in Canada;

and company-owned regional brands, which may be brewed only in one or two provinces. The national brands include Labatt 50 Ale (introduced as a special promotion in 1950), John Labatt Classic, Labatt's Light (Légère) and Labatt Select. The latter two are low-calorie beers introduced in 1978 and 1984, respectively. The first foreign brand to be brewed under license was Guinness Extra Stout, for which Labatt and Guinness Ltd of Dublin formed Guinness Canada Ltd in 1965. In 1980 Labatt's entered into agreement to brew Anheuser-Busch's Budweiser, the world's most popular beer, in Canada.

When Labatt's Edmonton brewery started brewing Budweiser, it was the first American beer to be brewed in Canada. Since 1980 Budweiser has been joined at Labatt's by Anheuser-Busch's Michelob and beers licensed by Carlsberg of Copenhagen, Denmark.

Labatt's major regional brands are Kokanee Pilsner Beer, which is popular in British Columbia; Club Beer in Manitoba; Crystal Lager Beer in Ontario; Blue Star in Newfoundland; and Alexander Keith's India Pale Ale, which is the largest selling brand of beer in the Maritimes. Other Labatt's regionals are Cervoise, Columbia Pilsner,

Cool Spring, Country Club Stout, Extra Stock Ale, Gold Keg, Grand Prix, IPA (India Pale Ale), Jockey Club Beer, Kootenay Pale Ale, Manitoba 200, Old Scotia Ale, Schooner, Skol, Super Bock, Velvet Cream Porter, Velvet Cream Stout and White Seal Beer. A recent addition to the product list includes Twistshandy, a lemon-lime flavored beer.

In addition to its activities in the field of brewing, John Labatt Ltd owns five packaged-food companies, agricultural products companies and Labatt Importers,

which exports its brewery products into the United States. John Labatt also has a 60 percent interest in McGavin Foods, a baked goods company in western Canada, and a 45 percent partnership interest in the Toronto Blue Jays baseball club of the American League.

Lethbridge (see **Sick's Lethbridge**)

Molson Breweries (**Brasserie Molson** in Quebec) is the oldest brewing company in

all of North America. The original brewery was established on its present site in Montreal, Quebec in 1786. The headquarters and the flagship three-million-barrel brewery are located in Montreal, and the company's other breweries are located in Barrie, Ontario (1.4-million-barrel capacity); Vancouver, British Columbia (700,000-barrel capacity); Edmonton, Alberta (400,000-barrel capacity); Winnipeg, Manitoba (300,000-barrel capacity); Prince Albert, Saskatchewan (240,000-barrel capacity); Regina, Saskatchewan (228,000-barrel capacity); and St John's, Newfoundland (200,000-barrel capacity). The Sick's Lethbridge Brewery in Lethbridge, Alberta has been a Molson subsidiary since 1958 and is listed separately below.

Molson's flagship brand is Molson Golden, which is a national brand in Canada and the biggest selling Canadian export brew in the United States. Other Molson beers include Molson Canadian Lager, Molson Light (Légère), Molson Export Ale and Export Light Ale. Special regional beers brewed by Molson's western breweries (British Columbia, Alberta, Manitoba and Saskatchewan) are Bohemian, Brador, Edmonton Export Lager, Frontier Beer, Imperial Stout, Old Style and Royal Stout. Regional beers brewed by Molson in eastern Canada include Molson Bock, Molson Cream Porter, Molson Diamond, Molson Oktoberfest, India Beer and Laurentide Ale.

Molson also brews Lowenbrau, a famous

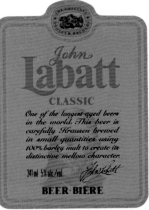

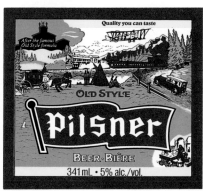

German lager, under license from Lowenbrau in Munich. (Lowenbrau is also brewed under license by Miller Brewing in the United States.) Since 1987 Molson has also brewed Coors in Canada, under license from the brewery in Colorado, and in 1988 Molson started contract production of Kirin Beer from Japan. The Kirin produced in Vancouver and Montreal is destined primarily for the United States market, but the fact that it is brewed in Canada permits Kirin to save money and time on shipping, and also to say that it is 'imported' without having to say that it is not imported from Japan. Ironically, the Kirin Brewery in Japan was actually founded by Americans.

Moosehead Breweries Ltd of St John, New Brunswick were founded by a family of Anglo-Swedish descent named Oland, who also founded Oland Breweries Ltd, now owned by Labatt's. Thanks in part to a successful export marketing campaign in the early 1980s, Moosehead's products are now extremely popular in the United States. They are, in fact, more popular in the United States than they are in Canada, where they are virtually unknown outside New Brunswick and Nova Scotia. Except for the Quebec and Ontario breweries of the big three, Moosehead's brewery, with a 1.4-million-barrel capacity, is the largest in Canada. Moosehead's flagship brands all carry the company name and the distinctive Moosehead logo. These include Moosehead Canadian Lager, Moosehead Pale Ale, Moosehead Golden Light, Moosehead London Stout and Moosehead Export Ales.

The brewery's other products are Alpine Lager, James Ready's Original Lager and Ten-Penny Old Stock Ale.

Mountain Ales of Surrey, British Columbia was another of the small breweries that started in the Vancouver area in the early 1980s. The brewery and bottle line are designed after the English model, as are the products, which include Mountain Amber Ale, Mountain Dark Ale and Mountain Light Ale.

Northern Breweries Ltd has more breweries in Canada's largest province than any other brewing company, although it is among Ontario's smaller breweries. Northern Brewing is headquartered in Sault Sainte Marie, where it operates an 80,000-barrel brewery. Its other three Ontario

breweries are in Sudbury (130,000-barrel capacity); Thunder Bay (60,000-barrel capacity); and Timmins (40,000-barrel capacity). The latter two breweries brew only draft, while Thunder Bay brews only Superior Lager and Thunder Bay, and Timmins brews only Northern Ale. Sudbury brews and bottles Northern and Encore Beer, while the Sault Sainte Marie plant brews and bottles Superior Lager, Northern Extra Light, Edelbrau, Encore, 55 Lager, Kakabeka Cream and Silver Spray.

Oland Breweries Ltd of Halifax, Nova Scotia was founded by the same Oland family that started Moosehead. The Oland

Breweries were sold to Labatt's in 1971. By the mid-1980s, SM Oland held the presidency of Labatt Brewing Company Ltd (a division of John Labatt Ltd) and Philip W Oland was chairman of Moosehead, while JR McLeod was president and general manager at Oland Breweries Ltd. (See labels pictured under John Labatt Ltd.)

Two Oland breweries operate; the one at Halifax is called Oland Brewery and the one at St John, New Brunswick is called Labatt's New Brunswick Brewery. The annual capacities of the two are 580,000 and 458,000 barrels, respectively. Both breweries produce Labatt's 'Blue,' Labatt's 50 Ale and Labatt's Schooner Beer, while Halifax brews Keith's India Pale Ale and St John brews Labatt's Light. Both breweries also brew Oland Export, and Halifax also produces two other Oland name brands, Oland Light and Oland Stout.

Pacific Western Brewing of Prince George, British Columbia was originally established on a freshwater spring in 1957 under

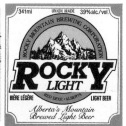

the name Caribou Brewing. Five years later it was bought by Carling O'Keefe and promptly auctioned off. It was purchased by Ben Ginter and rechristened Tartan Breweries. Ginter's popular products, Uncle Ben's Beer and Uncle Ben's Malt Liquor, carried the company successfully until he attempted to expand. He ran out of cash building a second brewery at Richmond, British Columbia, and Tartan Breweries went into receivership. The brewery was purchased in 1978 by Nelson Skalbania, who renamed it Canadian Gold Brewing. It was sold again in 1981 to WR Sharpe (formerly of Canada Dry) and his associates, who operated it as the Old Fort Brewing Company until 1984, when the name was changed to Pacific Western Brewing.

By 1984 Pacific Western had a seven percent share of the British Columbia market and had embarked on an aggressive marketing campaign aimed at the American West Coast. In 1989 Pacific Western purchased Simcoe Brewing in Ontario and Granville Island Brewing in Vancouver. Granville Island Brewing was among the largest of the smaller breweries that opened in British Columbia in the early 1980s. Its brands included Island Lager Beer and Island Bock Beer. Also in 1989 Pacific Western purchased the Calona Winery from Hublien.

The brewery's annual capacity stands at 200,000 barrels. Early products of the present owners included Old Fort Premium Beer, Pacific Gold Lager and Yukon Gold Premium Lager, which are no longer in production. Pacific Western does produce American Brand Lager, Iron Horse Malt Liquor, Pacific Pilsner Beer and Yukon Canadian Cream Ale. In October 1988 Pacific Western introduced Pacific Dragon Dry, becoming the first Canadian brewer to produce a 'dry' beer.

Rocky Mountain Brewing of Red Deer, Alberta (formerly owned by 'Uncle' Ben Ginter and now a subsidiary of Steeplejack Services in Calgary) operates the only independent brewery in the fast-growing, oil-rich province on the eastern side of the Canadian Rockies. Products of this 180,000-barrel capacity brewery include Gold Peak Premium Lager, 88 Pilsner, Steeplejack Pilsner, Steeplejack Special and Trapper Malt Liquor.

Sick's Lethbridge Brewery of Lethbridge, Alberta was founded by Fritz Sick in 1901. Though his son Emil built a Sick's brewery empire in the 1940s that crossed the border into the United States, dominated Seattle and ran from Montana to Oregon, today the original Lethbridge brewery is the only remaining Sick's brewery. The Sick's chain was sold to Molson in 1958, but the Lethbridge plant continues to carry its original name.

Sick's Lethbridge, with its 920,000-barrel capacity, is the largest brewery in Alberta. Products include Lethbridge Lager and Lethbridge Pilsner, as well as Molson Canadian, Molson Light, Molson Malt Liquor and Coors products for which Molson holds the Canadian license.

Spinnakers Brewpub was founded in Victoria, British Columbia in May 1984, and is owned by the Spinnakers Brewing Corporation of Victoria, which also owns the two Noggins brewpubs in Seattle, Washington. With brewing under the direction of master brewer Brad McQuhae, the brewery's 1989 capacity was 1200 barrels. The principal brands brewed here are Express Stout, Genoa Lager, Highland Scottish Ale, Imperial Stout, Mitchell's Extra Special Bitter, Mt Tolmie Dark, Ogden Porter, Spinnaker Ale, Spinnaker's India Pale Ale, Weizenbrau and other seasonal specialty beers. ∎

Strathcona Brewing of Edmonton, Alberta is a microbrewery that was founded in 1986 by Robert Herscovitch and Tom Daly. Under the direction of British brewmaster Frank Appleton, the brewery produces Strathcona Ale. ∎

Upper Canada Brewing was founded by Frank Heaps in Toronto, Canada in 1985. In 1988 the brewery's total capacity was 19,000 barrels, which was expanded to 25,000 barrels in 1989. Brewing is under the direction of brewmaster Klaus Antz. The brewery exports to Europe and the United States, and has been in negotiation over the possibility of Upper Canada products being produced under license in China, for sale throughout the Far East. The principal brands brewed here are Dark Ale, Lager, Rebellion Malt Liquor, True Bock and True Light. The brewery also brews Banks Beer, a popular Caribbean beer, under license from Banks DIH Ltd of Guyana. ∎

MEXICO

Though brewing in Mexico did not develop as quickly as it did in the United States and Canada, it has made great strides since the 1970s, when Mexico surpassed Canada as the continent's second largest brewing nation. Like Canada, Mexico's current brewing scene is overwhelmingly dominated by a 'big three,' of which two have merged to leave a 'big two.' Cuauhtemoc, Moctezuma and Modelo all developed from breweries established in the late nineteenth century by German or Swiss immigrants. In September 1985 Cuauhtemoc and Moctezuma joined under the umbrella of Valores Industriales, becoming the largest brewing company in Mexico and fifteenth largest in the world. Both partners continue, however, as separate operating groups, and are listed below in their pre-merger configurations. They have separate foreign distribution, but share a common distribution network within Mexico.

By the 1970s many of Mexico's brands were available as imports in the United States. Indeed, the largest growth by any imported brands in the American market has been among Mexican beers. In 1986 alone Moctezuma's Tecate enjoyed a 28 percent increase in popularity, while Modelo's Corona increased its share by an incredible *169 percent*, an unprecedented increase that made it second only to Heineken among imported beers in the United States market. Mexico is the third largest exporter of beer to the United States, with 1.5 million barrels annually, compared to three million for the Netherlands (mostly Heineken), two million for Canada, 1.3 million for West Germany and only .2 million for the United Kingdom.

Cervecería Cruz Blanca of Juarez, Chihuahua is the only existing Mexican brewing company founded since 1900. Located across the Rio Grande from El Paso, Texas (which hasn't had a commercial brewery since 1967 when Falstaff closed), the 400,000-barrel Cruz Blanca brewery, under the direction of master brewer

Arturo Rios, brews Austriaca, Chihuahua and Liston Azul, in addition to the flagship Cruz Blanca. Chihuahua is a popular product in the United States market.

Cervecería Cuauhtemoc, named for the Aztec emperor who died in 1521 and headquartered in Monterrey, Nuevo Leon was Mexico's second largest brewer prior to its being joined with Moctezuma under the Valores holding company. It is the brewer with the largest number of breweries (seven). These breweries are located in Toluca, DF (4.4-million-barrel capacity); Monterrey, Nuevo Leon (2.6-million-barrel capacity); Tecate, Baja California (2.5-million-barrel capacity); Mexico City (1.1-million-barrel capacity); Nogales, Veracruz (560,000-barrel capacity); Guadalajara, Jalisco (410,000-barrel capacity); and Culiacán, Sinaloa (300,000-barrel capacity). The company's flagship brand is Carta Blanca, but another important brand is Tecate, a lager beer frequently served, both in Mexico and in the United States, with salt and fresh lemon. Other cervezas from Cuauhtemoc are Bohemia, Brisa, Colosal, India, Kloster, Monterrey and Navidad Christmas Beer. In 1988 Cuauhtemoc introduced a pale lager called Simpatico into the American market. Intended to counter the success of Modelo's Corona,

which comes in a clear glass bottle, Cuauhtemoc *painted* the Simpatico bottles flat black. The Monterrey plant also produces 25,000 tons of malt annually.

Cervecería del Pacífico of Mazaltlán, Sinaloa was established in 1900 by Jacob Schuehle, who built the original Moctezuma brewery. The 1.4 million barrel brewery is today owned by Cervecería Modelo, but retains its original brands,

Pacifico Oscura, Pacifico Clara and Ballena. Pacifico Oscura is also brewed by Modelo in Guadalajara and Ciudad Obregón. The brewmaster is Abel Rodriguez Rivas.

Cervecería Moctezuma, headquartered in Mexico City, was established in 1894 at Orizaba, Veracruz by Adoph Borkhardt, Henry

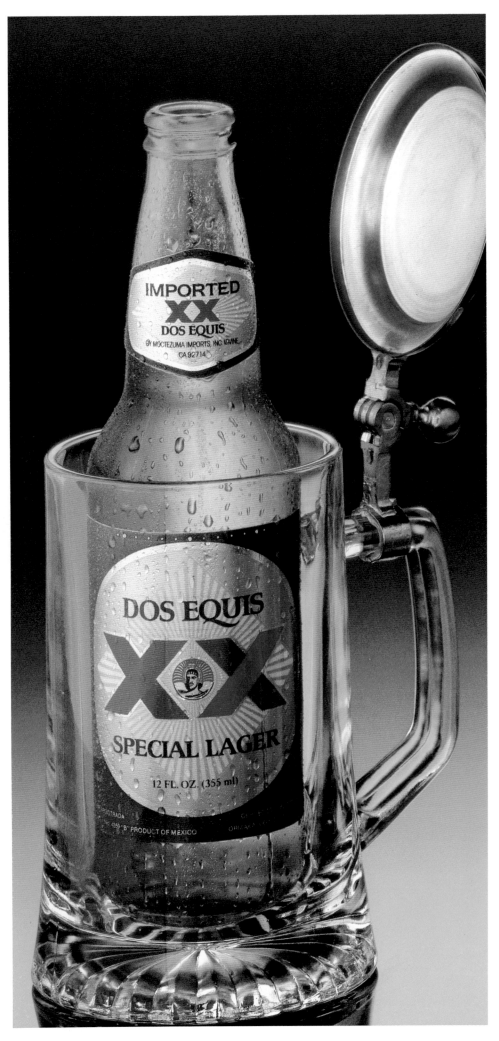

Manthey, Wilhelm Haase and C von Alten. In 1985 Moctezuma, along with Cuauhtemoc, became part of Valores Industriales. Orizaba brewery, with a 4.8-million-barrel annual capacity, is the second largest individual brewery in Mexico. The company's other breweries are a small 300,000-barrel brewery in Monterrey, Nuevo Leon and a 2.6-million-barrel brewery at Guadalajara. Moctezuma's flagship brands are Dos Equis (XX), which is extremely popular in the United States, and Superior. Other brands include Tres Equis (XXX), Sol Clara, Sol Oscura, Noche Buena and Bavaria, as well as two draft beers, Barril Clara and Barril Oscuro. In 1985, thanks in part to the marketing expertise of the company's American public relations firm, Moctezuma began a unique private label venture. Ensenada in Baja, California had been a popular destination for American tourists for over half a century, and no Ensenada watering hole had developed quite as widely known a reputation as Hussong's Cantina. In 1985 Moctezuma teamed up with Hussong's to produce a private label clara (lager) under the Hussong's name that would be available not only at the Cantina, but at retail outlets in the United States and Mexico as well.

Cervecería Modelo, headquartered in Mexico City, DF is Mexico's largest single brewing company. Modelo's annual production of 12 million barrels (1987) is greater than that of all but five American brewers and greater than any of Canada's brewers. Modelo's well-known Corona brand, which has been brewed in Mexico for decades and exported to the United States for years, became a phenomenal 'overnight' success in 1986 in the American market. Thanks to

skillful marketing, this pale Pilsen-style lager in its clear bottle increased its market share in the United States by 169 percent in just one year. Corona now sells about one million barrels annually in the United States, or about two-thirds of the total Mexican export market, and is in second place (behind Holland's Heineken) among imports to the United States.

Modelo operates a brewery in Mexico's Federal District of Toluca (one-million-barrel capacity), and one in Mexico City (6.5-million-barrel capacity), which is Mexico's largest brewery. Other Modelo breweries are located at Guadalajara, Jalisco (3.5-million-barrel capacity) and Ciudad Obregón, Sonora (850,000-barrel capacity). Modelo's flagship brand is Corona. Other brands include Ballenda, Estrella, Modelo Especial, a popular dark beer known as Negro Modelo, Victoria and a draft Corona appropriately dubbed Corona de Barril.

Cervecería Yucateca in Mérida, Yucatán was started before the turn of the century by José María Ponce y Cia and is today owned by the Modelo Group, though members of the Ponce family still manage the brewery. The brewmaster is Gabriel Lorel de Mola. The brewery has a six-million-barrel capacity, but in 1984 brewed just 270,538 barrels. This production is divided between Yucateca's house brands and the parent company's Corona. The Yucateca brands include Carta Clara, Leon Negra and Montejo.

CENTRAL AMERICA

The total beer production of Central America is less than six million barrels, but the area has a long brewing tradition. The Mayan-speaking peoples of pre-Columbian (before 1492) Central America favored a beer made by fermenting cornstalks, while the Uto-Aztecans and others (such as the Pueblo and Tarahumar) of northern Mexico and the border country brewed a sprouted maize beer. Known as *Tesguino* or *Tiswin*, this beer was produced in a manner that is more reminiscent of familiar brewing processes. For the tribes of the Yucatan peninsula, such as the Maya, corn and corn products were the central focus of their lifestyle, from food to religion. It is worth noting that the Mayan chiefs and clergy made a drink containing a specific number of grains (415) of toasted corn, which was called *Picula Kakla*.

Today, however, the tradition has shown more direct influence from German-trained brewers in the latter twentieth century than any of the nations to the north. German-style lagers and pilsens are much more common than in Mexico, owing to the region's more tropical climate. The Central American brewers are listed below in alphabetical order.

Belize Brewing Ltd is located in Belize City, Belize. In 1989 the brewery's total capacity was 44,000 barrels of beer and 650 tons of malt. With brewing under the direction of brewmaster Victor Tuicios Sr, the principal brands brewed here are Belikin Beer, Belikin Stout and Belikin Draft. Belize Brewing is owned 100 percent by Bowen & Bowen Ltd.

Cervecería Centro Americana in Guatemala City, Guatemala is one of Central America's oldest breweries, dating from the nineteenth century. With a two-million-barrel annual capacity, it is also potentially the largest brewery in the region, although in recent years production has been running at just over half of capacity, with about 850,000 barrels available for export. With brewing under the direction of master brewer José Bodensteiner, the principal brands brewed here are Durango, Cabrito Export, Gallo Cabro Moza, Monte Carlo, Monte Carlo Export and Victoria Medalla de Oro.

Cervecería Chiricana is located in the town of David (Chiriquí), Panama, a suburb of Panama City. In 1989 the brewery's total production was 60,000 barrels, with brewing under the direction of master brewer Eckart Schonleber. The principal brands brewed here are Atlas, Balboa, Dorada Light, Malta Vigor and Maxi Malta. The brewery is a subsidiary of Cervecería Nacional of Panama.

Cervecería Costa Rica is located in the city of San José, Costa Rica. In 1988 the brewery's total capacity was 640,000 barrels, with brewing under the direction of master brewer Joach Wagner and brewers Juan Batista Brenes and Rolando Coto. The brewery is a subsidiary of the Florida Ice & Farm Company of San José.

Cervecería Del Barú is located in the town of David (Chiriquí), Panama, a suburb of Panama City. In 1989 the brewery's production was 256,410 barrels, with brewing under the direction of master brewer Heriberto Graf. The principal brands brewed here are Cristal, Malta Del Barú, Malta Super Malta, Panamá and Soberana. Del Barú is associated with Cervecería Panamá of Panama City.

Cervecería Del Sur is located in the town of Escuintla, Guatemala. In 1989 the brewery's total capacity was 128,000 barrels. With brewing under the direction of master brewer Carlos Novotny, the principal brands brewed here are Gallo and Tocaná.

Cervecería Hondurena evolved through mergers with different companies that operated in the early years of the century (1915- 1965). These companies individually marketed the Salva Vida (1916) brand in La Ceiba, the Imperial (1930) and Nacional (1953) brands in Teguciagalpa, and the Ulva (1928) brand in San Pedro Sula.

Cervecería Hondurena's modern era started in 1965, when all breweries in Honduras came together to form one single company. Today owned by Castle & Cooke,

the American food processing company, Hondurena operates a 500,000-barrel brewery at San Pedro Sul and an 85,000-barrel satellite plant at Teguciagalpa. The brewmaster for both sites is Helmut Lutz. The products of the brewery include Imperial, Nacional, Salva Vida and Port Royal Export. The Port Royal and Salva Vida brands were exported to the United States beginning in 1985 and 1988, respectively. The company also produces Acti Malta, a malt-flavored soft drink, which was introduced in 1983.

Cervecería Nacional of Panama City was founded in 1909 and is Panama's largest brewer, with a 500,000-barrel annual capacity under the direction of master brewer Alfredo Arias. The company's

brands include Atlas, Balboa and Malta Vigor. The company also owns Cervecería Chiricana. Nacional is also the Central American licensee and brewer of Lowenbrau, the famous Munich brand.

Cervecería Nacional in Quezaltenango, Guatemala is the last brewery in a town that at the turn of the century had three breweries, more than any other city in Central America. The 250,000-barrel capacity brewery is under the direction of master brewer Juan Cortes and produces the brands Cabro, Coyote, Pilsen and Sol.

Cervecería Panamá is located in Panama City, Panama. In 1988 the brewery's total production was 170,000 barrels, with brewing under the direction of master brewer Heriberto Graf. The principal brands brewed here are Cristal, Malta Del Barú, Malta Super Malta, Panamá and Soberana. The company is the Central American licensee and brewer of Guinness Stout and is associated with Cervecería Del Barú of David (Chiriquí), Panama.

Cervecería Tropical is located in San José, Costa Rica. In 1984 the brewery's total production was 85,000 barrels, with brewing of Tropical Pilsen under the direction of master brewer Simón Buickl. This brewery is a subsidiary of Florida Ice & Farm Company of San José.

Compana Cervecería de Nicaragua is located in Managua, Nicaragua. In 1983 the brewery's total production was 300,000 barrels, with brewing under the direction of master brewer Gerardo Hausinger. The principal brands brewed here are Victoria and Victoria Light.

Industrial Cervecería is located in Managua, Nicaragua. In 1983 the brewery's total production was 118,000 barrels, with brewing under the direction of brewmaster Walter Hoai (who is listed as technical director). Industrial's only brand is Tona Beer.

La Constancia of San Salvador, El Salvador has a 300,000-barrel annual capacity for production of its Brisa, Malta, Noche Buena, Pilsen, Regia and Suprema brands.

Matus Brothers Brewery is located in Belize City, Belize. In 1989 the brewery's total capacity was 21,000 barrels. With brewing under the direction of Shelley Matus, the only brand brewed here is Shuster Beer.

THE CARIBBEAN

The brewing tradition of the little golden flecks which are the islands of Caribe is long and varied. In the beginning it was the aboriginal people and their *tesguino* beer and then the English with their imported beers. By the seventeenth century, when brewing was really taking hold on the mainland to the north, the isles of the West Indies had already gone over en masse to the warm embrace of rum.

By the nineteenth century there was the enigmatic Guinness West Indies Porter that may have been brewed there, perhaps in Barbados or possibly Jamaica. It may even have been brewed in the British Isles and brought to the Keys at high tide by wily traders who just pretended that it was the local brew. No lager could be brewed there because there was no ice, but then English tastes tended to give lager a wide berth in any event, and it was English tastes that formed the tastes of West Indian beer drinkers.

By 1898 there were just seven breweries in the entire region: one each in Barbados, Trinidad and Cuba, and four in Jamaica. When the United States defeated Spain in the Spanish-American War, Obermeyer and Liebmann came south from Brooklyn to open a second brewery in Cuba's capital, and then there were eight altogether, the same number as today, but the faces of the players have changed.

By the 1980s Cuban tastes included more Vodka than beer, and Obermeyer and Liebmann were as much a distant memory in Havana as they were in Brooklyn. In Jamaica, Desnoes & Geddes had been brewing Red Stripe (which had originally been ale but was reformulated as a lager in 1934) for 60 years. Red Stripe was the Caribbean's best known brand elsewhere on the continent. Holland's giant brewer, Heineken, the largest in Europe, has licensed its products to Desnoes & Geddes, and it owns breweries in the Antilles and Trinidad. From Denmark, Carlsberg is licensed in the Dominican Republic and Guinness is brewed in Jamaica. The breweries of the Caribbean are listed alphabetically.

Antilliaanse Brouwerij (Antillian Brewery) of Willemstad, Curacao in the Netherlands Antilles is owned by Amstel of Holland, which in turn is owned by Heineken. The brewery was officially opened in January 1960 as Prince Bernhard of the Netherlands ceremoniously tapped the 'first' foaming keg, although it had actually been producing beer for three months. In addition to Amstel, the 140,000-barrel-capacity brewery brews Green Sands beer, which is also brewed at Heineken-owned National Brewing in Trinidad. Antilliaanse Brouwerij has won several gold medals for its Antillian Amstel beer, including one awarded in Paris in 1960.

Banks Barbados Breweries of St Michael, Barbados has a 130,000-barrel annual capacity and an interesting roster of brands, including Banks Lager, Banks Strong Ale, Jubilee Stout, Tiger Malt and a sugary, nonalcoholic beer called Action Drink.

Brasserie Nationale d'Haiti is located in Port-Au-Prince, Haiti. In 1988 the brewery's total capacity was 13,000 barrels, with brewing under the direction of master brewer Alix Desvarieux. Brasserie Nationale d'Haiti produces Heineken Beer under license, and is also affiliated with Desnoes & Geddes of Kingston, Jamaica.

Brasserie Lorraine in Fort-de-France, Martinque, with its 85,000-barrel annual capacity, is the only French brewery in North America. The brewmaster is Paul Meertens. His brands include Lorraine, a lager reminiscent of the region of the same name in the mother country, Belorange, Cuptrohic and Mirinda.

Caribbean Development Ltd is located in Champs Fleurs, Trinidad. In 1989 the brewery's total capacity was 442,200 barrels, with brewing under the direction of master brewer JM Redhead. The principal brands brewed here are Carib Lager Beer, Carib Light Beer, Guinness Foreign Extra Stout, Malta Carib, Royal Extra Stout and Shandy Carib.

Cervecería Corona in Santurce, a suburb of San Juan, Puerto Rico, is the second largest brewer in the West Indies. The brewery's 1.3-million-barrel annual output is divided between the Cerveza Corona brand and Malta Corona, neither of which should be confused with the famous Modelo brand from Mexico of the same name.

Cervecería India in Mayaguez, Puerto Rico is the second largest brewery in Puerto Rico, with a one-million-barrel annual capacity. The brewmaster is Carlos Latoni. The company's brands include Cerveza Brewmaster, Cerveza India, Cerveza Medalla and Malta India.

Cervecería Nacional Dominicana operates two breweries in Santo Domingo, Dominican Republic, which have a total annual capacity of nearly two million barrels, and as such, is the largest brewer in the Caribbean. The two plants are Cervecería Nacional Dominicana (CND) and Cervecería Bohemia (CBSA). Its brands

include Cerveza Presidente, Coral, Morena Bohemia and license-brewed Carlsberg (Denmark), Heineken (Netherlands) and Lowenbrau (Germany).

Desnoes & Geddes of Kingston, Jamaica was founded in 1918 as a soft drink business by Eugene Desnoes and Thomas Geddes. It is today managed by their heirs, with Peter Desnoes as the most recent past

THE GREAT JAMAICAN BEER

chairman and Paul Geddes as the current chairman. Red Stripe Lager and Dragon Stout are the flagship brands for the 600,000-barrel brewery, which also produces Heineken and Mackeson Stout under license.

Guinness Jamaica Ltd is a subsidiary of Arthur Guinness and Son, London, and is located in Spanish Town. In 1989 the brewery's total capacity was 73,000 barrels. The principal brands brewed here are Guinness Stout and McEwan's Strong Ale.

National Brewing in Port of Spain, Trinidad is a 130,000-barrel subsidiary of Heineken that produces, in addition to the Heineken brand, National brews Green Sands (Shandy), Mackeson Milk Stout and Stag Beer.

GLOSSARY

Ale: A top-fermented beer that originated in England as early as the seventh century and made with hops after the sixteenth century. It is fermented at temperatures ranging between 55°F and 70°F, somewhat warmer than those used to ferment lager. Ale is darker (a translucent copper color) and more highly hopped than lager, but usually less so than porter and stout. Like all beers of the English tradition, it is served at room temperature. Ale is much more popular in England and eastern Canada than in most of North America, though its popularity saw an increase in the United States during the 1980s.

Altbier: A top-fermented beer very similar to ale, except that it originated in northern Germany while ale originated in England. Virtually unknown in the United States after Prohibition, it was reintroduced by several microbreweries in Oregon and California during the 1980s.

Barrel: A container for beer, at one time made of reinforced oak, now made solely of stainless steel. Also a unit of measuring beer which equals 31 gallons, or 1.2 hectolitres.

Beer: A fermented beverage with an alcohol content of between two and six percent by volume. Ingredients include malted cereal grains (especially, but not limited to, barley), hops, yeast and water, although early English beers were unhopped. Subtypes are classified by whether they are made with top-fermenting yeast (ale, porter, stout, wheat beer) or bottom-fermenting yeast (lager, bock beer, malt liquor). Generally, top-fermented beers are darker, ranging from a translucent copper to opaque brown, while bottom-fermented beers range from amber to pale yellow. Because of their English heritage top-fermented beers are usually drunk at room temperature, while bottom-fermented beers are served cold.

Bitter: A full-bodied highly hopped ale (hence the name) that is extremely popular in England but much less so elsewhere. Bitter (or bitter ale) is similar in color to other ales, but it lacks carbonation and has a slightly higher alcohol content.

Bock Beer: A bottom-fermented beer which is darker than lager and which has a relatively higher alcohol content, usually in the six percent range. A seasonal beer, it is traditionally associated with spring festivals. Prior to World War II, many American brewers produced a bock beer each spring, but the advent

of national marketing after the war largely eliminated the practice of brewing seasonal beers. In the 1980s several breweries began to reintroduce bock beer. The male goat (*bock* in German) is the traditional symbol of bock beer.

Brewing: Generically, the entire beer-making process, but technically only that part of the process during which the beer wort is cooked in a brew kettle and during which time the hops are added.

Cerveceria: The Spanish word for *brewery.*

Cerveza: The Spanish word for *beer.*

Draft (Draught) Beer: A term which literally means beer that is drawn from a keg rather than packaged in bottles or cans. Designed for immediate use, draft beer is not pasteurized and hence must be kept cold to prevent the loss of its fresh taste. Draft beer is generally better than packaged beer when fresh but not so as it ages. Some brewers sell unpasteurized draft-style beer, which must be shipped in refrigerated containers.

Fermentation: The process by which yeast turns the sugars present in malted grains into alcohol and carbon dioxide. Chemically the process is written as:

$$C_6H_{12}O_6 \rightarrow 2\,C_2H_5OH + 2\,CO_2$$
(glucose)　　(alcohol)　　(carbon dioxide)

Hops: The dried blossom of the female hop plant which is a climbing herb *(Humulus lupulus)* native to temperate regions of the Northern Hemisphere and cultivated in Europe, the United Kingdom and the United States. Belonging to the mulberry family, the hop's leaves and flowers are characterized by a bitter taste and aroma. It has been used since the ninth century as the principal flavoring and seasoning agent in brewing, although it had been prized before that for its medicinal properties. In addition to its aromatic resins, the hop also contains tannin which helps to clarify beer.

Different strains of hops have different properties and much of the brewmaster's art is in knowing how to use these properties. For example, one strain may be particularly bitter to the taste without being very aromatic, while another strain might be just the opposite. The brewmaster will blend the two in various combinations just as a chef will experiment with various seasonings before settling on just the right combination for a partic-

A female hop blossom, used in brewing beer to impart aroma and bitterness.

ular recipe. Hops also serve as a natural preservative.

Early North American brewers used indigenous wild hops, but European strains were later introduced and imported. Prior to World War II, many regions in North America grew hops. For example, California's fertile San Joaquin Valley once produced hops. Today, however, most of the hops produced in North America are the Cascade hops grown in the Yakima Valley of Washington State. Most major North American brewers use a mixture of Cascade and imported European hops.

Krausening (Kraeusening): The process of instigating a secondary fermentation to produce additional carbon dioxide in a beer. Some brewers will first ferment their beer in open containers where alcohol is produced and retained, but the carbon dioxide escapes. The second fermentation, or krausening, then takes place in closed containers after a first fermentation (whether that first fermentation took place in open or closed containers) and is used to produce natural carbonation or sparkle in the beer.

Lager: A pale bottom-fermented beer of moderate strength that originated in Central Europe, roughly in the area bounded by Munich, Germany; Vienna, Austria and Pilsen, Bohemia (now Czechoslovakia). Lager is the most popular beer type in all of North America, especially in the United States where it accounts for well over 90 percent of production. Lager is fermented at much colder temperatures than top-fermented beers (between 32°F and 50°F depending on the brand), and it is also served much colder. In order to conform to local laws concerning alcohol content, lager in the United States usually varies between 2.7 and 3.2 percent.

Lagering: The process of cold fermenting at temperatures close to freezing to produce lager beer.

The Beer-making Process:

The steps in the beer-making, or brewing, process can be briefly summarized as follows:

1. Malting to produce **malt.**

2. Mashing the Malt to produce **mash.** (Other cereal grains may be added to the Malt at this stage.)

3. Lautering the **mash** to produce sweet **wort.**

4. Straining the wort through **grant** prior to **brewing.**

5. Brewing the sweet **wort** (during which time the **hops** are added), to produce bitter or hopped **wort.**

6. Straining the **hops.**

7. Cooling the **wort.**

Lautering: The process of straining in a lauter tun.

Lauter tun: The vessel used in brewing between the mash tun and the brew kettle. It separates the barley husks from the clear liquid wort. The barley husks themselves help provide a natural filter bed through which the wort is strained.

Light Beer: Introduced in the mid-1970s by nearly every major brewer in the United States and Canada, light beers are by definition reduced-calorie lagers or ales. They also have a slightly lower alcohol content than comparable lagers or ales.

Malt: The substance produced by malting (also known as malted barley).

Malt Liquor: A bottom-fermented beer, it has a malty taste more closely related to top-fermented ale than to lager which is bottom-fermented. Malt liquor has a much higher alcohol content (5.6 to 6.5 percent) than lager.

Malting: The process by which barley kernels are moistened and germinated, producing a 'green malt' which is then dried. This renders the starches present in the kernel soluble. If pale beers are to be produced, the malt is simply dried. If dark beers are to be produced, the malt is roasted until it is dark brown. The malt is then subjected to mashing.

Mash: The substance that is produced by mashing.

Mashing: The process by which barley malt is mixed with water and cooked to turn soluble starch into fermentable sugar. Other cereal grains, such as corn and rice may also be added (rice contributes to a paler end-product beer). After mashing, the mash is filtered through a lauter tun, whereupon it becomes known as wort.

Near Beer: Nonalcoholic beer which originated during the Prohibition era in the United States and which is still in production.

Pasteurization: Though this term has come to mean the heating of a substance to kill harmful bacteria, the process was originally proposed by Louis Pasteur as a means of killing yeast to end fermentation and hence end the creation of alcohol and carbon dioxide (carbonation). Nonpasteurized beers are no less sanitary than pasteurized beers.

Pilsner (Pilsener): A pale bottom-fermented lager beer originally associated with the city of Pilsen, Bohemia (now Czechoslovakia) where it was first brewed. The term is often used interchangeably with the term lager although pilsners are technically the palest of lagers.

Porter: A traditionally top-fermented beer which originated in eighteenth-century London. It took its name from the city's porters who had taken an immediate fancy to it. Similar to but sweeter than stout, it is a dark beer of moderate strength (alcohol, five to seven percent by volume), made with roasted unmalted barley.

Prohibition: The process by which a government prohibits its citizens from buying or possessing alcoholic beverages. Specifically, *the* Prohibition refers to the period between the effective date of the 18th Amendment to the US Constitution (16 January 1920) and its repeal by the 21st Amendment. Repeal took effect on 5 December 1933, although it passed Congress in February and the sale of beer was permitted after 7 April 1933.

Reinheitsgebott: A German purity law that permits only malted barley, hops, yeast and water to be used in the brewing of beer. Though it has no jurisdiction outside Germany, many North American brewers follow it, and some use the fact that they meet its guidelines as part of their advertising.

Sake: A fermented beverage that is a cousin to the family of fermented beverages we call beer. Sake originated in Japan where it is an important national drink. Several sake breweries have existed in both California and Hawaii over the years, but the only remaining American commercial sake brewery is in Hawaii. Sake is brewed from unmalted rice and is not hopped. The resulting substance is clear and has a 14 to 16 percent alcohol content. In contrast to beer, which is drunk either chilled or at room temperature, sake is warmed before drinking.

Steam Beer: A term that originated in San Francisco during the gold rush era to refer to beer that was produced with bottom-fermenting yeast but fermented at 60° to 70° rather than the temperatures required for true lager fermentation. Fermentation was allowed to continue in the kegs and the escaping carbon dioxide that resulted from the tapping of the kegs is the possible source of the term 'steam' beer. In any event, the term steam

beer is now a registered trademark of The Anchor Brewing Company of San Francisco, brewers of Anchor Steam Beer.

Stout: A dark, heavy, top-fermented beer popular in the British Isles, especially Ireland (where Guinness stout is more popular than Budweiser lager is in the United States). It is similar to porter, though less sweet. Its alcohol content ranges from four to seven percent.

Tesguino: A type of corn beer produced by the Indians of Mexico and the American Southwest prior to their contact with Europeans.

Wheat Beer: A type of top-fermented beer in which malted wheat is substituted for malted barley. Originally brewed in Germany, it was produced by several small North American brewers in the 1980s.

Wort: An oatmeal-like substance consisting of water and mashed barley in which soluble starch has been turned into fermentable sugar during the mashing process. The wort is cooked, or brewed, in the brew kettle for more than an hour and for as much as a day, during which time hops are added to season the wort. After brewing, the hopped wort is filtered and fermented to produce beer.

Yeast: The enzyme-producing one-celled fungi of the genus *Saccharomyces* that is added to wort before the fermentation process for the purpose of turning fermentable sugar into alcohol and carbon dioxide.

Raw materials of the brewing process: hops, dark malt, malt and unmalted barley.

8. Adding the **yeast** to begin **fermentation.**

9. Fermentation of the **wort** to produce **beer.**

10. Optional **Krausening** or second ·**fermentation.**

11. Aging or settling.

12. Final filtration.

13. Packaging in bottles, cans or kegs.

14. Optional **Pasteurization** to stop the **fermentation.** (Unpasteurized beer must be kept cold after packaging to retain freshness.)

INDEX

PICTURE CREDITS

All pictures and labels are included through the courtesy of the specific brewing companies depicted therein, with the following exceptions:

Author's Collection 3, 6, 7, 102, 107, 118 top
Basso & Associates, Inc 85 top
Louis Bolis via Coors 49
Charles Finkel, Merchant du Vin 150 top
Jim Harter, Dover Publications 17, 36, 37, 38 top, 78 top two, 81 top, 82-83 all six, 93 right, 101 bottom
Fritz Maytag Collection 18-19, 20 bottom, 21 bottom, 24 left, 25, 79, 80, 208
Minnesota Historical Society 39, 40-41, 90 top

Molson Collection/ Public Archives of Canada 15, 112 both, 116 top, 117 top
Montana Historical Society 52-53, 53, 56-57, 58-59, 60-61
National Gallery of Art, Washington, DC 11
San Francisco Archives 1, 4-5, 62-63, 64, 66-67, 68-69, 70-71, 78 bottom, 91 top, 93 left, 96-97, 104-105
State Historical Society of Wisconsin 24 right both, 92
Washington State Historical Society 110 top
© Bill Yenne 2, 8, 9 left, 10 both, 12 both, 13 both, 14, 16 all three, 20 top three, 21 top three,

28 left both, 32 top, 41 top, 48 left, 56, 65 all three, 67, 69, 71, 72 top two, 73, 74 top right and bottom, 75 top left and bottom right, 81 bottom, 84 both, 85 bottom, 90 bottom, 91 bottom, 94 right and left and bottom both, 95 all eight, 101 top, 104, 105, 106 bottom, 110 bottom, 111 bottom and top, 116 bottom, 117 bottom, 130 bottom, 132-133, 134 all, 135 all, 136 all, 137 all, 140 all, 141, 149 right, 153 right, 154, 155 all

GREAT AMERICAN BEER FESTIVAL GOLD MEDAL WINNERS

	1987	1988	1989
American Light Lagers	Leinenkugel (Leinenkugel)	Boston Lightship (Boston Beer)	Hudepohl 14-k (Hudepohl-Schoenling Brewing)
American Lagers	Koch's Golden Anniversary Beer (Genesee)	Signature (Stroh Brewing)	Coors Extra Gold (Aldolph Coors)
American Premium Dark Lagers		Michelob Dark (Anheuser-Busch)	Lowenbrau Dark Special (Miller Brewing)
Continental European Pilsners	Samuel Adams Boston Lager (Boston Beer)	August Schell Pilsner (August Schell Brewing)	Manhattan Gold Lager (Manhattan Brewing)
Ales	Bigfoot Barley Wine Style Ale (Sierra Nevada Brewing)	TW Fisher's Centennial Pale Ale (Coeur d'Alene Brewing)	Sierra Nevada Pale Ale (Sierra Nevada Brewing)
Barley Wine Style Ales		Bigfoot Barley Wine Style Ale (Sierra Nevada Brewing)	
Porters	Great Northern Porter (Summit Brewing)	Anchor Porter (Anchor Brewing)	Tower Dark (Butterfield Brewing)
Stouts	Boulder Stout (Boulder Brewing)	Humboldt Oatmeal Stout (Humboldt Brewery)	San Quentin Breakout Stout (Marin Brewing)
American Cream Ales	Little Kings Cream Ale (Hudepohl-Schoenling Brewing)	Little Kings Cream Ale (Hudepohl-Schoenling Brewing)	Little Kings Cream Ale (Hudepohl-Schoenling Brewing)
Continental Amber Lagers	Golden Bear Dark Malt (Thousand Oaks Brewing)	Ambier (Ambier Brewing)	Schild Brau (Millstream Brewing)
Vienna Style Lagers	Vienna Style Lager (Vienna (Ambier) Brewing)		Market Street Oktoberfest (Bohannon Brewing)
Bocks/Doppelbocks	Chesbay Double Bock (Chesapeake Bay Brewing)	Sieben's Bock (Sieben Brewing)	Kessler Grand Teton Doppelbock (Montana Beverages)
Wheat Beers	Edelweiss (Val-Blatz Brewery)	August Schell Weiss (August Schell Brewing)	Stoudt's Weizen (Stoudt Brewery)
Alt Beers	Chinook Alaskan Amber Beer (Chinook Alaskan Brewing & Bottling)	Chinook Alaskan Amber (Chinook Alaskan Brewing & Bottling)	Samuel Adams Boston Stock Ale (Boston Beer)
Fruit Beers			Oldenberg Cherry Lager (Oldenberg Brewing)
Herb Beers			Christmas Ale (Anchor Brewing)
Consumer Poll (no medal)	Samuel Adams Festival Lager (Boston Beer)	Chinook Alaskan Amber (Chinook Alaskan Brewing & Bottling)	Samuel Adams Boston Lager (Boston Beer)